Mysterious Cup Marks

Proceedings of the
First International Cupule Conference

Edited by

Roy Querejazu Lewis
Robert G. Bednarik

BAR International Series 2073
2010

Published in 2016 by
BAR Publishing, Oxford

BAR International Series 2073

Mysterious Cup Marks

ISBN 978 1 4073 0634 6

© The editors and contributors severally and the Publisher 2010

The authors' moral rights under the 1988 UK Copyright,
Designs and Patents Act are hereby expressly asserted.

All rights reserved. No part of this work may be copied, reproduced, stored,
sold, distributed, scanned, saved in any form of digital format or transmitted
in any form digitally, without the written permission of the Publisher.

BAR Publishing is the trading name of British Archaeological Reports (Oxford) Ltd.
British Archaeological Reports was first incorporated in 1974 to publish the BAR
Series, International and British. In 1992 Hadrian Books Ltd became part of the BAR
group. This volume was originally published by Archaeopress in conjunction with
British Archaeological Reports (Oxford) Ltd / Hadrian Books Ltd, the Series principal
publisher, in 2010. This present volume is published by BAR Publishing, 2016.

Printed in England

BAR titles are available from:

           BAR Publishing
           122 Banbury Rd, Oxford, OX2 7BP, UK
EMAIL   info@barpublishing.com
PHONE +44 (0)1865 310431
FAX   +44 (0)1865 316916
           www.barpublishing.com

CONTENTS

Robert G. Bednarik: The first cupule conference: introduction and summary 1

(1) THE SCIENCE OF CUPULES

Robert G. Bednarik: Estimating the age of cupules 5

Marvin W. Rowe and Brandon Chance: Cupules in Qatar: potential for determining minimum ages 13

Giriraj Kumar: Lower Palaeolithic cupules obtained from the excavations at Daraki-Chattan in
India from 2002 to 2006 21

Robert G. Bednarik: Relevance of site lithology and taphonomic logic to cupules 33

(2) THE NATURE OF CUPULES

Robert G. Bednarik: Discriminating between cupules and other rock markings 41

Robert G. Bednarik: The technology of cupule making 53

Giriraj Kumar: Understanding the creation of early cupules, with special reference to
Daraki-Chattan in India 59

Robert G. Bednarik: The interpretation of cupules 67

(3) CUPULES AND OTHER TYPES OF ROCK ART

Gori Tumi Echevarría López: Circular concavities in the rock art of the Cachiyacu River basin,
Loreto, Peru 75

Alberto Bueno Mendoza: Pashash (Peru) cupules and significant figurations 85

Maarten van Hoek: The ambiguity of depressions in rock art 89

(4) CONTEMPORARY PERCEPTION OF CUPULES

Roy Querejazu Lewis: Cupules in Bolivia 99

Robert G. Bednarik: A short ethnography of cupules 109

Robert G. Bednarik: About lithophones 115

David Camacho: *Thok'os* or *thoketos* (cupules) 119

CONTRIBUTORS

Robert G. Bednarik
Convener, International Federation of Rock Art Organisations (IFRAO)
P.O. Box 216
Caulfield South, VIC 3162
Australia
robertbednarik@hotmail.com

Professor Alberto Bueno Mendoza
Calle Carlos A. Saco 180–182
Urbanización Apolo, Distrito La Victoria
Lima 13
Peru

David Camacho
Indigenous Quechua researcher
c/o Casilla 4243
COCHABAMBA
Bolivia
dcochullpa@hotmail.com

Professor Giriraj Kumar
President, Rock Art Society of India (RASI)
Faculty of Arts
Dayalbagh Educational Institute
DAYALBAGH, Agra 282 005
India
girirajrasi@yahoo.com

Professor Roy Querejazu Lewis
President, Asociación de Estudios del Arte Rupestre de Cochabamba (AEARC)
Casilla 4243
COCHABAMBA
Bolivia
aearcb@gmail.com

Professors Marvin W. Rowe and Brandon Chance
Department of Chemistry
Texas A&M University
College Station, TX 77843
U.S.A.

Gori Tumi Echevarría López
President, Asociación Peruana de Arte Rupestre (APAR)
Alameda Julio C. Tello 274
Dpto No. 303
Torres de San Borja
LIMA 41
Peru
goritumi@gmail.com

Maarten van Hoek
Independent rock art researcher
Laurier 20
5061 WS OISTERWIJK
Holland
mamvanhoek@home.nl

THE FIRST CUPULE CONFERENCE: INTRODUCTION AND SUMMARY

Robert G. Bednarik

Conferences dealing with rock art have become increasingly frequent in recent years, and now occur several times a year in one part of the world or another. In general, they address regional, methodological and particularly generic concerns in rock art research and protection, rather than highly specialised subjects such as one specific form of rock art. Professor Roy Querejazu Lewis, the President of the Asociación de Estudios del Arte Rupestre de Cochabamba (AEARC), has now presented an experiment breaking with this practice: an international conference dedicated exclusively to cupules, which would appear to be one of the simplest phenomena in the field. But he has managed to demonstrate two things: that such a specialised conference can be extraordinarily productive and pleasant, and that the subject of cupule research is significantly more complex than anyone had anticipated.

The International Cupule Conference was held in Cochabamba, central Bolivia, from 17 to 23 July 2007. Its first three days consisted of a series of symposia held at the Centro Pedagógico y Cultural Simón I. Patiño, a palatial, sumptuously furnished building surrounded by magnificent gardens. The second part of the conference offered participants the opportunity of visiting several sites of cupules and other, cupule-like phenomena in the Mizque valley and elsewhere in central Bolivia. The symposia were attended by almost one hundred tourism students of the Universidad Mayor de San Simon, filling up the venue's lecture hall to capacity. The international component of the participants included, besides many Bolivian researchers, representatives from Australia, Chile, India, Peru and Switzerland, and papers presented in absentia were contributed from Argentina, Greece, Holland and U.S.A.

The flawless performance of the conference was a credit to Professor Querejazu's superb planning and choice of secretariat personnel, and a seemingly effortless efficiency marked the proceedings throughout. From the pleasant welcoming of international visitors at the airport, to the impeccable continuous translation service (the outstanding quality of which deserves particular mention) for the full three days of lectures and discussions, to the well-orchestrated official events, even the perfectly organised and delightful tea breaks on the palace's terrace — the entire event was characterised by cordiality. It showed once again the advantages of smaller academic events, and one aspect that I found noteworthy is the expedience of combining academic content with didactic purpose. Querejazu had integrated the event in his teaching curriculum and his students were the most attentive participants.

Another outstanding factor was the participation of native Quechua speakers, especially David Camacho who presented one of the lectures (Figure 1). The involvement of indigenous people is one of the most consequential practices AEARC is developing, and is no doubt related to Querejazu's own studies of ongoing use of Bolivian rock art sites by traditional communities. Indeed, Camacho turned out to be a most fascinating scholar, a complete autodidact in every sense, and a self-taught archaeologist who researches Incan masonry, ceramics and cultural practices.

Another of Querejazu's 'trump cards' was Gori Tumi Echevaría López, a young archaeologist from the Universidad Nacional Mayor de San Marcos in Lima, Peru, one of a new breed of Andean scholars. He, too, has Quechua ancestry, and his approach to archaeology differs markedly from that of his traditional, neo-colonialist colleagues. Not only does

Figure 1. Quechua scholar David Camacho presenting his lecture at the Cochabamba cupule conference.

Figure 2. Fieldtrip participants examining natural, cupule-like features (potholes) at Chutu Kollu, near Tarata, central Bolivia.

he espouse a scientific and logical approach to the discipline, together with a deep personal commitment, his infectious enthusiasm will, I predict, ensure that we will hear much more from this young researcher. And he is not alone, Andean archaeology is developing rapidly into a modern discipline freeing itself of the intellectual vestiges of colonialism.

In every sense, this conference broke a great deal of new ground. Cupules are of course a significant feature in Andean rock art, as indeed they are in dozens of other major traditions around the world, from the Lower Palaeolithic in India to the 20th century in Australia. Perhaps one might have predicted that this will be a rather pedantic affair — after all, how much is there to be said about cupules? Yet this event has demonstrated that cupules are in fact a ferociously complex subject. Leaving aside the fairly obvious topics of their dating, and the perennial matter of their possible functions and meanings, a number of rather more interesting new facets emerged. For instance, there is no standardised methodology for their recording and study, yet there is an obvious need for its introduction. Then there are the great difficulties of distinguishing between cupules and natural features of a surprisingly great variety, or between cupules and other, perhaps utilitarian anthropic markings (such as mortars). These matters were highlighted and it emerged that they are in need of better resolution. This leads directly to the issue of distinguishing between cupules that relate to acoustic properties of the rocks they occur on (lithophones) and those that do not. Then there is the complex subject of the taphonomy of cupules. One of the most overwhelming impressions I took from the conference was that traditional interpretations, especially those one finds in European commentaries, are probably more misleading than we had thought. Cupules, ultimately, need to be seen as the surviving remnant of a highly specific but rather strange form of human behaviour, all the other traces of which have disappeared. Or, as they expressed it in Latin, '*ex ungue leonem*' ([to paint] 'the lion from the claw'): we have tended to deduce the whole from a small part or trace of it — which is what archaeology does at the best of times. The simplistic attempts to explain cupules (astronomical, receptacles of blood and so forth) that we have seen for a great many years are probably much further from the truth than even I, ever so sceptical of humbug explanations, had suspected. Cupules, most particularly, show us the impotence of ethnocentric interpretations. And they also show us that, in rock art, the perhaps most rudimentary phenomena might be far more complex research subjects than the celebrated 'naturalistic' zoomorphs that have been so much more popular (cf. Yann-Pierre Montelle's [2009] 'iconocentrism'). As we look at cupules, and other 'archaic' features in rock art, we catch a fleeting glimpse of the real intricacies of human worldviews that are of overwhelming remoteness from our own.

After this sacrilegious note I best round off my report of this particularly pleasant event with a brief account of the fieldtrips. They began with visits of several interesting sites near Tarata, a picturesque small town about 30 km from Cochabamba. The first three, of which only two were seen by the main body of the tour group (Chutu Kollu and Punku Cocha), were river sites of cupule-like phenomena and extensive rock fluting at a waterfall (Figure 2). These 'pseudo-cupules', also found at Rocas Rio Milloma, turned

Figure 3. Conference fieldtrip participants meet with the residents of Karakara, having been requested by the villagers to support their bid to have the nearby superb cupule sites protected and included in an archaeological park the community wants to see established. Their spokesman, Osvaldo Sanchez (with white beard) addresses the meeting, flanked by the spokesman of the community's Quechua speakers (left) and Professor Roy Querejazu Lewis (with book). Further to the right stands Enriqueta de Sanchez, who acted as Quechua interpreter, and seated on the far right is Dr Giriraj Kumar (India). Gori Tumi Echevarría López (Peru) is seated next to him.

out to be typical potholes (features caused by the water's kinetic energy released in quartz rocks caught in holes in soft schist rock), a veritable lesson in distinguishing between natural and artificial rock holes. A most memorable event was a meeting arranged between the tour group and the inhabitants of the small village Karakara, who had initiated a request that their rock art sites be protected and made the centrepiece of an archaeological park adjacent to their settlement. A community leader, Osvaldo Sanchez, whose family had lived there for 320 years, had made an impassioned speech to us in the town hall in Tarata, 'demanding' that the scholars turn their attention to 'his' valley (Figure 3). Querejazu will organise a thorough study of the cultural resources present, with the keen collaboration of the villagers (made up of both Quechua and Spanish speakers). There are at least two fascinating cupule sites near Karakara. In both cases the rock art occurs together with potholes now elevated more than 20 m above the river, and one of the sites is rich in archaic stone tools.

From Tarata, the fieldtrip continued to the Mizque valley, where the cupule sites at Inca Huasi, Lakatambo and Uyuchama 2 were visited. For the first of these three sites, I have provided limited dating information (Bednarik 2000). Meanwhile, Professor Querejazu and I undertook several days of fieldwork near Cochabamba, where we had previously commenced a study of a site complex at Kalatrancani. Here we had spectacular success: we located four new cupule sites in the general area, and one of them turned out to be the largest site currently known in the State of Cochabamba. It is now named Roca Fortunato 1, after the man who directed our attention to it. With this site alone, the number of cupules known in the entire region has virtually doubled, and the site also comprises hundreds of other petroglyphs.

I would like to express my gratitude to all who have contributed to the success and warmth of this most enjoyable event, people like Daniel Salamanca, Hugo Santa Cruz, Ana Maria Urquidi, Miguel Guzman, Pamela Rodríguez, Karim Mostacedo, Eliana Lizárraga, Melanie Delgadillo and Lorena Rojas; to the incredibly helpful Charles Disch, to Alfredo Palizza, Rodolfo Rodríguez, and particularly to Raquel Velasco. I am sure I express here the sentiments of each and every participant. We also thank Elizabeth Torres, the Director of the architectural marvel that was provided as the venue, the Centro Patiño. But, as is most obvious to everyone who had the good fortune of participating in this lovely conference, our principal thanks are to Roy Querejazu Lewis, who planned and executed this memorable experiment. He has demonstrated to the discipline that a small conference addressing a highly specific topic can be very successful, provided it is conducted with flair and a great deal of enthusiasm.

REFERENCES

BEDNARIK, R. G. 2000. Age estimates for the petroglyph sequence of Inca Huasi, Mizque, Bolivia. *Andean Past* 6: 277–287.
MONTELLE, Y.-P. 2009. Application of forensic methods to rock art investigations – a proposal. *Rock Art Research* 26: 7–13.

ESTIMATING THE AGE OF CUPULES

Robert G. Bednarik

Abstract. The dating of cupules presents the same challenges as does the dating of most petroglyphs, with the added difficulty that cupules, more than other petroglyphs, have often been subjected to reuse long after they were first created. This means that parts of their surface may derive from different periods, or all earlier surfaces may have been obliterated completely. Examples of this phenomenon are given, and a discussion of the currently available methods of estimating the antiquity of cupules is presented. It emerges that, since the dust created in making cupules or other petroglyphs is not realistically recoverable, the analytical possibilities in dating them are severely limited. One of the best options is not to date the rock art, but instead date the tools used in creating it. This has been successful in some cases. The use of field microscopy is shown to be indispensable in any analytical work with cupules.

Keywords: Petroglyph, Dating, Methodology, Early cupules, Microerosion analysis, Hammerstone

Introduction

While it is essential to establish some semblance of an initial working definition of cupules, this does need to be qualified by conveying that there are adequate ambiguities to banish any notion of finite or universal rules about such definition. Elsewhere in this volume I have explained the great difficulties archaeologists have in distinguishing cupules from other phenomena resembling them, both natural and anthropic. But even if these are resolved, there still remain concerns that cupules should be treated as a single class of evidence, and this needs to be borne in mind when considering issues of their spatial and temporal distribution. Cupules occur commonly in most parts of the world, and they can be found in astronomical numbers in many regions. Moreover, they first begin to appear in the Lower Palaeolithic period, and in some cultures, particularly in Australia, they were still made in the early 20th century. Their ubiquity, and especially their appearance so early in hominin history, renders it extremely unlikely that we are dealing with a culturally homogeneous phenomenon persisting through the ages. Rather, this class of artefact is probably only defined by its morphological homogeneity, and its apparently universal occurrence and characteristics are partly artefacts of our data-collecting strategies.

Cupules are unequivocally among the most perdurable of all non-utilitarian anthropic rock markings. It is of considerable significance that nearly all of the petroglyphs currently known of the Lower Palaeolithic are cupules (only four exceptions can be cited at present, three linear petroglyphs from Daraki-Chattan, one from Auditorium Cave, both sites being in India; Bednarik et al. 2005). Taphonomic logic (Bednarik 1994) decrees how very improbable it is that this was the first rock art produced, and it is highly likely that other forms of rock art were in use then, but have apparently not survived (see chapter in this volume on the taphonomy of cupules). This is confirmed by the occasional discovery of haematite crayons of the Lower Palaeolithic that were used to mark rock surfaces (Bednarik 1990), and by the finds from numerous sites of portable engravings and other palaeoart discoveries (Bednarik 2003).

The earliest object ever suggested to bear cupules is the pecked phonolite cobble from Olduvai FLK North 1 in Bed 1, Tanzania, about 1.74 Ma old (Leakey 1971: 269; cf. Bednarik 2003: Fig. 21). The rounded stone bears a deep cup-shaped, anthropic mark on one side, and a shallower such mark on the other. It does bring to mind a few very similar Middle to Upper Magdalenian quartzite and granite cobbles from France, from Laugerie-Basse and La Garenne (Lartet and Christy 1875; Tarel 1912, 1919; Peyrony 1918, 1920; de Beaune 1987, 1989). However, the Oldowan specimen may be the product of a utilitarian process. Vaguely cupule-like features on rock have on occasion been reported to be produced by chimps, and in South America even by monkeys, resulting from such activities as cracking nuts (McGrew 1992: 205, 1993). Joulian (1995: Fig. 5) presents a chimpanzee *percuteur* from Monogaga, Ivory Coast, that looks rather similar to Leakey's Olduvai specimen.

The first cupule demonstrated to be of the Lower Palaeolithic is one of two petroglyphs found on a quartzite

Figure 1. Exfoliated cupules excavated in a Lower Palaeolithic occupation layer at Daraki-Chattan, India.

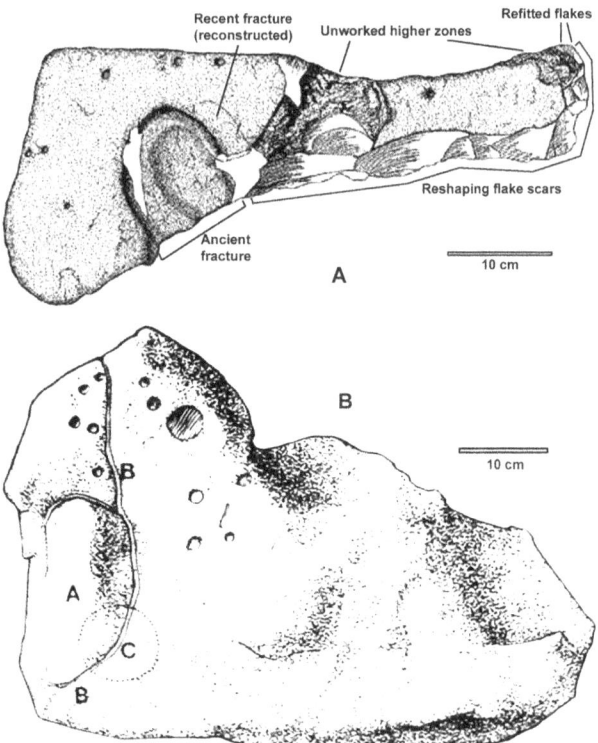

Figure 2. The Lower Palaeolithic slab with cupules from Sai Island, Sudan, and the sepulchral limestone block with cupules placed over a Neanderthal burial in La Ferrassie Cave, France (after van Peer et al. 2003 and Peyrony 1934).

boulder in an excavated trench in Auditorium Cave, Bhimbetka site complex, central India, covered by the top of the upper Acheulian horizon (Bednarik 1992a, 1993a, 1993b, 2001a, 2004) but probably of the lower chopping tool horizon. After detailed study of the site I proposed that nine further cupules nearby, but occurring above ground, were probably of similar antiquity (Bednarik 1996), but this was on the basis of largely circumstantial evidence. However, in the same year, Kumar (1996) reported the discovery of an assemblage of about 500 cupules in Daraki-Chattan, another Indian quartzite cave, which he suspected might also be of extremely great age. This was followed by further reports of Indian cupule sites of apparent Pleistocene antiquity, those of the Hathikheda sites (a series of outcrops of massive white quartz near Ajmer, including Moda Bhata), the large Morajhari cupule site (also in the vicinity of Ajmer), and the sites Bajanibhat and Jhiri Nala (near Kotputli). However, microerosion analyses at two of these sites has provided only Holocene ages so far (Bednarik and Kumar 2002; Bednarik et al. 2005), although the oldest phase of the complex Bajanibhat site does remain a viable candidate for Lower or Middle Palaeolithic antiquity. However, the substantial corpus at Daraki-Chattan has been clearly demonstrated to have been made by people with a chopping tool industry similar to the Oldowan, which underlies substantial Acheulian and Micoquian-like occupation layers. In the sediments at the entrance of this cave, some thirty exfoliated cupules (Figure 1) were excavated in and below the Acheulian deposit, extending all the way to the chopping tool layer, while numerous hammerstones used in the production of some of the approximately 540 cupules of the cave were concentrated in this lowest occupation deposit (Bednarik et al. 2005). This sound stratigraphical evidence suggests that the cupules in Auditorium Cave, too, are perhaps not of the Acheulian as previously suggested, but also belong to the chopping tool tradition found under the site's two Acheulian horizons, and separated from them by a sterile layer.

In addition to these two sites of Lower Palaeolithic cupules in India, a sandstone slab with seven small cupules and one very large cupule has recently been reported from Sai Island, Sudan, believed to be in the order of 200,000 years old (van Peer et al. 2003). This find from the Lower Sangoan (Figure 2A) immediately brings to mind the very similar limestone slab excavated in La Ferrassie, France, which had been placed over the grave of a Neanderthal child, with the cupules on the underside, i.e. facing the interment (burial No. 6; Peyrony 1934: 33–36, Fig. 33). The French specimen, which I have studied microscopically (Bednarik in prep.), bears one large cupule plus seventeen small ones, some of which are very faint, and sixteen of them are arranged in pairs (Figure 2B). It is usually attributed to the Mousterian, but this appears to be purely on the basis that the burial is of a

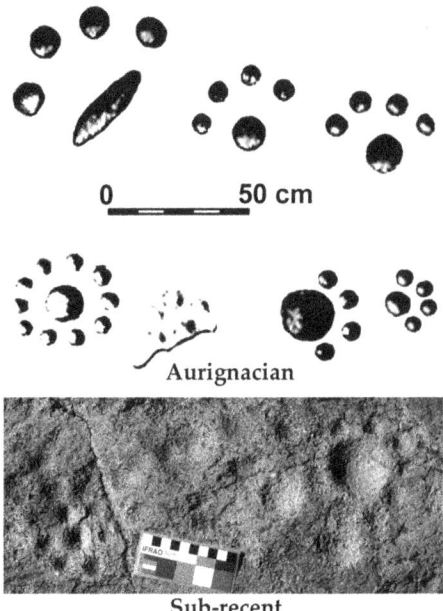

Figure 3. Arrangements of Aurignacian cupules from Abri Blanchard, France (top), compared with others of recent age at Llave Chico, Bolivia (Below). The age difference between the two groups is in excess of 30,000 years.

Neanderthal child. Since there are also Aurignacian cupules at this and other sites nearby, and since the Aurignacian also appears to be a tool tradition by robust humans rather than gracile moderns (Bednarik 2007a), the cultural placement of the sepulchral slab from La Ferrassie may need to be reconsidered.

Peter Beaumont has reported finding extremely early cupule sites also in the Korannaberg region, southern Kalahari (Beaumont in press; Beaumont and Bednarik in prep.; Bednarik 2003). Like those in India they occur on heavily metamorphosed and thus particularly weathering-resistant quartzite, and they appear to be either of the MSA (Middle Stone Age) or earlier. By the time of the Middle Palaeolithic, cupules had probably become very common. Tens of thousands occur just in Australia, where all Pleistocene and early Holocene rock art is necessarily associated with Mode 3 lithic industries (Foley and Lahr 1997), as is literally all rock art of Tasmania.

One might be tempted to see cupules as a '*Leitfossil*' of Middle Palaeolithic/MSA traditions, so dominant do they appear to be at that time, but they are found in even greater numbers in some of the most recent periods. They occur in the European Upper Palaeolithic, where they tend to be described as 'pitted blocks' because they are most often found on cave clasts or boulders. They seem to be particularly abundant in the earliest Upper Palaeolithic, and they are thought to be less common in the Upper Périgordian (i.e. the western Gravettian) than in the Aurignacian (de Beaune 1992). In all probability they were particularly associated with robust humans of the Final Pleistocene

Figure 4. Cupules on the truncation surface of a menhir of the Almendres cromlech, Evora, Portugal.

(Bednarik 2007a). Aurignacian examples (Figure 3) are abundant at Le Cellier, Castanet and Blanchard (Delluc and Delluc 1978). They have also been reported from sites of the Gravettian (Laussel), Solutrean (Badegoule) and from the Magdalenian, such as at Abri Reverdit (de Beaune 2000: 71). With the latter tradition, they even occur on small, round and very hard cobbles, such as the specimens from Laugerie-Basse and Abri de La Garenne (op. cit.: 101). Particularly noteworthy are two pieces, of the mid or upper Magdalenian, one of brown quartzite, one of granite, each bearing a cupule centred in a perfectly formed, deeply hammered circle. These well-rounded stones, under 10.5 cm, resemble the typical cup-and-ring features of much more recent times closely, and are thus unlikely to be utilitarian. At Limeuil cupules appear together with engraved lines (Capitan and Bouyssonie 1924: Pl. X), at La Ferrassie Peyrony (1934: 67–69, 75–78) reported them from the Middle Aurignacian levels, while in Cosquer Cave they occur on bedrock (Clottes et al. 2005: Figs 194, 195) and are probably of the mid-Upper Palaeolithic.

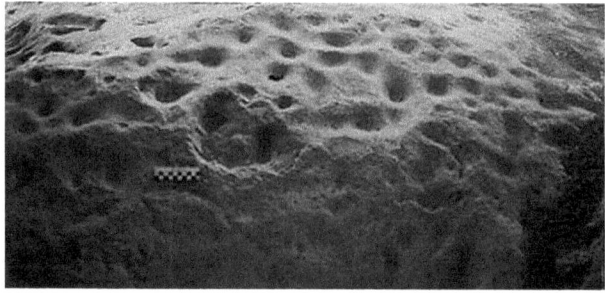

Figure 5. Cupules on sandstone at Sandy Creek Shelter 1, Cape York Peninsula, Australia, possibly up to 40,000 years old.

Cupules are much more common from apparent Holocene contexts, being most frequently described as Neolithic or Metal Ages features, for instance in western Europe (e.g. d'Arragon 1994; Steinbring and Lanteigne 1991). There they are frequently found with megalithic evidence (Figure 4). In some of these mid to late Holocene traditions it appears cupules were used with specific semiotic or syntactic meanings; for instance it is assumed that cupules placed between the legs of anthropomorphous petroglyphs denoted female sex. However, cupules are not restricted to pre-Historic times, they continue to be produced or re-used in Europe until well into the Historical periods (Mandl 1995; Rizzi 1995, 2007; Schwegler 1995: 112–113; Costas Goberna et al. 1999: 166). The most recently made cupules that have been convincingly dated in Europe are of the Middle Ages (Bednarik 2001b) and even more recent, up to the early 18th century C.E. (Rizzi 1995: 81).

In other continents, too, Holocene cupules are ubiquitous features of numerous rock art traditions. But before we consider these, it is appropriate to briefly return to the issue of 'Middle Palaeolithic' cupules. In accordance with Foley and Lahr's typological taxonomy, all of Australia's Pleistocene and early Holocene technological traditions are of 'Middle Palaeolithic' nature. The continent was initially settled by Middle Palaeolithic seafarers from Wallacea (Bednarik 1999), and the descendants of these colonisers retained their 'core and scraper' lithics until the mid-Holocene. Moreover, in Tasmania the human population became separated from that of the mainland about 12,400 years BP, i.e. when the sea-level passed about –56 m, and they retained this mode 3 technology right up to the time of British colonisation around 200 years ago. One may consider this tradition as the only 'Middle Palaeolithic culture' witnessed and described (however inadequately) in Historical times. More relevantly, in the present context, the petroglyph traditions of Tasmania seem to be dominated by mostly small cupules, among which occur rare large cupules (Bednarik et al. 2007), i.e. their pattern of occurrence resembles that found elsewhere with 'Lower' and 'Middle Palaeolithic' traditions. In some of the major petroglyph regions of mainland Australia, such as the Pilbara on the west coast, cupules are often very numerous, occurring in large numbers on individual boulders, and there is frequent evidence that they precede most or all other petroglyphs in those areas (e.g. McNickle 1991; Bednarik 1993a). On the other hand, the Jinmium controversy (Fullagar et al. 1996) demonstrated that it is impossible to generalise, and the weathered appearance of some of the cupules on softer sandstones may belie their true ages. Nevertheless, there can be no reasonable doubt that Pleistocene cupules occur in the tens of thousands in Australia, if not hundreds of thousands, from the Pilbara in the far west (especially the eastern Pilbara) via Carpenter's Gap in the Kimberley to the Cape York Peninsula in the east, where the cupule panel of Sandy Creek 1 (Figure 5) refers to an important Pleistocene site (Morwood 2002).

The age estimation of cupules

Globally there are not very many instances of the age of cupules having been estimated in absolute terms by credible methods. A few of them refer to archaeological predictions based on the excavation of cupules in roughly datable sediments. For instance in Africa, one vertical cupule panel has been minimum-dated by excavation. Clark (1958: 21–2) has obtained a carbon isotope age of 6310 ± 250 years BP from the sediment of Chifubwa Stream Rockshelter in northern Zimbabwe. At Daraki-Chattan in India, the two substantial cupule panels of the cave are securely linked to an occupation layer of Oldowan-like chopping tools occurring at the base of a deposit containing substantial handaxe-bearing deposits further up. This link is based on the presence of numerous exfoliated rock slabs from the wall panels, many with cupules, which occur down to this lowest occupation level. It is strongly reinforced by the presence of hammerstones within the chopping tool stratum, which are of the type used in cupule production. Although this link is secure, dating of the layer has not yet been accomplished, but the cultural attribution of the cupules by stratigraphy is adequate to designate this as one of the earliest of all known rock art sites.

Excellent archaeological dating of cupules has been achieved at several sites near Bressanone, in the northern Italian Dolomites. Egger (1948) excavated a cupule slab in the hearth of a middle Iron Age hut at Albanbühel. At a site in Plabach he managed to place another example in the middle Bronze Age (c. 3500 BP). Further excavations at the former site in 1989 yielded more cupule stones, dated to the 5th or 4th century B.C.E. (Rizzi 2007). Below the building foundation, five more occupation horizons were encountered, all of the middle Bronze Age, containing more cupule slabs. It was noted that some of the smaller specimens had been used as supports keeping pointed wooden posts in position, i.e. they were purely utilitarian. Much older are the small phyllite slabs found in the foundation of a Neolithic hut at the Plunacker site near Villanders, dating from the 5th to the mid-4th millennium B.C.E. (Rizzi 2007: 49). Stones with cupules have also been excavated from a Neolithic occupation floor at Feldthurn, in the same region. At that site, a Megalithic arrangement of the Chalcolithic

Figure 6. Petroglyphs of Rupe Magna, Grosio, Italy. One of the cupules has been subjected to microerosion analysis and is only about 1000 years old.

period included a block with cupules, and further small cupule-slabs were attributed to the Iron Age.

In a different part of northern Italy, Valtellina, microerosion analysis of a few petroglyphs of Rupe Magna, near Grosio, has included one fairly recent cupule (Figure 6). Its age has been estimated as being about E1030 years BP (Bednarik 2001b). Other preliminary microerosion results are available from two central Indian sites, Moda Bhata and Morajhari. Both are located in the vicinity of Ajmer, Rajasthan, but the former is unusual in that it occurs on a dyke of white crystalline quartz. It is part of a chain of several sites (Bednarik and Kumar 2002), the only reported occurrence of petroglyphs in the world on this hard rock. The gneissic rock of Morajhari is also quite hard, and both sites were considered to be good candidates for Pleistocene age. Both were subjected to microerosion analysis, which conclusively dispelled that expectation. One cupule at Moda Bhata yielded a microerosion histogram that clearly indicated the reworking of the feature long after it was originally created (Figure 7). Most of the fractures in this cupule were in the order of E9200 years old, but a small proportion centred on about E1800 BP. This raises a significant problem in the age estimation of such features that may have taken a long time to create, and that have been subjected to one or more episodes of reuse at a much later time. It is obvious that cupules on particularly hard rocks, such as granitic facies, heavily metamorphosed quartzite and crystalline quartz, were created over extended time spans. Once made, they may have been subjected to a variety of cultural uses, right up to the recent past in some cases, and these uses may have included more impact. Therefore the principal limitation of the use of microerosion analysis in estimating the age of cupules is not methodological, but relates to the fact that parts of the surface of a cupule can only date from the percussion it experienced most recently.

At the second Indian site yielding microerosion data, Morajhari, the ages of three cupule surfaces were estimated. One of them provided clusters of micro-wane widths

Figure 7. Cupules on white crystalline quartz at Moda Bhata, Ajmer, India.

Figure 8. Cupules on gneissic rock at Morajhari, Ajmer, India.

corresponding to E2600 years BP, E1750 years BP and E800 years BP, which again suggests re-working of this feature (Figure 8). Another cupule, on the underside of the same boulder, had to be made earlier because it was created before the boulder was turned upside down, and it yielded an estimate of about E5000 years BP. A third cupule 20 m away provided a tight cluster at about E1900 years BP.

Microerosion analysis has been applied since 1997 to cupules at several Bolivian sites in the region near Cochabamba, where it has yielded some surprisingly recent dates. In this case, the rocks the cupules have been hammered into contain no quartz or feldspar, and are therefore not amenable to the method. Consequently, a different approach has been introduced: instead of analysing the petroglyphs, quartz tools used in their manufacture, or tiny slivers that became detached from them at the time of impact, are analysed and the time of their fracturing is estimated (Bednarik and Querejazu Lewis in prep.). Unfortunately this approach, too, is limited by the fact that one can never securely relate the time of impact to any

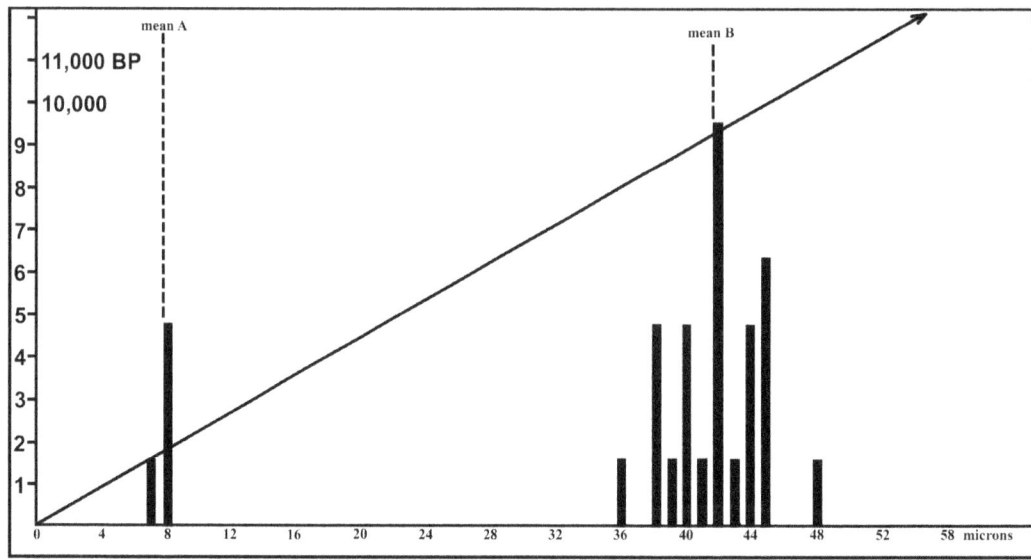

Figure 9. Microerosion histogram of micro-wanes, from one of the cupules at Moda Bhata, India. Note the widely separated clusters, indicating reuse of the cupule 7000 years after it was first made.

phase in cupule production: did it occur early in the making of the cupule, or late? All one can postulate with adequate veracity is that the tool damage dates from one episode in the cupule's creation, whereas the cupule surface typically relates to its most recent phase. However, even this may be problematic, as best shown by the example of the Moda Bhata specimen.

About methodology

The following methods of estimating the ages of cupules have so far been considered or applied:

1. *Archaeological*: through the age of sediments in which the rock art occurs. This can be either by:
1a. Naturally exfoliated rock slabs bearing cupules that have fallen to the ground and become covered by sediments. The enclosing sediment thus provides a minimum age, and a quite probably very conservative minimum age.
1b. Where no petroglyphs other than cupules occur, and these appear in a large number, it should be possible to locate and identify the hammerstones used in their production. If this succeeds, the enclosing sediment should offer an approximate relative or absolute age for the cupules.
1c. Where rock slabs bearing cupules had been placed on an occupation floor or in the foundation of a datable building, this event is probably datable. The cupules themselves may be older, or they may be of the same antiquity, but they cannot be younger in the absence of sedimentary disturbance.
2. *Scientific*: through determining the age of surface features by:
2a. Quantifying the microerosion experienced by the surface of a cupule. This usually determines the most recent time it was hammered, and probably not the time it was first made, especially on hard lithologies (Figure 9).
2b. Quantifying the microerosion experienced by specific surface aspects of either the hammerstone used in making a cupule, or of small fragments spalled from it in the process. Where the analysed material can be securely attributed to an event of cupule production, it provides an estimate of when that event occurred, but not of when production commenced or finished.
2c. Finding the dust created when a cupule was made, and dating it via the sediment by OSL or radiometric determination of some other component, has been attempted by one archaeologist (G. Susino) in respect of other petroglyphs but does not seem possible realistically.
2d. Finding lichens covering a cupule and estimating the age of the thallus. This has not been attempted so far, and it would only yield very conservative minimum ages. Lichenometry does not extend back much more than several centuries (Bednarik 2007b: 128).
2e. Colorimetry of patinae covering cupules has also not been attempted so far, and can only be considered as a supplementary method (Bednarik and Khan 2005).
2f. Sampling an accretionary deposit that has formed over the cupule and attempting to determine its age via one of the radiometric methods.

This last-mentioned alternative can again only provide very conservative minimum ages and is probably not worth the effort for a variety of reasons. Not only tend such accretions to be very significantly younger than the petroglyph they cover, the estimation of their age is fraught with many difficulties. All rock substrates are subjected to an open carbon system (Bednarik 1979), therefore unqualified bulk determination of their carbon isotopes (without reference to molecular or object determination of what is being analysed) is misleading and does not provide valid results for the purpose. Uranium-series analyses may be somewhat better suited but have not been attempted. All methods of this kind, in the absence of a taphonomic history of the accretion (accretionary skins tend to have complex histories), are plagued by severe limitations. This also includes the XRF or $^{40}Ar/^{40}K$ methods, unfortunately (for a more detailed discussion of these issues, see Bednarik 2007b: 115–144).

On that basis the age estimation of cupules is perhaps best served, for the time being at least, by archaeological excavation and microerosion analysis. The major drawback of the first method is that it can only be applied in vary rare circumstances. Worldwide, cupules have been found in reliable archaeological settings in very few cases. Moreover, the relation between the 'archaeological age', however derived, and the age of the cupule is far from secure. With microerosion analysis, the drawbacks are different (Bednarik 1992b). Although the method is unusually reliable and robust, it is very imprecise and tolerance margins of 20% can occur. Moreover, the method is currently limited to rock types containing quartz or feldspar, and preferably both. While many cupules do occur on suitable lithologies, the majority does not. Finally, the method's specific applications, for instance to hammerstones or their fragments, remain experimental and need to be tested at many sites.

In short: the estimation of cupule age is certainly possible in some cases, but it remains an underdeveloped field, which we can only hope to be developed further in the present century.

REFERENCES

BEAUMONT, P. B. in press. On a search for ancestral petroglyphs in the south-eastern Kalahari. *Rock Art Research*.

BEAUMONT, P. B. and R. G. BEDNARIK in prep. Pleistocene rock art from Africa.

BEAUNE, S. A. DE 1987. *Lampes et godets au paléolithique*. Supplement 23, *Gallia Préhistoire*, CNRS Éditions, Paris.

BEAUNE, S. A. DE 1989. Fonction et décor de certains utensiles paléolithiques en pierre. *L'Anthropologie* 93(2): 547–584.

BEAUNE, S. A. DE 1992. Nonflint stone tools of the Early Upper Paleolithic. In H. Knecht, A. Pike-Tay and R. White (eds), *Before Lascaux: the complex record of the Early Upper Palaeolithic*, pp. 163–191. CRC Press, Boca Raton, FL.

BEAUNE, S. A. DE 2000. *Pour une archéologie du geste*. CNRS Éditions, Paris.

BEDNARIK, R. G. 1979. The potential of rock patination analysis in Australian Archaeology — part 1. *The Artefact* 4: 47–77.

BEDNARIK, R. G. 1990. An Acheulian haematite pebble with striations. *Rock Art Research* 7(1): 75.

BEDNARIK, R. G. 1992a. The Palaeolithic art of Asia. In S. Goldsmith, S. Garvie, D. Selin and J. Smith (eds), *Ancient images, ancient thought: the archaeology of ideology*, pp. 383–390. Proceedings of the 23rd Annual Chacmool Conference, University of Calgary.

BEDNARIK, R. G. 1992b. A new method to date petroglyphs. *Archaeometry* 34(2): 279–291.

BEDNARIK, R. G. 1993a. About cupules. *Rock Art Research* 10: 138–139.

BEDNARIK, R. G. 1993b. Palaeolithic art in India. *Man and Environment* 18(2): 33–40.

BEDNARIK, R. G. 1994. A taphonomy of palaeoart. *Antiquity* 68(258): 68–74.

BEDNARIK, R. G. 1996. The cupules on Chief's Rock, Auditorium Cave, Bhimbetka. *The Artefact* 19: 63–72.

BEDNARIK, R. G. 1999. Maritime navigation in the Lower and Middle Palaeolithic. *Comptes Rendus de l'Académie des Sciences Paris*, Earth and Planetary Sciences 328: 559–563.

BEDNARIK, R. G. 2001a. Cupules: the oldest surviving rock art. *International Newsletter on Rock Art* 30: 18–23.

BEDNARIK, R. G. 2001b. Petroglyphs in Italian Alps dated. *Acta Archaeologica* 72(2): 109–114.

BEDNARIK, R. G. 2003. The earliest evidence of palaeoart. *Rock Art Research* 20: 89–135.

BEDNARIK, R. G. 2004. Cupules: the oldest surviving rock art (in Chinese). *Yan Hua* (Rock Art Research) 2004: 136–138.

BEDNARIK, R. G. 2007a. Antiquity and authorship of the Chauvet rock art. *Rock Art Research* 24: 21–34.

BEDNARIK, R. G. 2007b. *Rock art science: the scientific study of palaeoart*. Second edtn, Aryan Books International, New Delhi.

BEDNARIK, R. G., G. ANDREWS, S. CAMERON and E. BEDNARIK 2007. Petroglyphs of Meenamatta, the Blue Tier mountains, Tasmania. *Rock Art Research* 24: 161–170.

BEDNARIK, R. G. and M. KHAN 2005. Scientific studies of Saudi Arabian rock art. *Rock Art Research* 22: 49–81.

BEDNARIK, R. G. and G. KUMAR 2002. The quartz cupules of Ajmer, Rajasthan. *Purakala* 13(1–2): 45–50.

BEDNARIK, R. G., G. KUMAR, A. WATCHMAN and R. G. ROBERTS 2005. Preliminary results of the EIP Project. *Rock Art Research* 22(2): 147–197.

BEDNARIK, R. G. and R. QUEREJAZU LEWIS in prep. The Kalatrancani and Roca Fortunato petroglyph sites, Bolivia.

CAPITAN, L. and J. BOUYSSONIE 1924. *Limeuil. Son gisement à gravures sur pierres de l'Âge du Renne*. Libraire Nourry, Paris.

CLARK, J. D. 1958. The Chifubwa Stream rock shelter, Solwezi, northern Rhodesia. *South African Archaeological Bulletin* 13(49): 21–24.

CLOTTES, J., J. COURTIN and L. VANRELL 2005. *Cosquer redécouvert*. Éditions du Seuil, Paris.

COSTAS GOBERNA, F. J., J. M. HIDALGO CUÑARRO and A. DE LA PEÑA SANTOS 1999. *Arte rupestre no sur da Ría de Vigo*. Edición do Instituto de Estudios Vigueses, Vigo.

D'ARRAGON, B. 1994. Presenza di elementi culturali sui monumenti dolmenici del Mediterraneo centrale. *Rivista di Scienze Preistoriche* 46(1): 41–85.

DELLUC, B. and G. DELLUC 1978. Les manifestations graphiques aurignaciennes sur support rocheux des environs des Eyzies (Dordogne). *Gallia Préhistoire: Fouilles et monuments archéologiques en France métropolitaine* 21(1): 213–438.

EGGER, A. 1948. Schalensteine, eine volkskundliche Studie. *Schlern-Schriften* 53: 57–80.

FOLEY, R. and M. M. LAHR 1997. Mode 3 technologies and the evolution of modern humans. *Cambridge Archaeological Journal* 7: 3–36.

FULLAGAR, R. L. K., D. M. PRICE and L. M. HEAD 1996. Early human occupation of northern Australia: archaeology and thermoluminescence dating of Jinmium rock-shelter, Northern Territory. *Antiquity* 70: 751–773.

JOULIAN, F. 1995. 'Human and non-human primates': des limites de genre bien problématiques en préhistoire. *Préhistoire Anthropologie Méditerranéennes* 4: 5–15.

KUMAR, G. 1996. Daraki-Chattan: a Palaeolithic cupule site in India. *Rock Art Research* 13: 38–46.

LARTET, A. and H. CHRISTY 1875. *Reliquae aquitanicae, being contributions to the archaeology and palaeontology of*

Perigord and the adjoining provinces of southern France. Thomas Rupert Jones, London.

Leakey, M. D. 1971. *Olduvai Gorge. Vol. 3: excavations in Beds I and II, 1960–1963.* Cambridge University Press, Cambridge.

McGrew, W. C. 1992. *Chimpanzee material culture: implications for human evolution.* Cambridge University Press, Cambridge.

McNickle, H. P. 1991. A survey of rock art in the Victoria River District, Northern Territory. *Rock Art Research* 8: 36–46.

Mandl, F. 1995. Näpfchen, Schälchen und Schalen in der ostalpinen Felsritzbildwelt. *Mitteilungen der Anisa* 16: 63–66.

Morwood, M. J. 2002. *Visions from the past: the archaeology of Australian Aboriginal art.* Allen & Unwin, Sydney.

Peyrony, D. 1918. Gravure sur pierre et godet du gisement préhistorique du Soucy. *Bulletin de la Société historique et archéologique du Périgord* 45: 143–148.

Peyrony, D. 1920. À propos de lampes et galets à cupule de l'époque magdalénienne. Résponse à l'article de M. Tarel. *Bulletin de la Société historique et archéologique du Périgord* 47: 84–89.

Peyrony, D. 1934. La Ferrassie. Moustérien, Périgordien, Aurignacien. *Préhistoire* 3: 1–92.

Rizzi, G. 1995. Schalensteine, ein vielfältiges Phänomen? Überlegungen zum Forschungsstand in Südtirol. *Mitteilungen der Anisa* 16: 78–97.

Rizzi, G. (ed.) 2007. *Schweigende Felsen: Das Phänomen der Schalensteine im Brixner Talkessel.* Sudmedia Verlag, Brixen.

Schwegler, U. 1995. Datierung von Felszeichnungen und Schalensteinen. *Mitteilungen der Anisa* 16: 99–123.

Steinbring, J. and M. Lanteigne 1991. The petroglyphs of West Yorkshire: explorations in analysis and interpretation. *Rock Art Research* 8: 13–28.

Tarel, R. 1912. L'abri-sous-roche du Soucy (près la Linde, Dordogne) (Magdalénien supérieur). Nouvelles fouilles (MM. Délugin, du Soulas et Tarel). *L'Homme préhistoire* 5: 129–139, 6: 161–180.

Tarel, R. 1919. À propos de lampes et galets à cupule de l'époque magdalénienne. *Bulletin de la Société historique et archéologique du Périgord* 46: 67–71.

van Peer, P., R. Fullager, S. Stokes, R. M. Bailey, J. Moeyersons, F. Steenhoudt, A. Geerts, T. Vanderbeken, N. De Dapper and F. Geus 2003. The Early to Middle Stone Age transition and the emergence of modern behaviour at site 8-B-11, Sai Island, Sudan. *Journal of Human Evolution* 45(2): 187–193.

CUPULES IN QATAR: POTENTIAL FOR DETERMINING MINIMUM AGES

Marvin W. Rowe and Brandon Chance

Abstract. About 60 kilometres north of the capital city of Doha, Qatar, lays a petroglyph site with over 900 motifs. By far the most common petroglyphs are cupules, usually arranged in geometric patterns. Because there is little evidence to assign them to ages as old as 3000 years or more, or as young as a few hundred years old, we propose here a means of determining the lower limit on the age.

Keywords: Petroglyph, Limestone, Cupule, Meaning, Dating, Radiocarbon, Oxygen plasma, Qatar

Introduction

As elsewhere, for the Arabian peninsula the development of prehistoric research and its relevance for anthropology are strictly related to the capacity of recovering the indicators of chronology and subsistence from contextual associations of the primary layout. The poor consistency of the deposits and the devastating effects of erosion on the exposed surfaces have made the recovery of organic remains problematic everywhere.
....
A chronological skeleton remains, however, the priority issue, emphasized of course by the general scarcity of organic remains in safe context (Tosi 1986).

The Middle Eastern emirate of Qatar is a very small desert state, a peninsula extending off Saudi Arabia northerly into the Arabian Gulf (formerly the Persian Gulf). Figure 1 is a map of the Middle East with Qatar outlined by a box. Figure 2 shows a map of a closer view of Qatar. An arrow points out the approximate position of the petroglyphs discussed here.

Petroglyphs: cupules dominate

Initially, petroglyphs in Qatar were 'discovered' by Glob (1957). Virtually all the introductory and general material reported here about the petroglyphs, however, is taken from Nayeem's (1998) and Rice's (1994) books. Much is written, but little is known beyond a cataloguing of the petroglyphs, and some suppositions about the function of the petroglyphs that were ultimately rejected by both these authors. The petroglyphs

Figure 1. A map of the Middle East emphasising the position of Qatar, in the Arabian Gulf region (in the box).

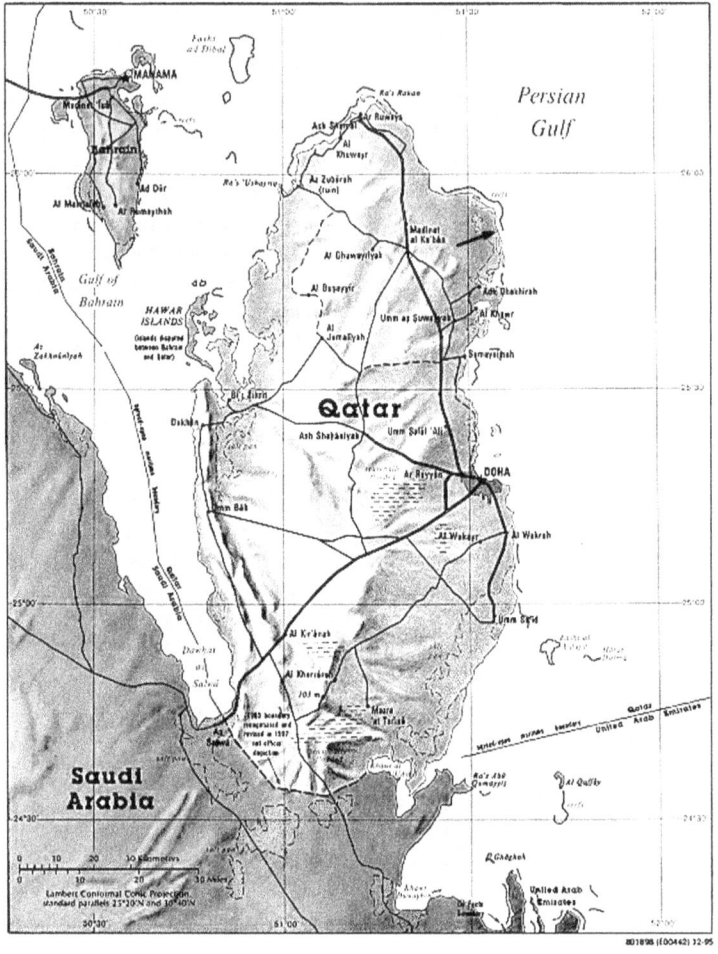

Figure 2. A map of Qatar. The approximate location of the Jabal Al Jassasiyah rock art site is shown by an arrow in the northeastern corner of Qatar.

are about 60 kilometres north of the capital city of Doha, nominally between the small villages of Safiyaa Fuwairit, Al Marrawnah and Al Huwailah. There are more than 900 petroglyphs of different figures carved on low-lying limestone outcrops (called *jabals*) among the sand dunes at the Jabal Jassasiyah site (Nayeem 1998). The rock art is carved on these more or less flat, parallel *jabals*. The outcrops are subtle, never rising more than a few meters above sea level and the sand dunes in which they are found. The entire site is encompassed in an area of about 1 × 5 kilometres. Figure 3a shows a view facing east of a rock art outcrop at Jabal Jassasiyah in the lower left hand corner of the picture, with the Arabian Gulf in the background near the horizon. Figure 3b is the view to the west where *jabals* are seen in the background, as well as in the left foreground.

Looking toward the east, a large villa is seen and near the horizon, the Arabian Gulf. One can see from this photograph just how close many of the petroglyphs are to the seashore — i.e. only about 0.5 to 3 kilometres from the Gulf. One also gets a feeling for the general lay of the land: low sand dunes alternating with more or less parallel limestone outcrops occur among flat caliche soil and stunted scrub brush. The view to the west (on the right) is instructive as it shows the shape of the *jabals* in the foreground and the background. One can see the very low rise of the *jabals* above the surrounding caliche and sand. The Jabal Jassassiya site is the most extensive of several sites in Qatar and is considered to be the most significant. There are various kinds of petroglyphs, including different kinds of boat images, geometric patterns and animals. But, as pointed out by Querejazu Lewis (2007), 'Cupules are one of the commonest forms of rock art throughout the world'. And that is certainly true for the tiny country of Qatar; by far the most common petroglyphs in Qatar are cupules, usually in arrangements of double rows of seven to nine cupules and roseate shaped patterns made up of

Figures 3a and 3b. Petroglyphs are on the limestone outcrop in the left foreground of both photographs. The photograph on the left is facing east; the one on the right is facing west. Low sand dunes, a villa and the Gulf are in the background of the left side. Jabals *are seen in the background of the right side figure. Limestone* jabals *on both the foreground and the horizon contain petroglyphs. In our observations of the petroglyphs we could see no reason why a particular site was chosen for them. Equally good, relatively smooth* jabals *are often free of rock art.*

(usually) nine cupules around a larger cupule. The photograph in Figure 4 includes cupules that are arranged in parallel rows as well as in a typical roseate form, this one with eight smaller cupules arranged in a circle around a larger central depression. R. G. Bednarik (pers. comm.) commented: 'The arrangements of cupules you mention ("rosettes", connected cupules) are very common in the southernmost parts of Saudi Arabia, where they occur in "fairly oldish" contexts. Yours, on the other hand, are clearly rather recent, being on limestone'. The paired cupules are far more numerous here than the average. There are also numerous apparently randomly placed cupules and a pair connected by a line. It appears that someone has been 'cleaning' these few petroglyphs as they appear devoid of the patina seen in all other areas — except in a few others that have also been 'cleaned'. Whether the 'cleaning' was physical or chemical is unknown at this time. Other examples occur for all these forms. Overall, cupules vary in size from ~1–25 cm in diameter and ~1–15 cm in depth.

Figure 4. Several groupings of cupules are depicted. Examples of several common motifs are shown: (i) paired parallel lines of cupules; (ii) circled smaller cupules around a central one, sometimes larger and sometimes similar size to the outside ones; (iii) cupules connected by grooves. Notice that this panel has been 'cleaned' for reasons and by techniques unknown to the authors.

The large basins you illustrate are clearly Kamenitza (*kamenitsa, kamenica, Opferkessel, Verwitterungswanne,* solution pan, pan hole, *tinajita, Kamenitza, lakouva, ythrolakkos, bljudce, cuenco, tinajita, erime tavasi, skalne kotlice, scalba, skalnica*), a typical karst phenomenon which archaeologists in the past claimed to be man-made and used for sacrifices. But this also occurs on non-carbonate rocks in various forms, including sandstone and granite. It occurs even on Uluru [Australia] (Bednarik, pers. comm.).

The next series of photographs shows some of the variety in the cupules.

Other possible cupules, larger than average for the site, but much smaller than the *Kamenitza* in Figure 5 are represented by the one shown in Figure 6. The grass and weeds were a new addition following a recent rain. Figure 7 shows a rectangle surrounded by cupules and a roseate form on the right along with more rectangular forms. Rectangular forms similar to the ones shown are rare. Figure 8 shows four cupules, the upper one larger than the others that are arranged in what could be described as a two-dimensional representation of a tetrahedron with the cupules forming the four corners. And finally, Figure 9 illustrates one of several images that feature a cupule with lines radiating outward in a downhill direction.

Figure 5. Large Kamenitza. The villa in the background on the Gulf is the same one seen in Figure 3. Brandon Chance is squatting to provide scale.

Figure 6. One of the few known larger cupules at this site, along with a single smaller one on the right.

Figure 7. One of the few known rectangular petroglyphs at the site, associated with a 'circle' of cupules surrounding one (on the left centre) and the others nearby, a roseate form with a larger cupule surrounded by nine smaller ones.

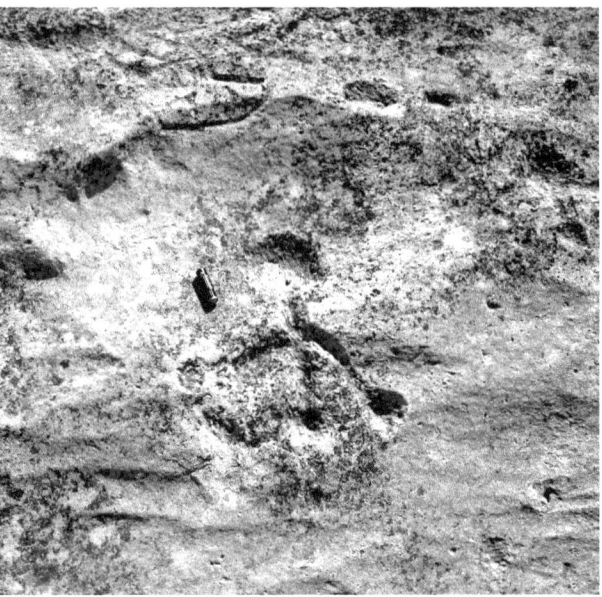

Figure 8. A photograph showing four cupules connected by grooves in a geometric shape that is reminiscent of a two-dimensional form of a tetrahedron. An AA battery is included for scale.

In an attempt to understand the meaning of the cupules in Qatar, three main propositions have been forwarded (Rice 1994): (1) That they represent a 'proliferation of vulvas'; (2) that they 'were boards for playing the game called in Arabia *huwais*, but which is known throughout the world under different names and many forms' and (3) that they 'were associated in some way with the pearl trade', possibly used to sort the pearls. Rice, however, rejects them all with convincing arguments. He also noted, as we have seen by our own observations, that 'They [the petroglyphs] seem to be distributed at random over the surface of the little hills; they appear to follow no evident orientation, neither solar, lunar or stellar'.

Ages of the petroglyphs

The ages of these features are thought to lie somewhere in the range from perhaps 3000 years old up to only a few hundred years old. But as Nayeem (1998) wrote, 'In Qatar there is no evidence of any kind to date these scores of cup-marks found as [sic] several places'. And this conclusion is fully supported by Rice (1994). But similar carved rows elsewhere are thought to be as old as the 15th century B.C.E.; we do not know how the antiquity of the latter was arrived at. Similar cupules in neighbouring Bahrain are considered to derive from the third millennium B.C.E. Again, we do not know how the antiquity of these was arrived at. However, the limestone outcrops on which the Qatari petroglyphs are made are soft and may likely erode rapidly, especially in view of the frequent sandstorms that occur in Qatar. If the latter is true, then a very long antiquity is unlikely. And probably the same could be said for the *jabals* in the neighbouring countries as well.

Potential for determining minimum ages

In many desert areas around the world, calcium oxalate (usually admixed with newly formed calcium carbonate [calcite]) forms anew as a layer over any carved figure. Numerous attempts have been made to constrain the ages of rock art using radiocarbon analysis of the oxalates (Edwards et al. 1998; Gillespie 1997; Rowe and Steelman 2003; Russ et al. 1995, 1999, 2000; Steelman et al. 2002; Watchman 1990, 1991; Watchman et al. 2000).

A schematic representation for the minimum age dating process is shown in Figure 10. While the exact mechanism for the production of oxalates is still unknown, there seems to be consensus that it forms from ambient carbon dioxide. That means that the carbon can be used to provide age information of associated rock art. Before the era of the petroglyph, the surface of limestone weathers, and an oxalate crust forms, often mixed with more abundant calcite (calcium carbonate). In Figure 10a, we depict a bare limestone surface that has aged with the formation of an oxalate-containing crust covering the entire surface. In Figure 10b, we see the effect of creating a cupule: the cupule is carved into limestone, removing the oxalate crust. From that time on, however, the weathering process again deposits oxalates onto all exposed surfaces. Then, at the present time, a sample is taken of the crust that has developed over the cupule surface (Figure 10c). Because the oxalate is on top of the surface of the petroglyph, it must have formed more recently than the freshly carved surface. In addition, the oxalate radiocarbon age is an average of the time of deposit of the new oxalate layer, presumably starting soon after the petroglyph was made and continuing up to the present time. These two factors mean that the age determined is a minimum age and is not directly related to the age of the rock art, i.e., the time it was created. But it can constrain the age. In an area where no idea of the ages is known, even such minimum ages would possibly yield useful information.

Figure 9. A photograph showing one of a few cupules that has radiating lines coming out. The radiating lines generally follow a downhill direction. There is an IFRAO Scale partially covered by a rock between the two right-most lines.

But are oxalates present in the cupules?

To investigate whether oxalates were present in this area, we took two samples from the limestone surface about a metre from two different petroglyphs separated by perhaps a hundred metres, to determine the presence or absence of oxalates. For the analysis, we used a Fourier Transform Infrared (FTIR) — Attenuated Total Reflectance (ATR) spectrometer. The instrument is a Perkin Elmer Spectrum One FTIR Spectrometer, Serial Number 9700, with Universal ATR Sampling Accessory. Spectra were taken using a 3 bounce diamond/zinc selenide crystal. The spectra were collected for four scans in the range 4000 – 650 cm^{-1} with a resolution of 4 cm^{-1}. One of the two samples contained evidence of calcium oxalate and that spectrum, shown in Figure 11, shows distinct negative 'peaks' that are attributable to the calcium oxalate on the limestone surface. Thus minimum dating of at least some the petroglyphs appears feasible.

Dating procedure

Thus, to actually obtain a minimum (radiocarbon) age of a

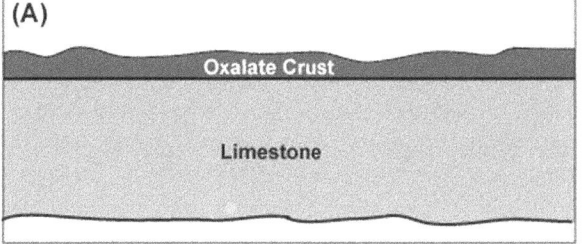

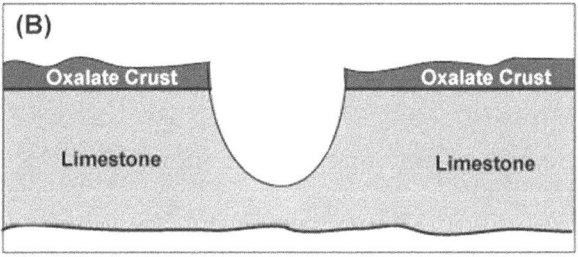

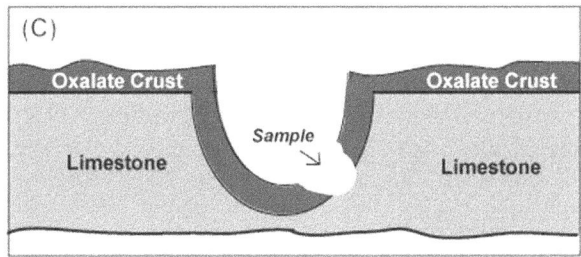

Figure 10. A schematic diagram depicting the process of deposit formation on a petroglyph. The oxalate that forms over a petroglyph and collects over time provides us the sample for radiocarbon dating. Its date gives a minimum age of the petroglyph.

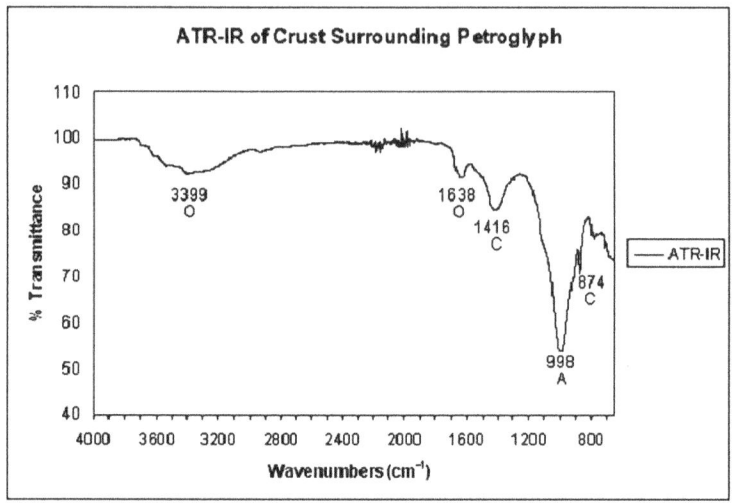

Figure 11. An FTIR-ATP analysis demonstrates the presence of calcium oxalate as marked on the figure. Here on the figure, O stands for calcium oxalate, C stands for calcite (calcium carbonate) and A stands for the rock mineral, apatite, $Ca_5(PO_4)_3(F,Cl,OH)$.

petroglyph, a sample taken by scraping the surface oxalate layer of the petroglyph must be acquired. We will limit this discussion to petroglyphs, although the same reasoning and procedure applies to paintings that have oxalate coatings. A very small aliquot of the powdered sample can be used to once again confirm that oxalates are present in the collected sample as described above. Then it is necessary to remove any carbonates that may be present in the sample (and they usually are, in amounts much greater than oxalates). That we can do by dissolving the calcium carbonate in 0.1 to 1 molar phosphoric acid (H_3PO_4). Phosphoric acid dissolves all calcium carbonate that is present in the sample, but leaves the calcium oxalate behind as an undissolved solid. Then the phosphoric acid/oxalate sample is filtered to remove and save the solid oxalates. The solid filtrate is washed well with doubly distilled, de-ionised water and dried in an oven at ~ 100°C. The solid may then be placed into a cold oxygen plasma (see Russ et al. 1990; Rowe 2005; 2007) to remove any organic contamination of the sample. Alternatively, it can also be cleaned in an oven exposed to the atmosphere at >250°C, usually overnight. At that point one is left with pure oxalate mineral (with only associated inorganic minerals that have no effect on the radiocarbon analysis). The sample is then sent to an accelerator mass spectrometer for radiocarbon dating. As mentioned before, that measurement yields a minimum age for two reasons: the sample was taken from over the carved surface, so the oxalate only began to form after the clean new surface was exposed. Because the oxalate may be deposited from the time of creation into modern times, the 'age' obtained for the oxalate will be a weighted 'average' that is less than the true age of the petroglyph. Researchers have been successful in obtaining such constraining dates from oxalates associated with rock art (Rowe and Steelman 2003; Russ et al. 1995, 1999, 2000; Steelman et al. 2002; Watchman 1991;

Watchman et al. 2000).

Conclusion

We found that one of two weathered surfaces of limestone in Qatar near cupules contain dateable calcium oxalate. The experimental procedure is well known and has been tested. We have just received permission from the proper Qatari authorities to sample some of the cupule surfaces to see whether oxalate crusts are common; if so, we will follow those analyses for oxalate with radiocarbon dating.

Acknowledgments

We thank Texas A&M University — Qatar for their support of this project. We are indebted to Lallah Howard, Lacey Martin, Kathleen Rowe; and Hans, Daniela, Josia and Rachel Schrodl for assistance in finding and photographing the various carved images at the Jabal Jassasiyah site.

REFERENCES

BEDNARIK, R. G. 2001 (2007). *Rock art science: the scientific study of palaeoart*. Brepols, Turnhout (2nd edn Aryan Books International, New Delhi).

EDWARDS, H. G. M., L. DRUMMOND and J. RUSS 1998. Fourier-transform Raman spectrometric study of pigments in native American Indian rock art: Seminole Canyon. *Spectrochimica Acta* A54: 1849–1856.

GILLESPIE, R. 1997. On human blood, rock art and calcium oxalate: further studies on organic carbon content and radiocarbon age of materials relating to Australian rock art. *Antiquity* 71: 430–437.

GLOB, P. V. 1956. *Reconnaissance in Qatar*. Kuml.

GLOB, P. V. 1957. *Prehistoric discoveries in Qatar*. Kuml.

KAPEL, H. 1983. *Rock carvings at Jabel Jusasiyah, Qatar*. Arrayan 8.

NAYEEM, M. A. 1998. *Qatar: prehistory and protohistory from the most ancient times (ca. 1,000,000 to end of B.C. era)*. Hyberadad Publishers, Hyberadad.

QUEREJAZU, R. 2007. Dialogues (3): Cupules in rock art. *La Pintura* 33: 4–5.

RICE, M. 1994. *The archaeology of the Arabian Gulf, c. 5000–323 BC*. Routledge, New York.

ROWE, M. W. 2005. Dating studies of prehistoric pictographs in North America. In L. L. Loendorf, C. Chippendale and D. S. Whitley (eds), *Discovering North American rock art*, pp. 240–263. University of Arizona Press, Tucson.

ROWE, M. W. 2007. Reflections on dating of rock art. In P. Chenna Reddy (ed.), *Exploring the mind of ancient man: Festschrift to Robert G. Bednarik*, pp. 218–231. Research India Press, New Delhi.

ROWE, M. W. and K. L. STEELMAN 2003. Comment on 'Some evidence of a date of first humans to arrive in Brazil'. *Journal of Archaeological Science* 30: 1349–1351.

RUSS, J., R. L. PALMA, D. H. LOYD, D. W. FARWELL and H. G. M. EDWARDS 1995. Analysis of the rock accretions in the Lower Pecos region of southwest Texas. *Geoarchaeology*

10: 43–63.

Russ, J., W. D. Kaluarchi, L. Drummond and H. G. M. Edwards 1999. The nature of a whewellit-rich rock crust associated with pictographs in SW Texas. *Studies in Conservation* 44: 91–103.

Russ, J., D. H. Loyd and T. W. Boutton 2000. A paleoclimate reconstruction for southwestern Texas using oxalate residue from lichen as a paleoclimate indicator. *Quaternary International* 67: 29–36.

Steelman, K. L., R. Rickman, M. W. Rowe, T. W. Boutton, J. Russ and N. Guidon 2002. Accelerator mass spectrometry radiocarbon ages of an oxalate accretion and rock paintings at Toca do Serrote da Bastiana, Brazil. In K. A. Jakes (ed.), Archaeological chemistry VI: materials, methods, and meaning, pp. 22–35. American Chemical Society 831, Washington, DC.

Tosi, M. 1986. The emerging picture of prehistoric Arabia. *Ann. Rev. Anthropol.* 15: 461–490.

Watchman, A. 1990. A summary of occurrences of oxalate-rich crusts in Australia, *Rock Art Research* 7: 44–50.

Watchman, A. 1993. Evidence of a 25,000-year-old pictograph in northern Australia. *Geoarchaeology* 8: 465–473.

Watchman, A. 1991. Age and composition of oxalate-rich crusts in the Northern Territory, Australia. *Studies in Conservation* 36: 24–32.

Watchman, A., P. Taçon, R. Fullagar and L. Head 2000. Minimum ages for pecked rock markings from Jinmium, north western Australia. *Archaeology of Oceania* 35: 1–10.

LOWER PALAEOLITHIC CUPULES OBTAINED FROM THE EXCAVATIONS AT DARAKI-CHATTAN IN INDIA FROM 2002 TO 2006

Giriraj Kumar

Abstract. Daraki-Chattan is a Palaeolithic cupule site in the Chambal basin in India. It is a small cave in the quartzite buttresses of Indragarh hill. It bears more than 500 cupules on its two walls and yielded Lower Palaeolithic artefacts from its floor surface. The front portions of both its walls are heavily exfoliated and are mostly devoid of cupules. These exfoliated cupule-bearing slabs and some of the hammerstones used for their production should be present in the sediments in front of the cave. Hence in order to test the antiquity of the cupule creation in the cave, excavations were carried out at Daraki-Chattan under the direction of Giriraj Kumar since 2002 to 2006. These excavations were the major part of the EIP Project ('Early Indian Petroglyphs: Scientific Investigations and Dating by International Commission'). It was commenced under the direction of Giriraj Kumar (RASI) and Robert G. Bednarik (AURA), the Indian and Australian directors of the project in 2001 and will continue for some more years into future. The excavations yielded slab pieces bearing twenty-nine cupules throughout the vertical depth of the cultural sediments of Lower Palaeolithic Age in the excavation. Besides, we also obtained hammerstones used for their production, and some linear form of petroglyphs. The paper presents the obtained evidence of Lower Palaeolithic petroglyphs from the excavation and their study.

Keywords: Lower Palaeolithic, Cupule, Excavation, EIP Project, Hammerstone, Daraki-Chattan, India

Introduction

Cupules are a simple form of human visual creations. They have the longest tradition of their continuity, right from the beginning of human cultures and up to the modern period in some of the tribal cultures. They are found generally in circular forms, sometimes in oval, elongated and conical forms also. Their creation is easy on soft rocks, but it becomes a very tedious and time-consuming task when executed on very hard rocks like quartzite and quartz.

Most of the literature on rock art presents Upper Palaeolithic rock paintings and finger flutings in the European caves as the earliest rock art in the world. But the evidence from central India has changed this perception. Early petroglyph sites have been discovered in the Vindhyas, Aravallis and in Chambal valley in central India during the last fifteen years. Mention may be made of the Auditorium Cave, Bhimbetka, Daraki-Chattan, Bajanibhats, Moda Bhata and other hill series in greater Ajmer. Out of these, Daraki-Chattan is the most important and has been excavated under the EIP project for five seasons from 2002 to 2006. It yielded slab pieces bearing twenty-nine cupules and a boulder with two engraved lines from Lower Palaeolithic sediments. Besides, the excavations have also produced hammerstones used to create cupules. It is an unambiguous evidence of extraordinary significance to world archaeology. It is going to rewrite the history of cognitive and cultural evolution of hominins

Daraki-Chattan

Daraki-Chattan is an extraordinary Palaeolithic cupule site in the Chambal basin in India (Figure 1). It is a small cave located in the upper strata of the quartzite buttresses on Indragarh hill. The cave is of tapered shape, both in its depth and height. It is 4.0 m wide at the dip line, and 1.4 m wide at its mouth (Figures 2 and 3). From here it continuously narrows down in width, to 34 cm at a depth of 7.4 m, it then becomes slightly wider, up to 40 cm, and finally closes at a depth of 8.4 m from its mouth. The cave is maximal 7.75 m in height. It bears more than 500 cupules on its both the walls (Figures 4 and 5) and yielded Lower Palaeolithic

Figure 1. Map of central India with principal early petroglyph sites: 1-Bajanibhat, 2- Modabhata, 3-Morajhari, 4-Daraki-Chattan (the early Palaeolithic cupule site excavated under the EIP Project), 5-Bhimbetka, 7-Raisen, and early human fossil site 6-Hathnora. Drawn by R. G. Bednarik.

Figure 2. A part of Indragarh hill with Daraki-Chattan in the centre of the buttresses. Photo by R. G. Bednarik.

Figure 3. Daraki-Chattan Cave.

artefacts from its floor surface.

Daraki-Chattan Cave was discovered by Ramesh Kumar Pancholi in 1993 (Pancholi 1994: 75) and was scientifically studied by Giriraj Kumar, assisted by his son Ramkrishna in 1995 (Kumar 1995). On the basis of archaeological remains obtained from the surface of the cave, cupule patterns and patination on them, Kumar claimed that the cupules in the cave belong either to the late phase of Lower Palaeolithic or the transitional phase of Lower Palaeolithic-Middle Palaeolithic (Kumar 1995). The same antiquity was also claimed for the Palaeolithic cupules discovered in 1990s and onwards first at Bhimbetka (Bednarik 1993), later at Bajanibhats, Moda Bhata and other sites on the same grounds (Kumar 1995). It brought a paradigm shift

Figure 4. *Southern wall of Daraki-Chattan Cave bearing cupules; also visible are the scars of the exfoliated cupule slabs in the front half of the wall.*

in rock art research in India (Figure 1). Their antiquity was claimed going back to the Lower Palaeolithic and Middle Palaeolithic age. It was a bold and extraordinary claim at that time (Kumar 2000–2001: 49–68).

The data reported from India contradict a great deal of the current model of Pleistocene archaeology. If they were being interpreted correctly, they would rewrite the history of cognitive and cultural evolution of hominins, just as the Pleistocene evidence of seafaring has recently revised the technological paradigm. It has become apparent that the language should be at least a million years old, and that a largely modern form of human cognition might have developed during the reign of *Homo erectus*. Most of the evidence these new data claims comes from the general area of southern Asia.

In view of their extraordinary importance to world archaeology, it was essential that the claims concerning India's extremely early petroglyphs be examined thoroughly and critically. It laid the foundation for the intensive and multidisciplinary research on early Indian petroglyphs with international collaboration through the EIP Project

The EIP Project

The EIP Project is a high profile multidisciplinary project on 'Early Indian Petroglyphs: Scientific Investigations and dating by International Commission'. It is a joint venture by the Rock Art Society of India (RASI) and Australian Rock Art Research Association (AURA) under the aegis of the International Federation of Rock Art Organisations (IFRAO). It was established by Giriraj Kumar, President, RASI and Robert G. Bednarik, President, AURA as the joint Project Directors in 2000 in Alice Springs, Australia. The work of the EIP Project has enjoyed the support from the Archaeological Survey of India, the Indian Council of Historical Research and the Australia-India Council. The Commission is to investigate all matters concerning the very early rock art of India including that of Daraki-Chattan thoroughly, using methods such as carbon isotope analysis, optically stimulated luminescence dating, microerosion analysis, uranium-thorium analysis and archaeological excavation. The Commission consists of geologists, archaeologists, rock art scientists and archaeometrists from India and Australia.

The fieldwork of the EIP Project was commenced in mid-2001 by Kumar and several colleagues and accelerated in

Figure 5. Cupules on the southern wall of Daraki-Chattan.

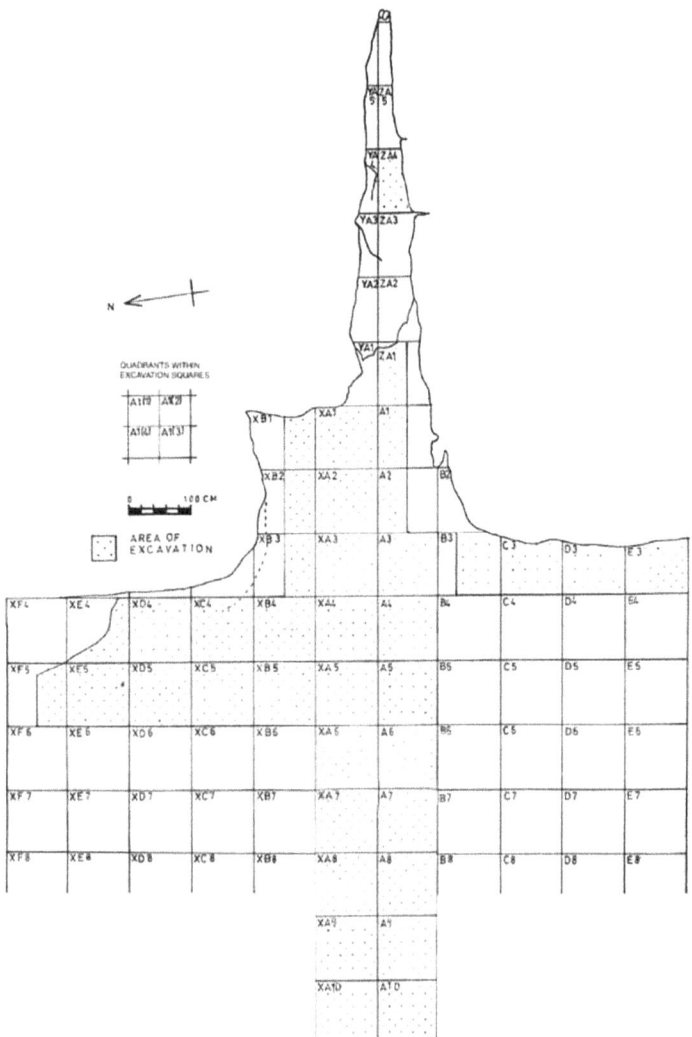

Figure 6. Floor plan of Daraki-Chattan Cave, with excavation squares indicated and the extent of the excavation shown.

the following years with an intensive campaign involving several specialists. A project web-page was established by Robert Bednarik at *http://mc2.vicnet.net.au/home/eip1/web/index.html*. The first tangible findings were presented at the RASI-IFRAO Congress in Agra at the end of November 2004 and have been published in 2005 (Kumar et al. 2002; Kumar et al. 2005; Bednarik et al. 2005), but fieldwork has continued, and will take several more years to complete.

Excavations at Daraki-Chattan, 2002 to 2006

The excavations at Daraki-Chattan form the major part of the EIP Project. The front portions of both the walls of Daraki-Chattan are heavily exfoliated and are mostly devoid of cupules (Figure 4). These exfoliated cupule-bearing slabs and some of the hammerstones used for their production were expected to occur buried in the sediments in front of the cave. Hence, in order to test the antiquity of the cupule creation in the cave, excavations were carried out at Daraki-Chattan under the direction of Giriraj Kumar since 2002 to 2006. Narayan Vyas was the official representative of the Archaeological Survey of India and was nominated as the co-director of the excavation. The area excavated was 33 square metres (Figure 6).

Stratigraphy

The excavations at Daraki-Chattan exposed sediments up to a depth of 311 cm from A1 in the main trench (Figure 7). The sediments slope towards west by 150 cm over a distance of 5 m, i.e. up to XB6(2). The nature of the sediments so far exposed in the excavations is fairly uniform with gradations of colour, size of the exfoliated flakes, stones, blocks and slabs. However, for convenience of study the sediments have been divided broadly into two parts, a lower deposit with pseudo-layers 6, 5 and 4; and an upper deposit with pseudo-layers 3, 2 and 1 (see Figure 8 and Table 1).

1. Lower deposit: The lowermost sediment is lateritic red soil that became slightly loose because of rainwater. It grades into the following compact brownish red soil and again into compact calcareous yellowish-brown soil (pseudo-layers 6, 5 and 4). These sediments also comprise fallen large slabs and stone blocks. Most of these slabs have been weathered deeply and became highly patinated with dark-brown mineral accretion. Such weathered rocks

Layer No.	Layer thickness	Nature	Associated cultural material
1	A few cm to 10 cm	Surface humus	Artefacts representing transitional phase from Lower Palaeolithic to Middle Palaeolithic
2	15–24 cm including layer 1	Loose brown soil	
3	37–110 cm	Loose brown soil with exfoliated flakes and stones	Lower Palaeolithic flake artefacts, some on pebbles and cobbles (Figure 10).
4	26–50 cm	Compact calcareous yellowish-brown soil	Lower Palaeolithic flake tools along with artefacts on pebbles and cobbles. Cupules, petroglyphs and arranged stones
5	25–28 cm	Compact brownish-red soil	Lower Palaeolithic. More artefacts on quartzite cobbles (Figure 9), pebbles and thick nodules, some also on natural flakes, split pebbles and humanly-made flakes on quartzite, a few on chert also. Rare occurrence of handaxe-like artefacts, only one cleaver, some hammerstones and slabs bearing cupules. Patinated chert flakes and artefacts continued. Hammerstones found from the upper part of the red laterite soil, layer 6, overlain by layer 5 (18-06-05)
6	25–76 cm	Comparatively loose lateritic red soil	Artefacts on quartzite cobbles and pebbles, some also on natural and human made flakes and split pebbles, a few on chert were also obtained from the upper part of the red laterite soil, layer 6, overlain by layer 5 (18-06-05). Otherwise most of the lower portion of this lateritic red soil is devoid of stone artefacts. It corroborates the evidence of Lower Palaeolithic artefacts obtained from only upper layer of laterite deposit at Barodia-Navali crossing (*Fanta*) on Gandhisagar road.

*Table 1. Stratigraphy and associated tool typology (section facing south, main trench).
Note: Layers 1 and 2 are visible only in the area of XB3 and XB4 and are almost indistinguishable.*

Figure 7. Section facing south exposed in the excavation of Daraki-Chattan Cave, 2006.

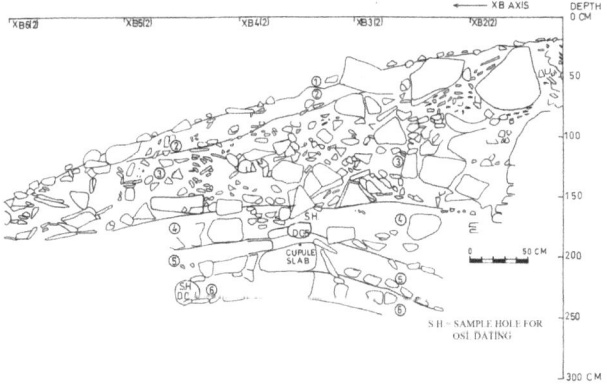

Figure 8. Daraki-Chattan excavations: section map facing south with pseudo-layer markings, 2005.

are locally known as *barbarya bhata*. These sediments bear Lower Palaeolithic artefacts. Their stratigraphic-typological variation has been given in Table 1.

2. Upper deposit: It is composed of loose brown sediment with exfoliated flakes and stones, generally of comparatively small size and progressively of lower number. It consists of the upper three pseudo-layers (3, 2 and 1). The top 20 to 24 cm sediment grades into greyish-brown pseudo-layer 2 and thin humus layer 1. At places, pseudo-layers 1 and 2 have been washed away by rainwater.

Observations

Excavations have proved that Daraki-Chattan cave is a Lower Palaeolithic site. Initially it was used by humans using artefacts made on big quartzite cobbles and pebbles, a few on flakes, both natural and humanly-made. Patinated chert flakes are also found. Stratigraphically these were obtained from the upper part of layer 6 of lateritic soil, and a portion of layer 5 of compact dark-brown soil immediately lying on layer 6. Artefacts are highly patinated and weathered. Handaxes or cleavers were absent.

In the second phase in layer 5, intensity of these artefacts increases considerably. Handaxes and cleavers appear but rarely. Artefacts are patinated and comparatively less weathered. In the following layer 4 of compact calcareous yellowish-brown soil, we have discovered many artefacts, both on cores and flakes of Acheulian industry. Still the handaxes and cleavers are rare. Layers 3, 2 and 1 yielded late Acheulian industry. Artefacts are generally patinated and in mint condition. Only a few show a minor wear from transport. It means most of the artefacts were either manufactured at the site or brought here by some human agency.

Figure 9. Chopper on quartzite cobble in situ lying on bedrock.

Thus, preliminary observations indicate that the early Acheulian artefact industry is preceded stratigraphically by an industry of artefacts made on cobbles, pebbles and flakes, both natural and man-made (Figures 9 and 10). Such an early cultural horizon preceding early Acheulian bifaces stratigraphically has also been observed by V. S. Wakankar in the excavations in the Auditorium Cave at Bhimbetka (Wakankar 1975). Besides, similar observations were also made by Z. D. Ansari at Nittur (1970) and by J. Armand at Durkadi (1980) in central India.

Excavated cupules

The excavations yielded twenty-nine cupules on sixteen slab pieces exfoliated from the cave wall throughout the vertical depth of the cultural sediments of Lower Palaeolithic age. Generally cupules obtained from the lower layers are heavily patinated and weathered as compared to those obtained from the upper layers. Their diameter ranges between 30.7 mm to 51.9 mm and depth between 4.7 mm to 8.8 mm.

Excavated cupules, 2002

Many slab pieces were recovered from squares A2, XA2, XA1 and A1, distributed mostly around point A2 at depth -26 cm to -43 cm from A2 (-38 cm to -55 cm from A1). Out of these, seven fragments joined perfectly to form a slab measuring 95 × 50 × 5–10 cm (Figure 11). Its three big pieces bore seven cupules. One of its large pieces was covering a portion of another one in the excavation. These were found with a southward orientation at an inclination of nearly 25°. The inclination might indicate a former hollow space below. After removing them, one more piece was discovered 10 cm below them.

Besides, four more slab pieces (including the vertical slab in the southeast corner of the trench) were found bearing

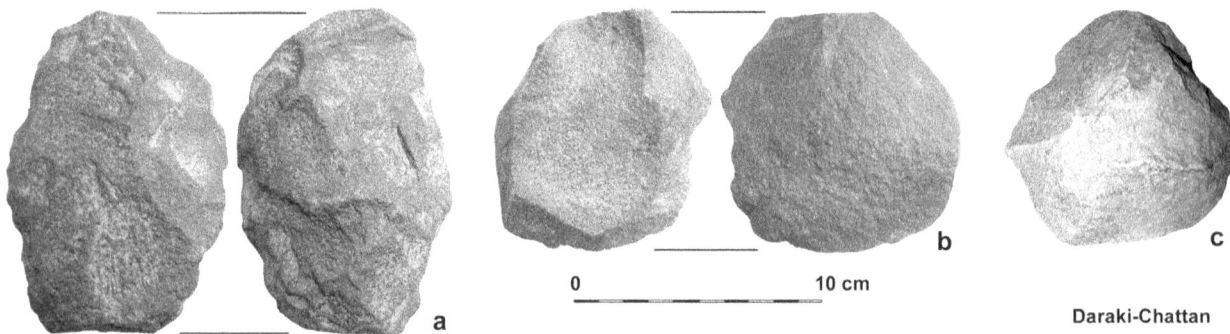

Figure 10. Other artefacts from Daraki-Chattan excavations. Photograph by R. G. Bednarik.

Figure 11. Exfoliated cupule slab, assembled from seven fragments excavated separately in Daraki-Chattan in 2002.

one cupule each. The dimensions of the cupules range from 26.1 × 29.0 × 1.85 mm to 50.5 × 51.9 × 7.4 mm. Stone artefacts representing the transitional phase from the Lower Palaeolithic to the Middle Palaeolithic were discovered both above and below these slabs

Another slab piece bearing three cupules was discovered from A2(2) at the time of collecting soil sample No. DC-1 on 27 September 2002. The soil sample was collected at a depth of -50 cm from the surface. The cupule slab fragment came out while digging horizontally into the section facing north. This fragment is roughly rectangular in shape, with one corner curved and another side obliquely cut towards the end. The maximum dimensions of the slab are 22.0 × 13.5 × 5.5/2.6 cm. The upper surface of the slab is sloping, while its lower surface is almost plain with a shallow depression in the centre. The slab piece bears three cupules:

1. At the 'left' side, 45.8 × 37.7 (broken) × 6.7 mm.
2. In the 'right' half of the slab, 41.0 × 35.0 (broken) × 8.8 mm.
3. At the extreme end of the 'upper right' corner. The cupule is broken, only one-quarter of it remains. It is 16.0 mm deep.

Excavated cupules, 2003

1. A piece of cupule-bearing slab was found in XB(3) at depth –63 cm to -70 cm from A1. It is 18 × 16 cm in size and was inclined towards north. It bears two deep cupules and two shallow ones. It comes from slightly below the level from which cupule slabs were obtained from the Daraki-Chattan excavation last year. Stone artefacts obtained from around it were of quartzite. In the month of December 2003, a team of Stone Age archaeologists, consisting of S. B. Ota, R. K. Ganjoo, G. Kumar and A. Pradhan, studied the material. The team came to the conclusion that the assemblage obtained in the excavation until 2003 represents a late Acheulian tradition. Two fine chalcedony blades were also obtained close to this slab, one from towards its east and another from towards its south. They might have sunk down from above with rainwater.

2. A small piece of cupule slab was found lying upside down in XB2(2) at a depth of -72 cm from A1. Two stone artefacts of quartzite were obtained close to it.

3. Another small slab piece with two broken cupules was obtained from XA2(1) at a locus 55 cm from XA2, 81 cm from XA3, at a depth of -85 cm from A1 (-55 cm from surface).

Excavated cupules, 2004

1. A slab piece of quartzite bearing two cupules was found upside down in XC5(1) in the adjacent rockshelter at a locus 36 cm from XC5 and 74 cm from XB5, at a depth of -17 cm from the surface (-127 cm from A1 datum), in a Lower Palaeolithic context. The cupule surface is weathered, the cupules' dimensions are as follows: cupule 1, 31.0 × 25.0 mm (broken) × 4.7 mm; cupule 2, 40.6 × 36.8 mm (broken) × 5.0 mm.

2. A small cupule slab piece of quartzite was found in XC4(1) at a locus 59 cm from XB5, 59 cm from XC5, at a depth of -36 cm from XC4 (-142 cm from A1 datum). The cupule surface is smooth and patinated. It was found in the Lower Palaeolithic level. The dimensions of the cupule slab piece are 70 × 69.4 × 20.7 mm, and those of the cupule are

Figure 12. Daraki-Chattan excavations, 2005-06: large cupule slab in situ lying close to bedrock.

Figure 13. Close up of the cupule on cupule slab of Figure 12.

30.7 × 19.2 mm (broken) × 6.4 mm.

3. An irregularly broken thick slab was found lying along the slabs of the floor along the section facing south in XA3(1)/XB3(2) on 28 May 2004). The locus of the slab is 79 cm from XB4(2), 110 cm from XA4, depth -93 cm from surface and -164 cm from A1 datum. The sediment covering it yielded four Lower Palaeolithic artefacts, out of these three were of quartzite and one of highly patinated chert. When we removed this slab, we observed two broken cupules on its patinated and slightly weathered surface. The cupules are smooth and appear to be equally patinated with a little light-brown encrustation on them. The dimensions of the slab are: upper surface 13 × 13 cm, lower surface 26 × 17 cm. It bears two cupules: cupule 1, 42.5 mm × 42.7 mm (broken) × 7.8 mm, ovoid in shape; cupule 2, 41.7 mm × 30.7 mm (broken) × 7.0 mm. A little distance from it, a multifaceted hammerstone was found.

Cup marks on slabs still lying in the main trench

On 19 June 2005 we observed a cupule on a quartzite slab projecting from the section facing south in XB3(2) (Figures 12 and 13). The locus of the cupule is 39 cm from XA3, 70 cm from XA4, 119 cm from A3, depth -129 cm from XB4 and -184 cm from A1 datum. The dimensions of the cupule are: 32 mm (broken) × 29 mm × 6 mm. The thickness of the cupule-bearing slab is 20 cm and its remaining size is 49 × 45 cm. It is resting on another slab, thus making the cupule-bearing surface 32 cm above bedrock in layer 5 (early phase). So far, it represents the earliest cupule from the Daraki-Chattan excavation. Soil sample No. DC-5 for OSL dating was collected just above this slab on 9 and 10 December 2004.

Another cupule was observed on a very big fallen slab in 2004. It is still lying in A2, A3 and A4 in layer 4 and is slanting in northwest direction. The cupule is slightly diagonal, with dimensions 32 (broken) × 34 × 16 mm. It is located just close to the section facing north, at locus 83 cm from A3, 124 cm from A4 and at depth -58 cm from surface of section facing north and -240 cm from A1 datum. The remaining slab size is 118 × 93 × 34 cm.

Hammerstones

The excavations also produced ten hammerstones used for the production of cupules. They are mostly on quartzite cobbles, some on pebbles with hard dark-red core.

A hammerstone fragment of a quartzite river cobble in XA2 (2) is from a locus 53 cm from XA2(3), 28 cm from XA2(2), at depth -37 cm from A1. It has a broad striking surface, which has been worn smooth by impact, obtained just 5 cm below the two major Acheulian artefacts in the same quadrant. It was found on 8 June 2002. The same sort of smooth crushed surface on hammerstones has been produced in the replication of cupule production.

Figure 14. An early hammerstone obtained from close to bedrock in the eastern part of the trench in Daraki-Chattan. Lower Palaeolithic.

A big sturdy hammerstone of quartzite from XA1(2) at a locus 50 cm from XA1, 50 cm from XA2, at depth -63 cm from the surface and A1 datum was discovered on 28 May 2003. In the same year, a second hammerstone of quartzite used for cupule production was also found. It had been split after use to produce a secondary artefact, and occurred in XA1(2), 70 cm from XA1, 85 cm from XA2, at depth -127 cm from A1 (Figure 14). It was lying just on the bedrock; hence it represents one of the earliest evidence of cupule production in the cave. It was discovered on 16 June 2003. This level yielded a rich concentration of Lower Palaeolithic artefacts; one of them is a 30-cm-long flake of quartzite.

Five more hammerstones were recovered in 2004. In XA3(1), a pointed hammerstone of quartzite from the Lower Palaeolithic floor level was left in situ for inspection by members of the EIP Commission, and removed in their presence. It comes from layer 4 and was found 5 cm from XA3, 96 cm from XA4, at depth -111 cm from surface (-164 cm from A1 datum). In XA3(4)/XA4(1), a quartzite hammerstone was obtained from the extended trench at 30 cm in line from XA4 towards A4, at depth -107 cm from A1 datum. Another specimen was found in association with large Lower Palaeolithic artefacts of quartzite in XA4(1), at a locus 86 cm from A4, 65 cm from XB4(2), at depth -42 cm from the surface in XB4(2). A long quartzite hammerstone was excavated in XA3(2), in association with Lower Palaeolithic quartzite artefacts at 51 cm from XA3, 51 cm from A3, at depth -145 cm from surface (-190 cm from A1 datum). The fifth specimen found in 2004 came from XA5(1). It was a long hammerstone of quartzite, Lower Palaeolithic, also left in situ for reference. It was found 60 cm from XA5, 85 cm from XA6, at depth -67 cm from XA5.

Finally, three further hammerstones were discovered in the lower strata in 2005. The first was an example with a good battering facet obtained from XA4(3) at a depth of -10 cm to -20 cm from surface, found in loose sediment on 30 May 2005. This was followed by a hammerstone of a quartzite cobble from XC4(2) at a locus XB4 -42 cm, XC4 -80 cm depth, -40 cm from surface, found 14 cm south of a fallen big rock in the rockshelter and 8 cm below it (obtained on 3 June). The most recently secured hammerstone, also on a quartzite cobble, was found in XB4(4) at locus XB4 -80 cm, XA5 -80 cm, on 18 June. It occurred at a depth of -140 cm from XB4, where the sediment changes from lateritic red to brownish-red soil. It is another example of the hammerstone coming from the lower-most level of the cultural deposit in the excavations. Its dimensions are 97 × 81 × 64 mm. It was found along with a Lower Palaeolithic artefact made from a quartzite cobble, a haematite pigment nodule and another cobble tool. All of these four objects come from an area measuring 17 × 16 cm in XB4(4), at -132 to -140 cm depth from XB4. One more Lower Palaeolithic artefact of a quartzite flake comes from nearly 20 cm away from the hammerstone. All these artefacts were found surrounded by decomposed quartzite stone blocks (*barbarya bhatas*).

Observations

Daraki-Chattan is a unique Lower Palaeolithic cupule site in the world. More than 500 cupules on its two walls represent different phases of cupule creation in the Lower Palaeolithic, beginning in the first phase by the users of cobble tools and pebble tools, preceding the early Acheulian. This is evident from the occurrence of hammerstones and cupule slabs from the very beginning of the deposition of layer 6. The activity of cupule creation continued in the following phases of the Lower Palaeolithic also, as we have discovered twenty-nine cupules throughout the vertical depth of the sediments exposed in the excavations. Besides cupules, early humans also produced engraved linear petroglyphs. So far, we have not observed rock paintings or any other iconic form of rock art created in the cave in a terminal phase of the Pleistocene or Holocene periods.

The lack of cupules on exfoliation scars on the cave walls implies that the remaining wall cupules are of ages similar to those in the excavation. The actual age of the cupules must have been much greater than that of their archaeological-stratigraphic age, as they must have been exfoliated much later after their production on the cave wall.

Cupule surface in the cave

The thin exfoliation of the rock surface has resulted in the loss of cupule dimensions and ultimately the cupules. The loss of cupules is clearly visible on both walls of the cave. Generally, the smaller diameter and shallowness of the round cupules is because of exfoliation of the surrounding surface. Hence, any metrical analysis based on simply cupule dimensions will not help in reaching the proper conclusion.

Why younger AMS ^{14}C dates?

Why we obtained comparatively young AMS ^{14}C dates (nearly 12,000 BP) for encrustation collected from outside the cupule by Alan Watchman in 2002 (Kumar et al. 2005: 63–64) was a question to be answered scientifically. Kumar minutely studied the cave walls from 12 to 14 June 2006, and observed that the surrounding surface of the cupule has been continuously exfoliating in thin layers. Hence, the older deposits of encrustation flake off with the small-scale exfoliation of the rock surface. A new process of encrustation then commences. It has been better observed at one place on northern wall where recent deposit of encrustation is overlapping or concealing both the older and new surfaces of the rock. Deposition on the new surface means comparatively younger deposits, hence younger AMS ^{14}C dates are to be expected.

Other petroglyphs

We also found a block with two engraved lines. They are heavily patinated, bearing dark-brown patina and thick encrustation in the groove. U/Th dating of the latter will be attempted. When this block was removed, twenty Lower Palaeolithic artefacts were found from above and along its sides

Nature of the sediments

The study of the sediments in the sections exposed in the excavation indicates that most of the sedimentation at the site is due to exfoliation of the standing and overhanging rocks. A little portion of the sediment is in situ development, while a small component has been deposited by rainwater in the form of a narrow strip of loose soil particularly in the north-east corner, visible in the corner of Sq XB1(2) and XB 2(2), then in the narrow gully running slightly diagonally from south to north-west, along the side of the big and thick slab bearing a cupule. The flow of both the channels joins and then runs diagonally through XB4 from where we took soil sample DC4 for OSL dating in December 2004. That is why we are getting loose soil along this course. This narrow course of run-off water was there even before the visit of the humans to this site. That is why there is a deposit of lateritic red soil on the bedrock in the sections facing east and north in XA4, while in the section facing south in XA4 the soil is loose yellowish-red.

Activity area

The major activity area in front of the cave and in the shelter as revealed by the concentration of the Lower Palaeolithic artefacts obtained in the excavations appears to be the area covered by Sq XD4,5, XC4,5, XB3,4,5, XA1,3,4,5 and A1,4,5, in 11.5 sq m.

The extended trench in the west revealed the thick and high, step-like bedrock/slabs on bedrock approaching the cave. They grade 200 cm over a distance of 4 m.

Conclusion

For the first time in the history of world archaeology, excavations at Daraki-Chattan Cave in India have from 2002 to 2006 produced confirmed evidence of cupules and hammerstones used for their production in the Lower Palaeolithic period (Kumar et al. 2005). It also endorsed the occurrence of Lower Palaeolithic petroglyphs (a deep cupule and a meandering line) from the excavation carried out in the Auditorium cave, Bhimetka by V. S. Wakankar in 1970s, and were recognised later on by Robert G. Bednarik in 1990 (Bednarik 1993). At Daraki-Chattan, petroglyphs recovered from the excavations consist of a total of twenty-nine cupules exfoliated from the cave wall, and two linear grooves. The lack of cupules on exfoliation scars on the cave walls implies that the remaining wall cupules are of ages similar to those in the excavation. The actual age of the cupules must have been much older than that of their archaeological-stratigraphic age, as they must have been exfoliated much later after their production on the cave wall. The same relationship has been suggested for the cupules above ground in Auditorium Cave.

The recent research has shown that our understanding of art origins is rapidly changing. More than any other evidence during the last 100 years, the evidence produced by the EIP Project, especially from the excavations at Daraki-Chattan, has shown that we have misjudged the time depth of palaeoart and human cognition, creative ability and symbolism. Now the time has come to change our mindset. The evidence is so important that it is set to affect not only our concepts of Pleistocene hominin development in southern Asia, but it will influence the way we view cognitive evolution generally.

The present evidence from the Daraki-Chattan excavations has shattered the biased conception of the Eurocentric origin of art and culture beginning in the Upper Palaeolithic period. It strongly supported the view that rock art is a global phenomenon and non-iconic rock art precedes the iconic art in the Pleistocene period. In Australia, hundreds of thousands of petroglyph motifs are considered to be of Middle Palaeolithic age on technological grounds (cf. Foley and Lahr 1997). Even in Europe itself, we have at least one instance of Middle Palaeolithic rock art in the form of eighteen cupules executed on the underside of a large limestone slab placed on top of La Ferrassie burial No. 6, the grave of a Neanderthal infant (Peyrony 1934). This, however, is an isolated case, whereas in other continents, pre-Upper Palaeolithic rock art and portable palaeoart are much more common (Bednarik 1992, 1993a, 1994, 2001a, 2002a, 2003). While we have huge numbers of 'Middle Palaeolithic' rock art motifs, mostly from Australia, the incidence of Lower Palaeolithic cases remains very rare, and confirmed cases of it are limited to India.

Acknowledgments

I am sincerely thankful to Robert G. Bednarik for his guidance, co-operation and support for research in rock art with a new vision as a friend and as the co-director of the EIP Project with me.

The EIP Project is a joint venture by the Rock Art Society of India (RASI) and the Australian Rock Art Research Association (AURA) under the aegis of the International Federation of Rock art Organisations (IFRAO) and enjoying the support of Archaeological Survey of India (ASI), Indian Council of Historical Research (ICHR) and Australia-India Council, Canberra. I thank the heads and staff of these three sponsors, especially Prof. M. G. S. Narayanan, Dr R. S. Bisht and Dr R. C. Agrawal. My special thanks are due to the Director General, Archaeological Survey of India, for granting us permission for the excavation at Daraki-Chattan and for sample collection from the early Indian petroglyph and rock painting sites. We have also benefited greatly from the collaboration of Dr Narayan Vyas, Dr P. K. Bhatt, Arakhita Prahran, Dr A. Sundara, Dr S. P. Gupta, Dr R. K. Sharma, Dr Amarendra Nath, P. B. S. Sengar, Ram Krishna, Dr S. Pradhan, K. K. Muhammed, Alok Tripathi, Dr B. L. Bamboria and Dr Ashvini Kumar Sharma. I heartily thank Dr Alan Watchman and Professor Richard G. Roberts for carrying out scientific investigations of samples for AMS ^{14}C and OSL dating respectively. I also wish to thank the visiting scholars for their invaluable participation and contributions: Dr Ewan Lawson (carbon isotope analysis), Dr Carol Patterson (rock art research), Professor V. N. Misra (Pleistocene archaeology), Dr R. K. Choudhury (nuclear physics), Professor S. N. Behera (nuclear physics), R. K. Pancholi (rock art research), Dr G. L. Badam (palaeontology), Dr R. K. Ganjoo (geology), S. B. Ota (archaeology), M. L. Sharma and M. L. Meena (both rock art research). Their co-operation has greatly facilitated the success of this endeavour. My special thanks are due to my wife Gita Devi with out whose co-operation this project could not have been done smoothly.

REFERENCES

Ansari, Z. D. 1970. Pebble tools from Nittur. In S. B. Deo and M. K. Dhavalikar (eds), *Indian antiquary 4: Professor H. D. Sankalia felicitation volume*, pp. 1–7. Popular Prakashan, Bombay.

Armand, J. 1980. The Middle Pleistocene pebble tool site of Durkadi in central India. *Palaeorient* 5: 105–144.

Bednarik, R. G. 1992. Palaeoart and archaeological myths. *Cambridge Archaeological Journal* 2(1): 27–43.

Bednarik, R. G. 1993a. Palaeolithic art in India. *Man and Environment* 18(2): 33–40.

Bednarik, R. G. 1993b. About cupules. *Rock Art Research* 10(2): 138–139.

Bednarik, R. G. 1994. The Pleistocene art of Asia. *Journal of World Prehistory* 8(4): 351–375.

Bednarik, R. G. 2000/01. Early Indian petroglyphs and their global context. *Purakala* 11/12: 37–47.

Bednarik, R. G. 2001a. Cupules: the oldest surviving rock art. *International Newsletter on Rock Art* 30: 18–23.

Bednarik, R. G. 2001b. The Early Indian Petroglyphs Project (EIP). *Rock Art Research* 18(1): 72.

Bednarik, R. G. 2002a. An outline of Middle Pleistocene palaeoart. *Purakala* 13(1–2): 39–44.

Bednarik, R. G. 2003. The earliest evidence of palaeoart. *Rock Art Research* 20: 89–135.

Bednarik, R. G. and G. Kumar 2002. The quartz cupules of Ajmer, Rajasthan (with Giriraj Kumar). *Purakala* 13(1–2): 45–50.

Bednarik, R. G., G. Kumar and G. S. Tyagi 1991. Petroglyphs from central India. *Rock Art Research* 8: 33–35.

Bednarik, R. G., G. Kumar, A. Watchman and R. G. Roberts 2005. Preliminary results of the EIP Project. *Rock Art Research* 22(2): 147–197.

Chakravarty, K. K. and R. G. Bednarik 1997. *Indian rock art and its global context*. Motilal Banarsidass, Delhi and Indira Gandhi Rashtriya Manav Sangrahalaya, Bhopal.

Foley, R. and M. M. Lahr 1997. Mode 3 technologies and the evolution of modern humans. *Cambridge Archaeological Journal* 7: 3–36.

Galbraith, R. F., R. G. Roberts and H. Yoshida 2005. Error variation in OSL palaeodose estimates from single aliquots of quartz: a factorial experiment. *Radiation Measurements* 39: 289–307.

Ganjoo, R. K. and S. B. Ota 2002. EIP Project report-III: preliminary geoarchaeological study on Quaternary deposits of river Rewa near Indragarh, Madhya Pradesh. *Purakala* 13: 29–36.

Kumar, G. 1996. Daraki-Chattan: a Palaeolithic cupule site in India. *Rock Art Research* 13: 38–46.

Kumar, G. 1998. Morajhari: a unique cupule site in Ajmer District, Rajasthan. *Purakala* 9: 61–64.

Kumar, G. 2000–01. Early Indian Petroglyphs: scientific

investigations and dating by international commission, April 2001 to March 2004. *Purakala* 11/12: 49–68.

KUMAR, G. 2002. EIP Project report-I: archaeological excavation and explorations at Daraki-Chattan-2002: a preliminary report. *Purakala* 13(1–2): 5–20.

KUMAR, G. 2003. Preliminary report of the excavation at Daraki-Chattan for the session 2002–2003, for the office of the D.G. Archaeological Survey of India. Unpublished.

KUMAR, G. 2004. Preliminary report of the excavation at Daraki-Chattan for the session 2003–2004, for the office of the D.G. Archaeological Survey of India. Unpublished.

KUMAR, G. 2005. Preliminary report of the excavation at Daraki-Chattan for the session 2004–2005, for the office of the D.G. Archaeological Survey of India. Unpublished.

KUMAR, G., R. G. BEDNARIK, A. WATCHMAN, R, G. ROBERTS, E. LAWSON and C. PATTERSON 2002. 2002 progress report of the EIP Project. *Rock Art Research* 20: 70–71.

KUMAR, G. and M. SHARMA 1995. Petroglyph sites in Kalapahad and Ganesh Hill: documentation and observations. *Purakala* 6: 56–59.

KUMAR, G., R. G. BEDNARIK, A. WATCHMAN and R.G. ROBERTS 2005. The EIP Project in 2005: a progress report. *Purakala* 14–15: 13–68.

KUMAR, G., PRADYUMN, K. BHATT, A. PRADHAN and RAMKRISHNA 2006. Discovery of early petroglyphs in Chambal valley, Madhya Pradesh. *Purakala* 16: 13–34.

MISRA, V. N. 1978. The Acheulian industry of rock shelter IIIF-23 at Bhimbetka, central India — a preliminary report. *Australian Archaeology* 8: 63–106.

MURRAY, A. S. and J. M. OLLEY 2002. Precision and accuracy in the optically stimulated luminescence dating of sedimentary quartz: a status review. *Geochronometria* 21: 1–15.

PANCHOLI, R. K. 1994. Bhanpura khetra me navin shodha (Hindi). *Purakala* 5(1–2): 75.

PEYRONY, D. 1934. La Ferrassie. *Préhistoire* 3: 1–92.

SHARMA, M. L., V. KUMAR and P. T. SHARMA 1992. New rock art sites discovered in Sahibi valley, Rajasthan. *Purakala* 3: 84.

TRIVEDI, H. V. and V. S. WAKANKAR 1958–59. Excavations at Indragarh, M.P. *Indian Archaeology 1958–59: A Review*, New Delhi.

TRIVEDI, H. V. and V. S. WAKANKAR 1959–60. Excavations at Indragarh, M.P. *Indian Archaeology 1959–60: A Review*, New Delhi.

TURNEY, C. S. M., M. I. BIRD, L. K. FIFIELD, R. G. ROBERTS, M. SMITH, C. E. DORTCH, R. GRÜN, E. LAWSON, L. K. AYLIFFE, G. H. MILLER, J. DORTCH and R. G. CRESSWELL 2001. Early human occupation at Devil's Lair, southwestern Australia 50,000 years ago. *Quaternary Research* 55: 3–13.

WAKANKAR, V. S. 1975. Bhimbetka — the prehistoric paradise. *Prachya Pratibha* 3(2): 7–29.

RELEVANCE OF SITE LITHOLOGY AND TAPHONOMIC LOGIC TO CUPULES

Robert G. Bednarik

Abstract. Most reports of cupules, and for that matter other petroglyphs, fail to provide adequate information on the lithology on which the rock art occurs. The relevance of such data is explained in terms of the taphonomy and technology of the cupules, of their dating and, ultimately, their interpretation. Similarly, the principles of taphonomic logic and their application to cupule research are briefly explained. It is shown that the patterns of cupule occurrence, in any period, environment or lithology, are largely determined by their taphonomy. This renders it impossible to determine the significance of variables relating to cupules, e.g. their apparent distribution or statistics, without first consulting their taphonomy. The principles of applying taphonomic logic to cupules are briefly presented.

Keywords: Lithosphere, Rock hardness, Cupule, Taphonomy, Taphonomic logic

Hardness of the rock

Here we will review the considerations concerning the influence the lithology has on cupules, on their dimensions, their morphology, on distribution and taphonomy. To create a scientific base from which to validly speculate about the cultural roles of cupules, it is essential that these topics be explored first and the relevant variables are understood. Moreover, the lithology of cupules is certainly crucial to such subjects as their scientific dating, or age estimation, also to issues concerning their preservation and site management, as well as a host of other issues. It needs to be remembered that the perspective of, for instance, the archaeologist of cupules is only one of many. It differs significantly from that of the rock art scientist, which is perhaps midway between that of the geomorphologist and the archaeologist. Geologically, cupules and other petroglyphs are a form of biological weathering: anthropically induced weathering. And then, of course, there are the perspectives of the traditional owner or custodian of rock art, the anthropologist, the ethnographer, the semiotician, the art historian and many others who claim a stake in rock art. Thus the scientific study of rock art is a multidisciplinary task, and has relatively weak links with archaeology, a non-scientific pursuit.

I begin the task of reviewing the roles of lithology and taphonomy by considering a cupule site I named after the late Howard McNickle, who drew my attention to it in the 1980s. McNickle's Shelter is located near Wittenoom, a 'ghost town' in the Pilbara of Western Australia. This very large shelter, formed along horizontally bedded rock strata of various types, contains one of the very few painting panels of the entire Pilbara, on the underside of one of the eroding laminae. Between 0.5 m and 1 m above the floor runs a layer of mudstone for the full 50 m length of the shelter's wall. It is significantly softer than the many facies above and below it, and it was apparently this quality that attracted the production of hundreds of pit-shaped markings (Figure 1). Many of these bear distinctive tool marks, which are perfectly preserved, suggesting that these cupules may be of relatively recent ages. The tool marks, both within the cupules and in their vicinity, are readily visible at the macroscopic level, but their microscopic study reveals even more detail about the production of these features. The site is superbly suited for forensic reconstruction of the gestures involved, and if there is a scientific way to

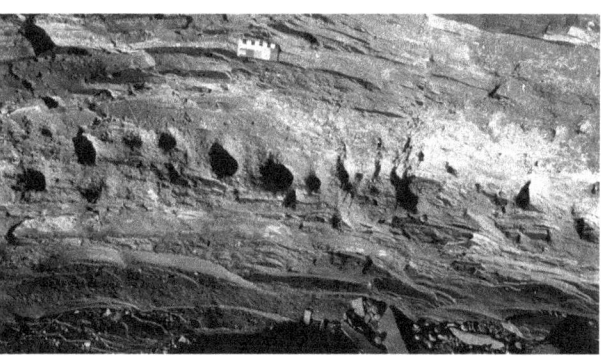

Figure 1. Vertical cupules on mudstone seam in McNickle's Shelter, Pilbara, Western Australia.

Figure 2. Impact and scraping activity marks with cupules in McNickle's Shelter.

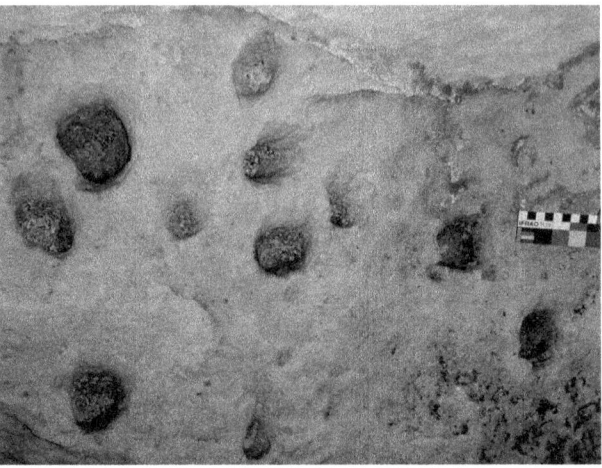

Figure 3. Deep and large cupules on exceedingly soft limestone wall of Ngrang Cave, South Australia.

determine the physical circumstances of cupule creation, such work has to be at its core.

The most obvious characteristics are the following two. In addition to the randomly arranged cupules along the narrow horizontal band of soft rock, there are also thousands of impact marks, scrape marks, incisions, and some broad abrasion marks, apparently of ages similar to those of the cupules (Figure 2). This suggests that the making of the cupules was perhaps only one aspect of behaviour manifested at the site, and that those traces would not have survived on much harder rock, or at sites that suffered extensive subsequent weathering. Secondly, the cupules are on average deeper relative to their rim diameter than they are on harder rock. There is a distinctive endeavour evident of keeping the diameter small, because on such a relatively soft medium, it would be easy to gouge deeper by allowing the hole to be larger. Therefore one of the most distinctive characteristics of these cupules is that the makers deliberately kept the diameters small, but tried to dig as deeply as possible into the rock.

Much the same has been observed also on very hard rock types, and when we test the underlying proposition by turning to examples on even softer rock, we find the same principle manifested. In the entrance part of Ngrang Cave, a limestone site in Victoria (Bednarik 1990), there are forty-five 'extraction pits' on a single wall, many of them bearing corroded but still recognisable tool marks. This rock is so workable that the holes have been gouged up to 17.5 cm deep, and they are mostly deeper than wide (Figure 3). Naturally this was not possible to achieve by direct percussion, but Yann-Pierre Montelle and I have by replication established the types of tools most likely used. What I wish to emphasise here is that these pits certainly do not look like typical sandstone or granite cupules, and some observers would probably reject their inclusion under the rubric of cupules. In my view, they were created by the very same behaviour patterns as the more 'conventional' cupules, and our definition merely refers to *our convention* of taxonomy, and not necessarily to objective classes. It is easy to become trapped in our own nomenclatures, and in this case, the CCD (crucial common denominator) of the phenomenon category (Bednarik 1994a) may well not be apparent from our preconceived idea of the concept 'cupule' (e.g. a specific diameter/depth ratio or shape or size). Instead of focusing on what we are inclined to formulate as 'the type' — which we can only base on a taphonomically distorted sample under the best possible circumstances — we need to ask: which forms of the phenomenon would be expected to be under-represented in the total available sample? We also need to ask: if we had the 'total living sample' (i.e. all cupules ever made), how would it affect our conjectures about the CCD?

Since it had become apparent to me that there might be a causal relationship between cupule depth and lithology, and since the ratio of cupule depth to rim diameter seemed to matter greatly to most cupule makers, I decided to test that relationship. Cupules are found on rocks of up to hardness 7, so I secured random samples of cupule depths from rocks ranging in hardness from very soft limestone through to massive crystalline quartz and fully metamorphosed quartzite. The result (Figure 4) seems to indicate a strong correlation: the softer the rock, the deeper the cupule, on average. While my samples may be judged too small to offer conclusiveness, and greater refinement of the method is certainly desirable, the trend is far too distinctive to ignore. Nevertheless, I believe that future work of this type should employ different criteria. In particular, we might use the ratio of diameter to depth against hardness of rock, instead of simply plotting cupule depth against hardness. With that method, we are likely to find the trend even more pronounced.

The implications of these observations are of considerable consequences to the interpretation of cupules, even to their identification. If I had had no data on cupules of the softest rock type, of hardness 1, I could have predicted their mean dimensions and ratio on the basis of the quantified trend. As the sample from Ngrang and other caves in the

Mt Gambier region shows, I would have been correct had I extrapolated the curve in Figure 4. Therefore the inclusion of these particularly large pits in the category 'cupules' is fully justified, and one can begin to formulate what appears to be a more 'objective' definition of 'cupule'. We are also beginning to realise that what we describe as cupules is essentially the result of specific behaviour patterns, and that these can, in fact, be examined scientifically. That does not mean that all things we currently call cupules were made for the same reasons, or by the same cultural behaviour or motivation, but when it comes to biokinetic behaviour, the empirical evidence narrows the possible range down quite considerably.

Specific issues of cupule lithology

A phenomenon sometimes observed in cupules requires special attention under the heading of 'lithology'. It was first commented upon in relation to a small cupule site located on the plateau above Daraki-Chattan Cave in central India, a few hundred metres north of the cave (Bednarik et al. 2005: 186). A geometric arrangement of cupules, thought to be of the Holocene, bears a remarkable laminar surface feature within each cupule. This resembles an accretionary deposit of some kind (Figure 5), yet microscopic examination excludes that possibility. The cutaneous lamina consists of the original floor of the cupule, rather than a deposited mineral crust, and is exfoliating. The rock surface surrounding the cupules has been subjected to granular exfoliation, whereas in the cupules much of the original surface at the time of their execution has been preserved through this feature. It appears as if the sustained application of kinetic energy during cupule production has somehow created a cutaneous zone that was more resistant to weathering than the unmodified surface. In a nearby palaeo-riverbed, boulders that were heavily polished by fluvial action show precisely the same phenomenon: a surface lamina that is slightly more resistant to erosion than the very dense quartzite.

Moreover, Francaviglia's (2005) photographs of cupules from Umm Singid and particularly from Jebel as-Suqur (Sudan) seem to illustrate the very same phenomenon (Francaviglia 2005: Figs 2, 7, and especially the close-up in Figure 5). I have observed a similar instance of cutaneous consolidation in cupules in northern Saudi Arabia, at Shuwaymas 1 (Bednarik and Khan 2005), on much less metamorphosed sandstone (Figure 6). Closer examination of these features is warranted and their origins need to be established. They seem to differ from

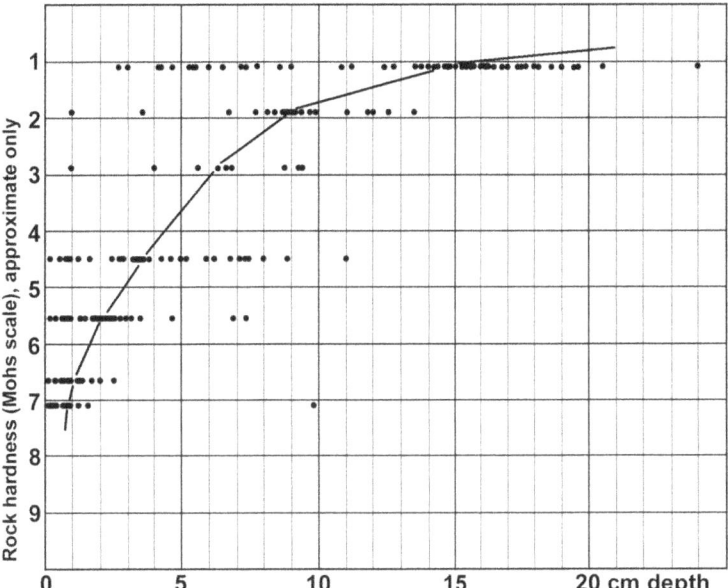

Figure 4. The depths of 221 cupules on rocks ranging in hardness from 1 to 7. The graph illustrates a distinctive trend.

case hardening in that the resistant skin is very thin, and the phenomenon may be relevant to issues of dating. One possible explanation would be that the great kinetic energy brought to bear on a cupule has somehow converted (slightly metamorphosed?) the colloid silica cement. I cannot cite a process by which this could have occurred, but as it seems the most reasonable explanation, I place the possibility before the reader and perhaps someone may care to comment.

Walsh (1994: 35) contends that some Kimberley cupules

Figure 5. Cutaneous surface feature in a cupule on eroding quartzite, Indragarh Hill, near Daraki-Chattan, central India.

are what he terms 'pebraded', i.e. first pecked and then abraded, 'to create a very smooth recess and perimeter'. Although he acknowledges the very great investment of time and energy in making cupules, he goes on to suggest that they were made before the sandstone had fully metamorphosed. This implies that he misunderstood both the technology and the relevant petrography. Taphonomy (see below) ensures the preferential survival of cupules on the hardest rocks, which it would be impossible to abrade in the fashion Walsh imagines. The 'abraded' appearance he observed is the result of the pounding action: as the crystals or grains are literally crushed into fine dust particles, the cupule surface and its rim take on a macroscopically polished appearance. But under the binocular microscope, no evidence of abrasion has so far been observed in any genuine cupule anywhere in the world. Not only is the term 'abraded' clearly inappropriate here, the term 'pecked' (Maynard 1977) in Walsh's portmanteau word is so also. There is no evidence whatsoever that cupules were made by pecking (indirect percussion), except on soft rock types. Moreover, Walsh's assumption that the rock had not been fully metamorphosed at the time of cupule production is geologically naive. The metamorphosis of these rocks to quartzite takes many millions of years, indeed hundreds of millions of years. The earliest cupules of Australia can, according to present knowledge, be no more than a few tens of thousands of years old. In fact Walsh's pronouncement comes close to the view of Aborigines that petroglyphs were made 'when the rocks were soft' (Flood 2006). It is far more likely that his 'pebraded cupules' are relatively unweathered specimens still showing the sheen of the crushing, whereas his 'pecked cupules' are weathered examples that experienced some degree of granular exfoliation.

All cupules on hard rock (hardness 4 to 7 on Mohs scale) can safely be assumed to have been created by direct percussion, i.e. pounding with a hand-held hammerstone. We may reasonably assume that the type of tools used in their production were similar to those observed not only ethnographically, but were also used in all recorded replication work (see article by G. Kumar, in this volume). Moreover, they are identical to the tools recovered in excavations at petroglyph sites, as well as from the surface at or near major concentrations of petroglyphs. Of greater technological interest are cupules on very soft rock, because in favourable circumstances, good traces of their production have remained intact. The chance of detecting such traces is best on softest rock types, offering the potential of securing valuable technological data. The softest rock on which I have recorded cupules is moisture-containing Miocene limestone in caves, which is soft enough to be easily marked by a fingernail (hardness 1 or 1½). Such instances show that indirect percussion has often been used on soft types of rock, but with non-lithic tools. Cupule-like pits in cave walls in the Mt Gambier region of southern Australia are the subject of detailed forensic studies, examining not only tool traces on limestone, but also the gestures involved in the making of these features.

Figure 6. Eroding cutaneous feature in a cupule on sandstone, Shuwaymas Site 1, Near Ha'il, northern Saudi Arabia.

The taphonomy of cupules

Reference has already been made to the importance of taphonomic considerations. The first demand in any pursuit that professes to be a scientific study of palaeoart is always the *coherent identification of that part of the extant characteristics of the evidence that is not the result of taphonomic processes* (Bednarik 1993). Taphonomic logic (Bednarik 1994b) requires that we expect a significant part of the empirical evidence about cupules to be greatly distorted, most especially variables related to degradation. In much the same way that it takes perhaps a thousand times longer to create a cupule on quartzite than to make an identical one on chemically very similar siliceous sandstone (several days vs two minutes, in fact; see my chapter on technology, this volume), it may take a thousand times longer to wear away the quartzite cupule by natural processes of erosion. To understand the scale of the effects of taphonomy, the great magnitude of these ratios must be fully appreciated. The probability that a cupule of a specific depth would survive for a given period of time might be a thousand times greater if it occurred on a very hard rock rather than a much softer rock. But rock hardness is certainly not the only variable determining longevity;

others are location, climate (e.g. precipitation pH, which is variable through time), rock chemistry, site morphology or hydrology, biological factors and so forth.

It is certainly no coincidence that the oldest cupules so far discovered occur on extremely weathering-resistant rock and are located in caves, safe from atmospheric water. At Daraki-Chattan (Bednarik et al. 2005), very faint traces of probable cupules occur on one boulder outside the cave, but they were only found in the course of careful examination of the site and would not be noticed *or* accepted elsewhere. They suggest that the site's cupules only survived in good condition because they were not exposed to rain. Similarly, cupules in a sandstone shelter should not be expected to have survived for such a great time span (i.e. since the Lower Palaeolithic), even though they were not exposed to rain. At the other end of the scale it would be absurd to expect cupules on, say, schist exposed to rainfall to survive for more than a few millennia — notwithstanding the belief of many European archaeologists that even very shallow, perfectly preserved rock engravings in the Côa valley of Portugal survived practically unweathered on schist for more than twenty millennia. And it would probably be futile to expect finding cupules of much more than 2000 years age on exposed limestone (Mandl 1995; Bednarik 2007: 164), unless it was metamorphosed (to marble). It is thus very apparent that the interdependence of lithology and taphonomy is a great deal more important to the scientific study of cupules than anything archaeology can provide, and that the potential effects of these variables tend to be significantly greater than their cursory consideration might imply. Another important taphonomic conclusion is that cupules, despite being the oldest rock art found, cannot be the earliest rock art made (Bednarik 1997). If the earliest examples of a phenomenon category in archaeology are the most deterioration resistant possible, it is illogical to assume that they are the earliest produced.

It follows also that cupules on soft rock are greatly under-represented on the surviving record, and that their frequent occurrence on basaltic, granitic or harder rocks is a taphonomic phenomenon. The more typical cupules should be those found on, say, limestone or mudstone, and as expected, these tend to be relatively recent, unless occurring in well-sheltered locations. Clearly, then, we need to apply taphonomic logic to the surviving corpus of cupules.

The term *taphonomy* (Efremov 1940; Solomon 1994) is only a recent introduction in archaeology. It cannot even be found in an archaeological dictionary that is more than a few decades old, and yet it is of crucial importance to understanding how the archaeological record relates to what happened in pre-History. In archaeology, taphonomy refers to the study of the processes that have transformed those materials, which archaeologists consider to constitute the archaeological record. Initially, taphonomy defined merely some of these many processes, particularly those affecting skeletal remains: animal scavenging, chemical decay, trampling and other mechanical processes. Today

we mean by taphonomy any process that affects any characteristics of those remains deposited in the past that now form what we regard as the surviving record. If a multitude of processes combine to distort the record, one would not initially be capable of isolating the effects of any one of these many processes. Some taphonomic processes are related to preservation, other forms concern selective deposition; others again are attributable to selective recovery, and by extension, some even to selective reporting (cf. metamorphology; Bednarik 1995). It is therefore clearly impossible to separately address the effects of any one of these factors a priori, i.e. before we understand their interplay with all of the others. In short, it would be advisable to address the entire range of taphonomic processes together, at least initially.

It is fairly self-evident that most rock art ever produced has not survived to the present time. What is now found on the rocks is but a minute fraction of what was once produced. The extant record is the result of a highly complex interplay of natural deterioration, cultural factors such as art techniques and site selection, which affect survival chances, and even predispositions of researchers. The extant record must be massively distorted in favour of rock arts of better survival properties and of more advantageous locations, such as deep caves, especially the older an art is. Consequently any statistical characteristics of a corpus of rock art or a rock art tradition are so heavily distorted that they are of no value to interpretation. Such statistical data are purely descriptive of a current state. They must not be used in any form of interpretation without being taken through a 'taphonomic filter' first.

Most interpretative studies of palaeoart have been conducted with an implicit assumption that the surviving remnants are an accurate reflection and a representative sample of the symbolic production of a given culture, tradition or period. In reality, nearly 100% of the symbolic production of all past societies does not survive, and the characteristics of the tiny fraction of a per cent that does survive are almost entirely the result of taphonomic processes. The geographical distribution, the colour, groove depth, motif type, rock type, site type profile — in short, all quantifiable variables of the surviving remnant of rock art — may be and often are the result of selective processes. Ignoring these will almost certainly lead to the invention of non-existent traditions, or whole sequences of traditions. The normative laws determining the effects of taphonomy have been explained and quantified, at least as integral functions (Bednarik 1994b). *Taphonomic logic* thus deals with quantifying the idea that the characteristics of a record of past events or systems are not an accurate reflection of what would have been a record of the live system or observed event.

In rock art science, taphonomy is the study of the processes affecting rock art after it has been executed, determining its present appearance and statistical properties. Taphonomic logic is a form of logic viewing rock art as the surviving remnant of a cumulative population that has been subjected

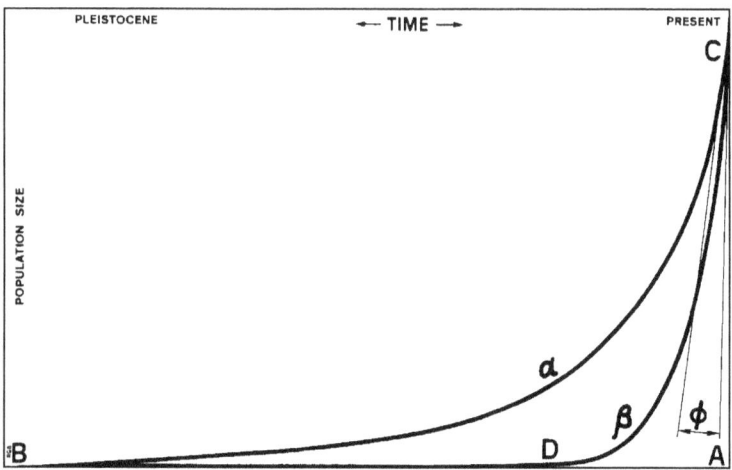

Figure 7. Principles of the relationship of total cumulative production of phenomenon category s_α to its surviving instances s_β as a function of angle φ, depicting the basis of taphonomic logic.

to continuous degradation that selects in favour of specific properties facilitating longevity (Figure 7). It inevitably leads to the concept of the *taphonomic threshold*, which is the point in time at which instances of a specific class of material remains ('phenomenon category') either begin to appear, or begin to appear in significant numbers. Before their respective taphonomic thresholds, all classes of material remains experienced a *taphonomic lag time*. This is the period during which the phenomena resulting in the material remains in question did exist, but from which we have found no such evidence — or so little that it is usually explained away as a 'running ahead of time' (Vishnyatsky 1994), or as incorrectly dated or identified. Until examined closely this may seem a minor issue, but for most classes of material remains, the taphonomic lag times are well in excess of 90% of the phenomenon's historical duration. Indeed, taphonomic lags in excess of 98% and 99% are quite common in archaeology.

In rock art, taphonomic lag times remain largely undetermined, but they would certainly differ greatly according to the climate, type of rock art and type of support rock. The taphonomic threshold of beeswax rock art in the Northern Territory of Australia (Nelson et al. 2000) has been estimated to be about 800 years BP (Bednarik 2001). One of the most common forms of surviving rock art consists of red paintings in sandstone shelters, and their threshold is believed to be in the order of 8000 years. For most other rock paintings the taphonomic threshold is lower. However, there are notable exceptions, especially rock art sites located in deep limestone caves offering extraordinary preservation conditions. In other words, the Palaeolithic 'cave art' traditions of Europe are known to us *only* because some of the art of the societies concerned was placed in 'fluke preservation conditions'. That evidence would probably not have survived elsewhere.

The ability of petroglyphs to survive in the open, i.e. exposed to precipitation, is governed largely by the rock they were made on, besides the ambient environment. Those on limestone have a taphonomic threshold of well under 2000 years (Mandl 1995), while those on granite can easily survive from the Pleistocene, and recent dating evidence suggests that their threshold might be in the order of 30,000 or 50,000 years under arid conditions (Bednarik 2002). Other relevant variables are climate and geochemistry. Taphonomic logic demands that rock art of the respective types was produced before all of these thresholds, but evidence of it should be either unavailable or extremely rare. Since occurrence, distribution and other characteristics of surviving corpora are all determined by taphonomic factors, it would be meaningless to state that a particular tradition produced only deep line petroglyphs, or painted only in caves, or left no open-air engravings. All characteristics of rock art that might contribute to their longevity (e.g. groove depth, location, type of rock support, morphology of site, composition of paint) are of no relevance to defining a tradition, because taphonomy skews their statistics systematically. For instance, the probably most common technological form of petroglyph is the sgraffito, made by the removal of a patina or weathering zone to reveal a differently coloured surface beneath. Sgraffiti tend to be obliterated by repatination processes within three or four millennia; therefore it is pointless to observe that the earliest petroglyphs of a region are consistently those that are deeply engraved. This observation, while valid, leads to misinterpretation of the sequence, unless moderated by taphonomic logic.

The mechanics of taphonomic logic are rather more complex than indicated in the present brief comments, but it must be emphasised that they are of crucial importance to the interpretation of primary data about rock art. This is the most important methodological tool so far developed in the interpretation of rock art data, and indeed, in archaeological interpretation of data and in hypothesis building. Its importance to the study of cupules cannot be overstated, as the following example illustrates.

If we compare my experimental shape predictions of the β-curve (surviving component of the phenomenon category) for quartzite, basalt and limestone cupules (Figure 8), ignoring here other taphonomic variables, we see that it is difficult to avoid the conclusions that increasing over-representation is a function of (a) the rock's resistance to erosion and (b) antiquity. For the sake of simplicity I assume here that the cumulative population (α-curve) of each of the three groups is identical. That taphonomy selects in favour of any properties facilitating longevity is obvious, but how effective is this selection quantitatively? If we focus mainly on the right part of the graph we see that the logic clearly demands that, for the duration of the time with appreciable numbers of surviving limestone specimens, nearly all quartzite ones and most of the basalt ones would have survived. Naturally we do not know the total population numbers, or how production varied through time, but even this preliminary model implies that we must expect the over-representation factor to be far more effective than a common sense prediction might suggest. Taphonomy eliminates nearly all populations on some rock types during a time period that registers very little impact on certain other types. In fact the difference may be a thousandfold, as we noted above.

This may sound over-theoretical, but it provides a timely warning that, when we consider the world's surviving cupule repertoire, we see a sample that must be assumed to be greatly distorted, and the phenomenon it is intended to represent would need to have appeared very differently if we only had access to the entire population. Therefore, our construct of 'cupule' is not set in stone; it is a tentative working hypothesis that remains very much in need of testing of the type I have implied here. I have teased out a whole list of reasons for this scepticism, which stands in stark contrast to the brash but unfounded interpretation attempts we have seen for much more than a century (addressed in my chapter on interpretation, this volume).

The perhaps most obvious factor preventing a development of such a scientific approach to cupules is the distinctive lack of systematic empirical information about the subject. No standardised forms of comprehensive data are available, which means that we even lack proper description of what has presently survived. In surprisingly many cases, we lack the most basic descriptions of petrography, metrics and statistics, therefore no attempt has been made to even rudimentarily describe the sites, apart from their locations and some possibly inconsequential archaeological pronouncements about them (e.g. presence of other signs of human activity, which may date from a different period). This is not a criticism of those who have collected field data, but of those who created the conditions that determined what data ought to be collected. While the field researcher needs to know what types of data are required, a rudderless discipline, relying on archaeology's bootstrapping epistemology, has not determined this and left the site surveyor to his or her own devices. This has been a monumentally wasteful exercise, in the sense that enormous efforts have been invested in securing data that are not adequate for scientific purposes.

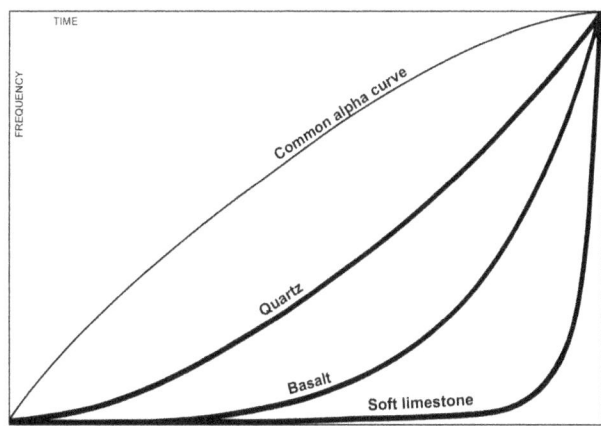

Figure 8. Prediction of β-curves for cupules on hard (quartz), intermediate (basalt) and soft rock (limestone) according to taphonomic logic (Bednarik 1994b).

REFERENCES

Bednarik, R. G. 1990. The cave petroglyphs of Australia. *Australian Aboriginal Studies* 1990(2): 64–68.
Bednarik, R. G. 1993. Refutability and taphonomy: touchstones of palaeoart studies. *Rock Art Research* 10: 11–13.
Bednarik, R. G. 1994a. On the scientific study of palaeoart. *Semiotica* 100(2/4): 141-168.
Bednarik, R. G. 1994b. A taphonomy of palaeoart. *Antiquity* 68(258): 68–74.
Bednarik, R. G. 1995. Metamorphology: in lieu of uniformitarianism. *Oxford Journal of Archaeology* 14(2): 117–122.
Bednarik, R. G. 1997. Rock art, taphonomy and epistemology. *Purakala* 8: 53–60.
Bednarik, R. G. 2001. The taphonomy of beeswax figures. *Rock Art Research* 18(2): 91–95.
Bednarik, R. G. 2002. About the age of Pilbara rock art. *Anthropos* 97(1): 201–215.
Bednarik, R. G. 2007. *Rock art science: the scientific study of palaeoart* (2nd edn; 1st edn 2001). Aryan Books International, New Delhi.
Bednarik, R. G. and M. Khan 2005. Scientific studies of Saudi Arabian rock art. *Rock Art Research* 22: 49–81.
Bednarik, R. G., G. Kumar, A. Watchman and R. G. Roberts 2005. Preliminary results of the EIP Project. *Rock Art Research* 22(2): 147–197.
Efremov, J. A. 1940. Taphonomy: a new branch of paleontology. *Pan American Geologist* 74(2): 81–93.
Flood, J. 2006. Copying the Dreamtime: anthropic marks in early Aboriginal Australia. *Rock Art Research* 23: 239–246.
Francaviglia, V. M. 2005. Le copelle dell'area di El-Geili (Sudan). Rapporto preliminare. *Sahara* 16: 169–172.
Mandl, F. 1995. Näpfchen, Schälchen und Schalen in der ostalpinen Felsritzbildwelt. *Mitteilungen der Anisa* 16: 63–66.
Maynard, L. 1977. Classification and terminology of Australian rock art. In P. J. Ucko (ed.), *Form in indigenous art: schematisation in the art of Aboriginal Australia and prehistoric Europe*, pp. 385–402. Australian Institute of Aboriginal Studies, Canberra.
Nelson, D. E., J. R. Southon and C. Takahashi 2000. Radiocarbon dating the wax art. In D. E. Nelson (ed.), *The beeswax art of northern Australia*, pp. 44–59. CD-ROM, Archaeology Department, Simon Fraser University, Burnaby.
Solomon, S. 1990. What is this thing taphonomy? In S. Solomon, I. Davidson and D. Watson (eds), *Problem solving in taphonomy: archaeological and palaeontological studies from Europe, Africa and Oceania*, pp. 25–33. Tempus 2, University of Queensland, St Lucia.
Vishnyatsky, L. B. 1994. 'Running ahead of time' in the development of Palaeolithic industries. *Antiquity* 68: 134–140.
Walsh, G. L. 1994. *Bradshaws: ancient rock paintings of northwest Australia*. The Bradshaw Foundation, Edition Limitee, Carouge-Geneva.

DISCRIMINATING BETWEEN CUPULES AND OTHER ROCK MARKINGS

Robert G. Bednarik

Abstract. A number of natural processes are discussed that may result in phenomena archaeologists have found difficult to distinguish from cupules. In particular, erosion phenomena of several types are presented and their distinguishing characteristics are discussed in adequate detail to facilitate their identification in the field. Similarly, cupules on horizontal surfaces may resemble grinding hollows (mortars, querns, metates) and their discrimination is also discussed. The use of field microscopy is emphasised in discriminating cupules from natural or other artificial rock markings.

Keywords: Cupule, Pothole, Solution pan, Tafone, Solution scallop, Mortar, Metate

Numerous commentators have found it difficult to discriminate between natural rock markings resembling cupules, humanly created features that look somewhat like cupules (or large versions of them), and those features the word 'cupule' is intended to describe. Unless we can be certain that we include in our studies of cupules only those instances or phenomenon populations that we intend to deal with, any further elaboration, interpretation or discussion seems pointless. For instance, there would seem to be no value in considering the orientation of natural rock hollows to determine their astronomical function. Before we can hope to explore our subject productively we will have to master the distinction between natural and 'cultural' rock markings, and determine that what we are considering are indeed non-utilitarian features of quite specific and distinctive morphological characteristics.

Natural rock markings resembling cupules
Potholes

These are fluvial abrasion hollows caused by the grinding action of clasts caught in rock depressions, scouring the bedrock in eddying or swirling water (Figure 1). They range in shape from cylindrical to hemispherical and sub-conical or test-tube shaped, and they can vary considerably in size (Gilbert 2000), but are most commonly in the order of 5 cm to 20 cm in diameter. Except for the smallest specimens, their depth usually exceeds their diameter. The largest reported pothole in the world, Archbald Pothole in Pennsylvania, is 18 m deep, larger examples reported are the result of other processes. These phenomena occur especially along turbulent rivers of high kinetic energy, but they can also be found along marine and lacustrine shorelines. Kayser (1912) distinguishes between *Flusstöpfen* (fluvial potholes), *Gletschertöpfen* (glacial potholes)

Figure 1. Potholes

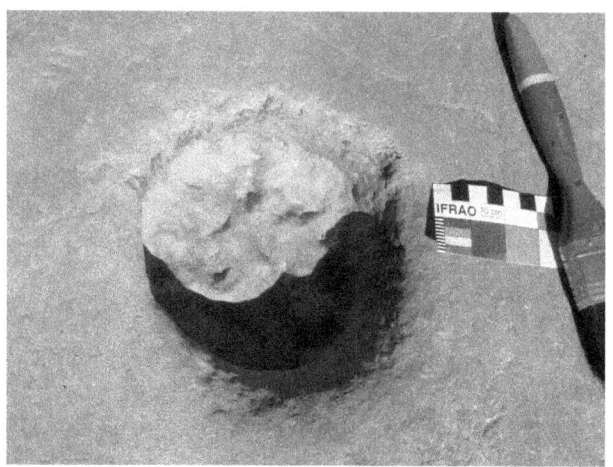

Figure 2. Convex-floor pothole at Rocas Rio Milloma, near Tarata, central Bolivia.

Figure 3. Small initial potholes in river bed, Punku Cocha, near Tarata, Bolivia.

and *Meermühlen* (marine potholes). Morphologically, he divided these phenomena into three types: shallow with a *Weinflaschenboden* (convex floor), deeper with a flat floor, and very deep with a bowl-shaped floor and spiral-shaped furrows in the wall. Fluvial potholes develop preferentially in rock channels, at waterfalls and at rapids, and they can only begin to form where an initial hollow exists that retains swirling sand or clasts (Elston 1917–1918). Rehbock (1917, 1925) initiated the complex study of hydraulic energy in potholes. Richardson and Carling (2005) limit the term explicitly to round depressions eroded by approximately vertical vortexes and through mechanisms other than plucking, thereby excluding one of the two types Rehbock had established experimentally. The convex floor pothole (Figure 2) is thought to result from the centrifugal force of the abrasive material (*Schleifmaterial*) (Ljungner 1927–1930).

Springer et al. (2005, 2006) have examined the potholes on streambeds using empirical analyses of field data and geometric constraints. They report that radius and depth of such features are strongly correlated, using a simple power law, which they explain. Erosion efficiencies within small, hemispherical potholes (Figure 3) must be high if the potholes are to survive in the face of streambed fluvial incision. As potholes deepen, the necessary efficiencies decline and increasing concavity through growth imposes stricter constraints. Thus hemispherical potholes are gradually converted to cylindrical potholes, the geometries of which favour enlargement while they are small. More substrate is eroded by volume from cylindrical pothole walls during growth than from cylindrical pothole floors (Figure 4). Clasts acting as grinders (called 'tools' by pothole researchers) play a secondary role to suspended sediment entrained within the vortices that occur in potholes.

Marine potholes (Swinnerton 1927: Note 5) are found in places where the bedrock is exposed in the zone of wave action, chiefly due to the breakers' action. The favoured locations in the formation of fluvial potholes are the upper levels of waterfalls, but the perhaps most important prerequisite is the presence of relatively soft bedrock (particularly sedimentary rocks, even those lightly metamorphosed) and the involvement of very hard abrasive clasts, sand and silt (e.g. quartz). The identification of these rock markings is particularly difficult when they are found high above a present river course, and heavily weathered corresponding to their great antiquity. For instance at Hoover Dam in the United States, 'fossil' potholes occur in a palaeochannel 275 m above the present Colorado River bed (Howard 2004). However, even relatively recent and unweathered examples have been misidentified as anthropic markings by archaeologists on many occasions.

Of particular relevance is that potholes sometimes co-occur with cupules, and in such cases it is reasonably assumed that it was the very presence of the potholes that prompted the production of the more recent anthropic markings (Figure 5). This raises interesting issues concerning the functional context of the latter, but it also demonstrates that the discrimination between the two forms of rock markings is well outside the domain of archaeologists who have

Figure 4. Cylindrical pothole, Rocas Rio Milloma, Bolivia.

Figure 5. Potholes co-occurring with cupules, near Karakara, Bolivia.

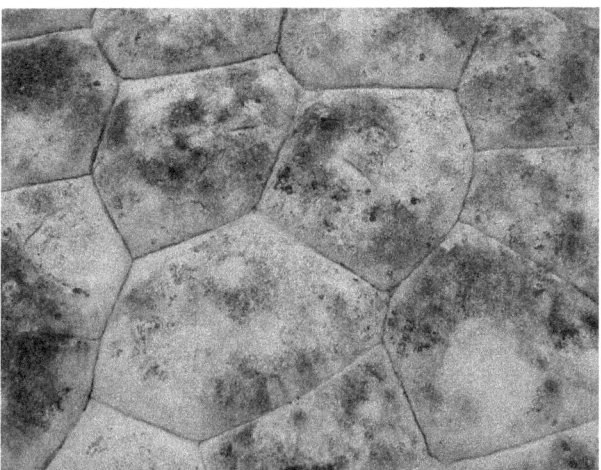

Figure 6. Tesselation on sandstone pavement at Elvina Track site, Ku-ring-gai Chase National Park, near Sydney, Australia.

misidentified the potholes as mortars, *tacitas* or cupules in many cases. Examples are the extensive concentrations featuring cupules, other petroglyphs and potholes at El Valle de El Encanto and El Valle del Sol (Iribarren 1949, 1954; Klein 1972; Ampuero and Rivera 1964, 1971; Ampuero 1993; Van Hoek 2003), or the potholes in the Coquimbo Region (Gallardo Ibáñez 1999), all in Chile (see also Gajardo-Tovar 1958–59). The issue, as far as I have been able to ascertain, seems to have its origins in Menghin's (1957) pronouncements. Similar cases of misidentification can be cited, however, from many other countries, e.g. Azerbaijan (Anati 2001: Fig. 10) or Greece (Papanikolaou 2005).

On the other hand, an illiterate Quechua man of Karakara, Bolivia, has insisted that these phenomena were not created by human hand. He has explained that they are perhaps the result of lightning strikes, presumably because the specific examples he referred to where located on exposed rock outcrops so high above the current riverbed that he could not conceptually relate them to the river. While his explanation is not correct, it does demonstrate, as I have observed on numerous occasions, that the explanations of 'ethnoscientists' (sensu Mark P. Leone) are sometimes closer to those of science itself than to those of archaeologists. Non-archaeologists frequently outperform archaeologists in the identification of supposedly archaeological phenomena (Bednarik 1994), and this also applies to potholes.

Lithological cupmarks

Only two types are briefly mentioned here. In the first, thousands of pit markings on tesselated sandstone pavements in the Sydney region, Australia, are the subject of an ongoing controversy (Cairns and Branagan 1992; Branagan and Cairns 1993a). Extensive lattices of deeply eroded natural grooves divide some twenty-five known pavements into mosaics of geometric shapes, most often hexagons.

The tesselation has not been explained satisfactorily by geologists (Branagan and Cairns 1993b), but it is evident that the vertical disconformities causing it extend well into the substrate (at least 20 cm, but probably much deeper). In my view, the tesselation (Figure 6) has been caused by cumulative stresses of a susceptible facies, and the reason for the geometric shapes is much the same as the laws causing the way a drying mud cover in a floodplain breaks up into hexagonal or other geometric features: in both cases the layer consists of a sediment of randomly oriented grains. In both cases the shapes of the tesselation polygons represent Voronoi cells, and their sizes are determined by the spacing of Voronoi sites (Voronoi 1907). These inherent tessellation characteristics of Sydney sandstones have given rise to selective weathering which formed the grooves separating the polygons, whose natural character is generally accepted. The largest of these pavements, the Elvina Track site, measures about 6500 square metres. Many of its thousands of polygonal panels bear a number of pits of 20–50 mm diameter. These pits closely resemble

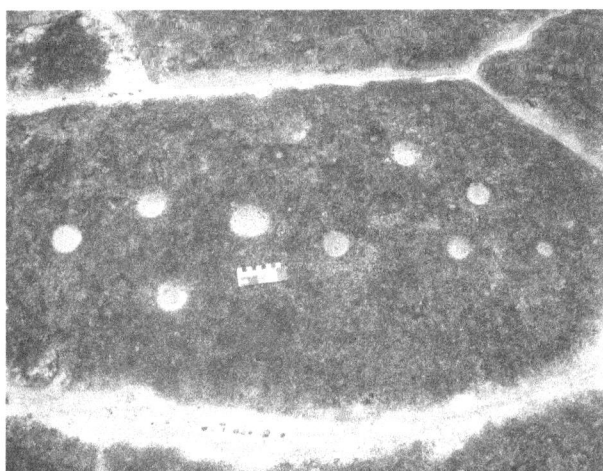

Figure 7. Cup-marks that have formed naturally on a tesselation polygon at Elvina Track site.

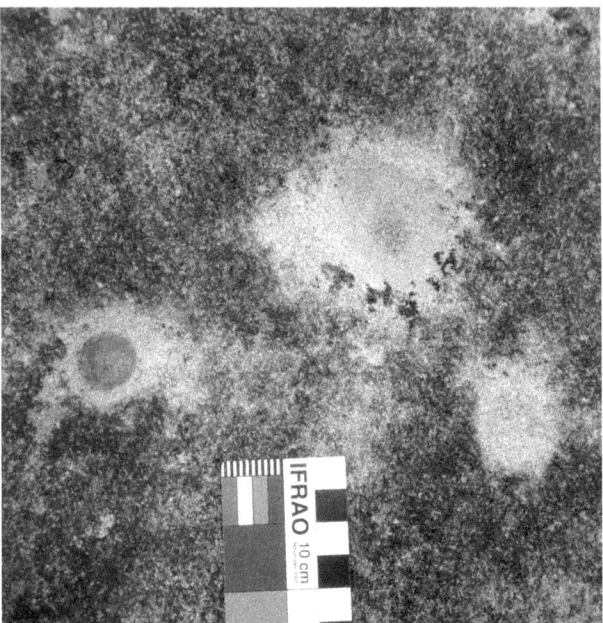

Figure 8. Natural cup-shaped pits, close to 20 mm deep. Elvina Track site, near Sydney, Australia.

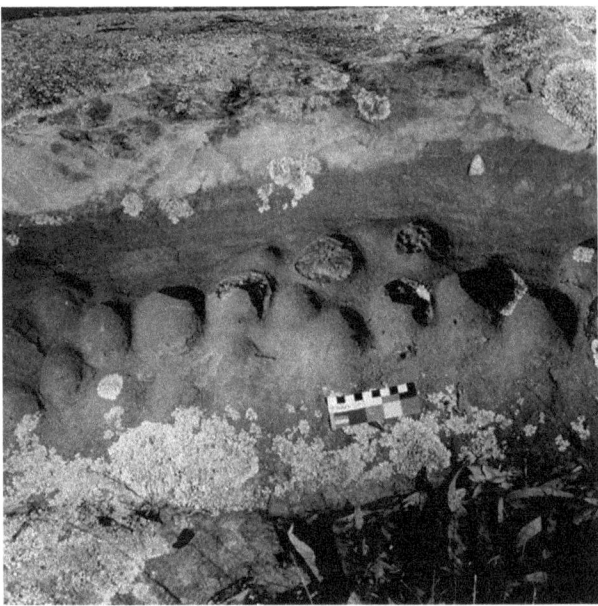

Figure 9. Natural erosion pits south of Horsham, Victoria, Australia.

small cupules, and it is possible that humans have modified some, because a number of genuine petroglyphs occur also at the site, located in a region rich in rock art. However, the pits are essentially natural phenomena (Bednarik 1990). Each polygon has similar run-off characteristics: near the borders, the profile curves gently towards the surrounding groove, into which rainwater drains readily (Figure 7). Drainage is slower in the more central parts of the polygon, and water will remain in even the slightest depressions there. Differential granular exfoliation is the result, leading to drainage towards the gradually deepening depression. This process favours regular spacings as watersheds are established in the micro-topography of each polygon. Once under way, it leads inevitably to foci of erosional activity, and ever-accelerating rates of erosion in just one location — the pit forming in the middle of each 'local drainage zone' (Figure 8). The result is a natural pattern of regularity, which the uncritical observer is likely to interpret as intentional.

While the process responsible for this example can be observed frequently in nature, my second example, also from Australia, refers to circumstances that are more unusual. Several vertical panels of hard but very weathered siliceous sandstone south of Horsham, Victoria, are densely covered by cup-shaped marks of typical cupule appearance. There are several hundred such marks at the site, all measuring between 5 and 10 cm in diameter, and a few centimetres deep (Figure 9). Superficially the exposures seem indistinguishable from anthropic cupule panels, and yet they are entirely natural products of geological antiquity. I consider them to be the result of a complex lithological process at the time the rock formed, in which a layer of highly water-sorted, evenly sized, near-spherical cobbles was deposited on quartz sand. The sand bed was metamorphosed to a slightly quartzitic sandstone. Erosive processes then removed the pebble conglomerate completely, presumably because it was less weathering resistant than the silica cement of the sandstone. This facies was replaced by a highly ferruginous conglomerate of maximal very-coarse-sand/small-pebble-fraction fluvial detritus, filling in the hollows left by the cobbles. Most of this second conglomerate eroded subsequently, and the remaining negative impressions of the cobbles were exposed to weathering action. Once weathered, the dense groups of hemispherical depressions became almost indistinguishable from cupules. However, significant remains of the ferruginous facies still adhere to many areas of the panels (Figure 10).

Figure 10. Remains of ferruginous conglomerate in some of the natural pits near Horsham, indicating their geological antiquity.

Solution phenomena

A variety of rock types, most especially sedimentary facies, can be susceptible to pitting by localised granular or mass erosion. This can take many forms (Bednarik 2007: 20–3), but one distinctive example is found on carbonate rocks, especially limestone, the *Kamenitza*. Numerous examples, often occurring together with cupules, are illustrated by Papanikolaou from Greece (2005: 87, 91–94, 98, 105, 109, 110, 120–125, 134–46). Less pronounced forms of smaller sizes occur, and where such phenomena are well developed they can resemble cupules. A specific weathering phenomenon, the tafone, is defined as a 'roughly hemispherical hollow weathered in rock at the surface' (Jennings 1985). It has been documented in sandstone, dolerite, limestone, rhyolite tuff, metamorphosed conglomerate, and particularly in granitic rocks (Dragovich 1969; Martini 1978; Smith 1978). Tafoni can occur in many climates, from the Antarctic to hot arid regions, and are also found on Mars (Cooke et al. 1993). Their development tends to commence from zones of differential weathering on a rock surface, attributable to variations in lithology, structure, composition, texture or biota (Dragovich 1969). Once a tafone has begun to form, the interior of its concavity tends to erode faster than the visor. There are two schools of thought on the formation process: one holds that there are inherent differences in the rock hardness and moisture content between the interior and exterior parts (the 'core softening' theory, e.g. Conca and Rossman 1985; cf. Matsukura and Tanaka 2000), while the other attributes the process to microclimatic differences between the interior and the exterior, specifically of humidity and salinity (e.g. Dragovich 1969).

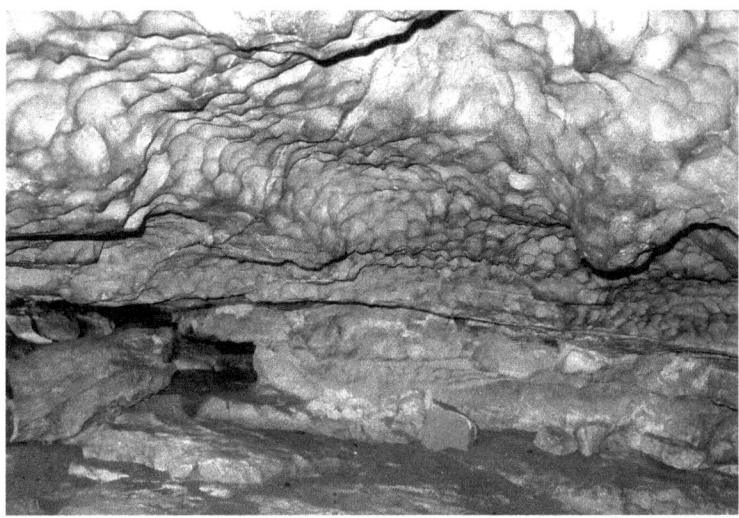

Figure 11. Solution scalloping on the walls and ceiling of Mawanga Cave, Kenya (photograph courtesy of Jean Clottes).

Both are perhaps partially right: the core softening (particularly pronounced on some sandstones) is probably the result of how rock surface geometry affects moisture retention, especially in arid regions (Bednarik 2001 [2007]: 22). More prominent rock aspects dry faster than those sheltered from wind and insolation, and they weather slower (through case hardening). The process leads logically to cavernous, deeply alveolar features that could not be mistaken for anthropic phenomena. However, in the early stages, small tafoni may well resemble eroded cupules or similar anthropic features. Although large specimens measure several metres, the smallest tafoni do fall within the size range of cupules.

Another solution phenomenon found particularly on granite is the gnamma, a rock-hole on a horizontal rock exposure that is of particular importance in Australia, where it commonly served as a water source (Bayly 1999: 18–20, Fig. 2). Forming from initially cup-sized depressions, gnammas can measure several metres across, after gradual enlargement by chemical weathering. Found especially on the top of domed inselbergs (Twidale and Corbin 1963), the name of this geomorphological feature derives from Western Desert Aboriginal languages and means 'rock-hole' (Bayly 1999: 20). Gnammas were of great importance to the Aborigines (and European explorers; Giles 1889: Vol.1: 211, 217; Lindsay 1893; Calvert 1897; Carnegie 1898), who protected them against evaporation and fouling by animals (Helms 1896), and who sometimes diverted water into them from nearby rock surfaces by pounding channelling grooves (Tindale and Lindsay 1963: 65; such hydraulic grooves have also been reported from axe grinding panels, see Bednarik 1990). In practice, most gnammas are too large to be mistaken for cupules or other anthropic markings, but it is thought that, in Australia at least, humans contributed to the enlargement of some specimens by removing loose and weakened rock (Jutson 1934). Gnammas are closely related to *Kamenitza*, the main difference being in the role of the rock's impermeability in the case of the former. Both of these phenomena are *Verwitterungswannen* (solution basins)

Another solution phenomenon resembling cupules has been reported by Campbell et al. (2007), who illustrate dense concentrations of natural 'cupules' from the ceiling, walls and to some extent even the floor of a limestone cave (J. Clottes, pers. comm. Dec. 2007) on Mfangano Island in Lake Victoria (Kenya). The phenomenon illustrated is solution scalloping, commonly observed in limestone caves that have been subjected to vadose water flow (Figure 11). Solution scallops are concavities formed through erosion by eddies in flowing water (De Serres 1835: 24; Monroe 1970; Lowe and Waltham 1995; Mihevc et al. 2004: 522). They are separated by sharp ridges, they can range from 1 cm to 1 m in size, and they are asymmetrical in horizontal section. The latter characteristic allows flow direction to be established, because the upstream slope is always steeper (Figure 12). Their size indicates flow velocity, smaller scallops being formed by faster flowing water. The French names of solution scallops are *cannelure* and *vague d'érosion*, while

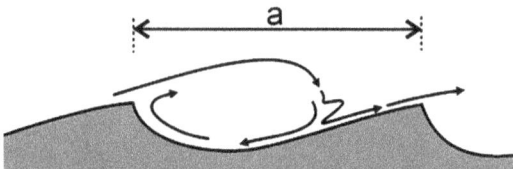

Figure 12. Section through solution scallop in the direction of water flow, showing flow and eddy current.

in German the phenomenon is known as *Fließfacette*, and in Spanish as *huella de corriente*.

Clegg's 'snames'

Clegg (2007) has recently described a phenomenon he calls 'snames'. He defines these as 'shallow, approximately circular, flat-bottomed depressions, a metre or so in diameter', which he has found on Sydney sandstone. His illustrations depict them as being several centimetres to perhaps 10 cm deep, and clearly unrelated to the site's tesselation. He is baffled by them and reports that several geologists could not explain them and had never encountered such features before. But the phenomena he describes are well known (e.g. Cremeens et al. 2005), including in Australia (Figure 13). They have been described as '*Opferkessel*' (another severely misleading archaeologist's term) and their correct geomorphological name is *Verwitterungswanne* or solution pan (cf. pan hole, *tinajita, Kamenitza, kamenica, kamenitsa, lakouva, ythrolakkos, bljudce, cuenco, tinajita, erime tavasi, skalne kotlice, scalba, skalnica*; see Bednarik 2001 [2007]: 21). This biochemical phenomenon occurs on flattish horizontal rock surfaces lacking drainage and it can be found on many lithologies. It occurs most commonly on sedimentary rocks, but similar forms occur also on granitic facies (see gnamma) and other rock types. After the nature of his 'snames' was explained to Clegg he continued to insist that they are a new phenomenon, because if they were solution basins they would have to be horizontal, whereas those he checked had slopes ranging from 0 to 0.2%, i.e. they were not precisely horizontal (Clegg 2008: Fig. 5). That is indeed the case, but again Clegg is mistaken: the sandstone slab on which his 'snames' are located is unstable and has changed its inclination since the time these *Verwitterungswannen* formed, long before the arrival of humans. Recently, Rowe and Chance (this volume) have described a few similar examples on limestone in Qatar, which are best defined as *Kamenitza*. *Verwitterungswannen*, the generic phenomena defining Clegg's 'snames', have distinctive features by which they can be identified, and their formation processes are understood. It is not appropriate to invent a new name for them, there already are far too many names because other commentators have done so without realising that the phenomenon has a name and has been defined and explained scientifically.

I have examined many of Clegg's 'snames' at the Elvina

Figure 13. Verwitterungswannen (solution pans) on Uluru (formerly Ayers Rock), central Australia.

Track site and other, nearby locations in Ku-ring-gai Chase National Park, Sydney (Figs 14 to 16). Some of

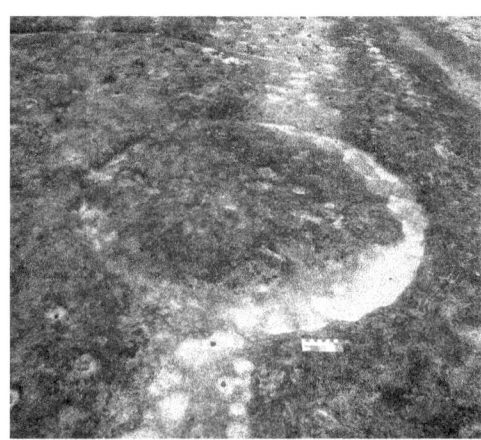

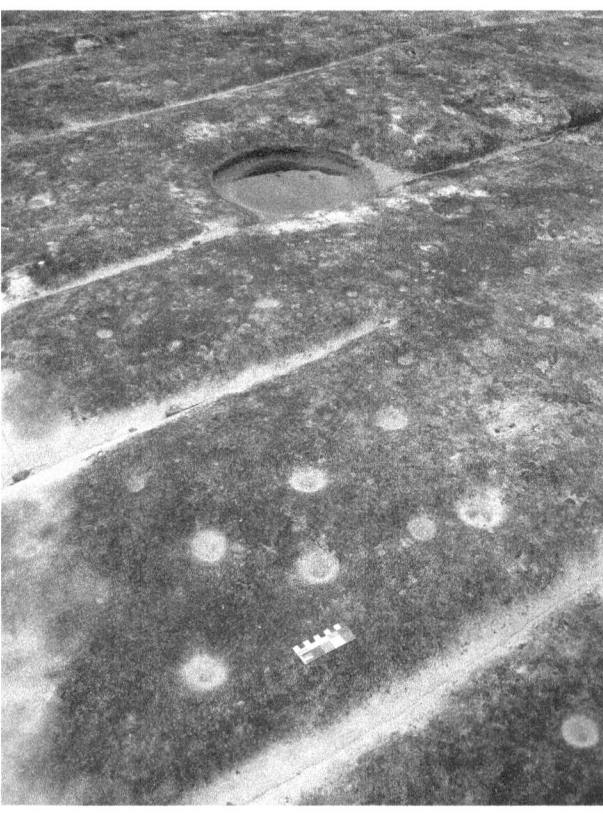

Figures 14 and 15. Solution pans, Elvina Track site, near Sydney.

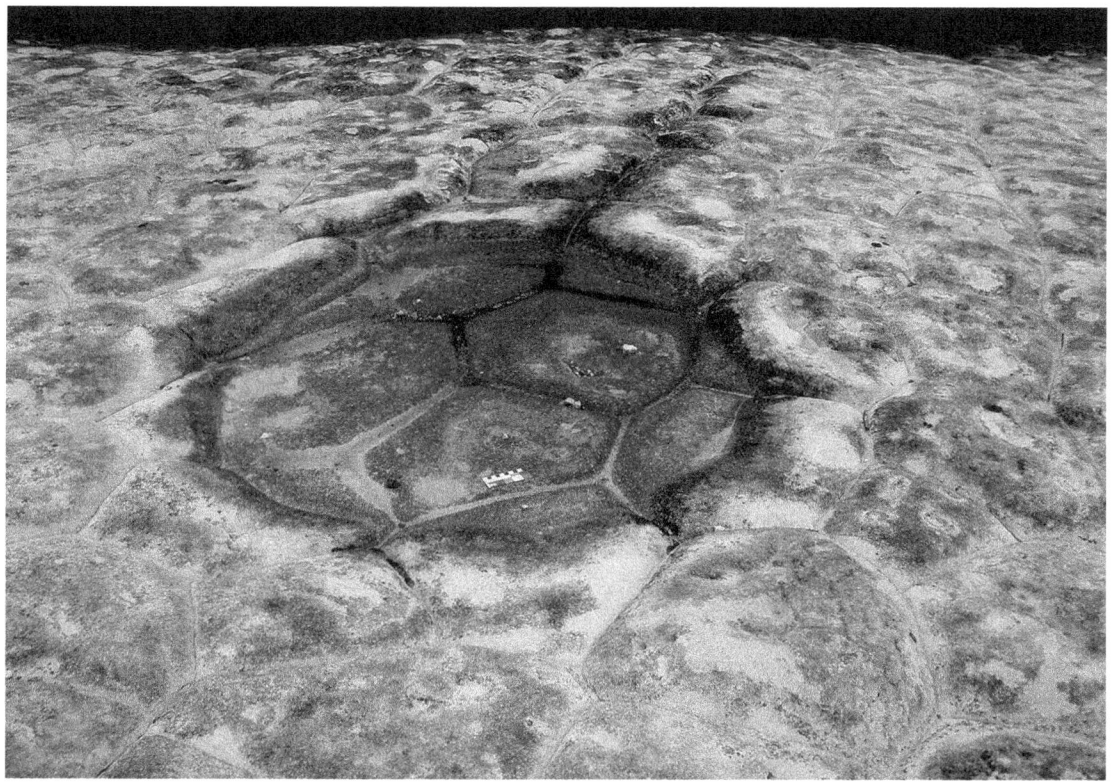

Figure 16. Solution pan, Elvina Track site, near Sydney, truncating several tesselation polygons. Scale in cm.

them are roughly circular, but irregular shapes also occur. They range in size up to 4 m and are without exception horizontal, because it is the retention of rainwater that causes their formation. Any variation from the horizontal position is entirely due to the dip in the sandstone slab, the southern part of which is gradually being lowered as its support facies gives way. It is wrong to separate them taxonomically from other solution phenomena at the site, on the basis of size or shape. In reality, there is a continuum ranging in size from 20 mm to 4 m, and in shape from circular to any random shape, the most common sizes being between 5 cm and 20 cm (Figure 17). While the smaller fraction has been falsely defined as cupules (see above), some of the larger examples, which can extend across several tesselation polygons, constitute Clegg's 'snames'. All of these phenomena are natural features, as shown by field microscopy (Figure 18).

The difficulties in discriminating between natural and artificial features have spawned countless confrontations between archaeologists and other researchers, in many areas of archaeology (beginning, perhaps, with Boucher de Perthes' 'worthless pebbles' of well over a hundred years ago). An early example involving rock depressions featured Leiden professor K. Martin who ridiculed C. A. van Sypesteyn (a later Governor of Suriname) over this issue (Martin 1887; see also Bubberman 1977: 566) — who turned out to be right.

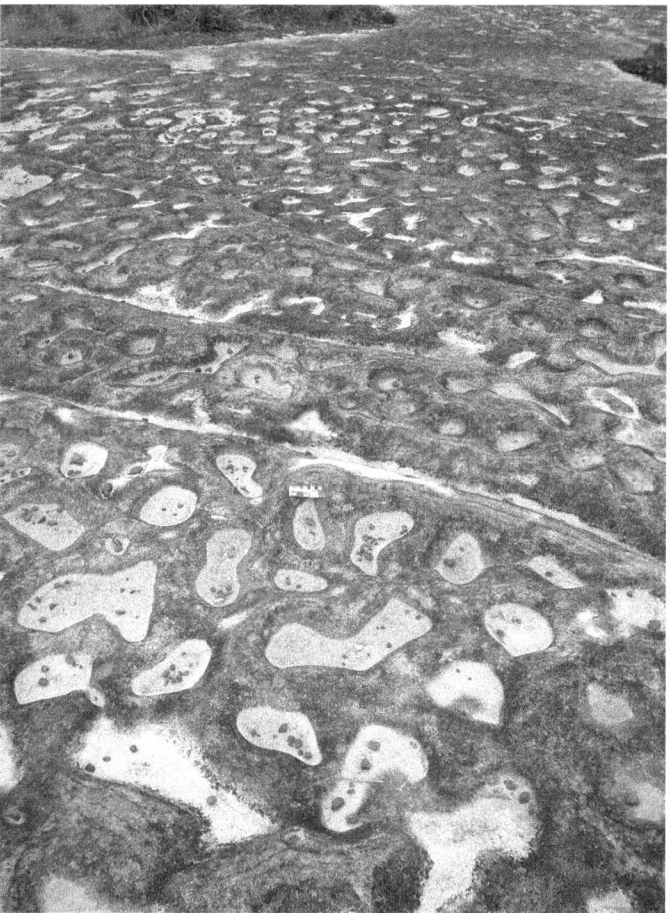

Figure 17. Sandstone pavement with a great diversity of solution phenomena, Elvina Track site.

Figure 18. Microphotographs of the heavily weathered surface of one of Clegg's 'snames'.

Artificial rock markings resembling cupules

In addition to the many *natural* features that have been misunderstood or misidentified as cupules or cupule-like phenomena (the above list is not complete) there are also various anthropic rock markings they have been

Figure 19. Stone slab with mortars resembling cupules, central Niger.

confused with. In particular, rock mortars and metates can resemble large cupules (Figure 19). A metate typically consists of a stone slab with a ground depression, which may be elongate or circular, depending on the direction of movement of the grinding stone (called *mano*), used generally in grinding materials such as foodstuffs (e.g. Lange 1996). In Mesoamerica, especially Costa Rica, decorated ceremonial metates made of volcanic rock have been described. In North America, the term 'grinding slab' has been used to define large rocks bearing a number of anthropic hollows that were used, for instance, to grind acorns, and these features can resemble cupule boulders rather closely (Alvarez and Peri 1987: 12). The term metate is an American variation of the more widely found quern stones, which occur especially among the remains of agricultural societies. The term mortar also is more general, describing essentially a rock hollow, portable or non-portable, that was used in conjunction with a pestle to crush, grind and mix substances (grain, meat, ochre, medicines or numerous others). It is obvious that distinctions between these various terms are fairly arbitrary, depending mostly on assumed economic activities, and that in reality the surviving traces of these features tend to grade into other types. The only major technological distinction might be that metates are most often the result of to-and-fro abrasion, while mortars or querns relate more to rotating or crushing motions.

Similarly, there is no obvious or self-evident separation between some of these economic features and non-utilitarian cupules; rather, the discrimination can only be made after exhaustive study of the features in question, and after detailed consideration of various aspects. This is usually beyond archaeological taxonomisation endeavours and involves a whole host of considerations, concerning lithology, macroscopic and microscopic traces, orientation, inclination, spatial context and so forth. These are discussed in other parts of this volume. Similarly, many cupules occur on lithophones, and it is then questionable whether they could reasonably be described as non-utilitarian, as cupules are generally presumed to be. The proper recognition of lithophone cupules is in itself a complex subject that will need to be considered in any identification of cupules (see chapter on lithophones). Indeed, an absolute separation between utilitarian and non-utilitarian cupule-like features is in the final analysis impossible, even if we had reliable ethnographic information. A cupule could only be entirely non-utilitarian (symbolic) if no practical consideration were involved in its production. We cannot determine this with finite precision in the extremely sparse ethnographic instances of interpretation available to us, so it would be correspondingly much more difficult to make such distinction in the countless cases we have that lack any form of ethnography. Clearly, science cannot involve itself in such issues, on the basis of the sound data currently available to it.

Other types of anthropic and utilitarian rock markings vaguely resembling cupules of various types occur. One

Figure 20. Deep and large utilitarian pits on soft tuffaceous rock, near La Paz, Bolivia.

example are large and deep rock depressions in soft rock that have been suggested to have served as storage pits (Figure 20). Modern tool marks have sometimes been mistaken for petroglyphs by archaeologists (Bednarik 1994), including markings by rock drills, core drills and other modern equipment. Some of these traces can resemble cupules and similar phenomena, especially when they have been subjected to rapid weathering. An example are the several dozen rock holes at Blue Tier in Tasmania, arranged in an alignment that is 19.5 metres long (Sharland 1957; see Bednarik et al. 2007: Fig. 2).

Discussion

What emerges from this paper is that archaeologists have often found it difficult to discriminate between cupules and other anthropic rock markings, and especially to recognise natural markings. The latter have not been summarised before, and the above is intended to assist in such discrimination. However, by itself an appreciation of these alternatives may not suffice to generate reliable identifications in the field. The best analytical tool in this quest is field microscopy — the use of specially adapted binocular microscopes or digital microscopes at the sites in question (Figure 21). Unfortunately field microscopy is widely eschewed by both general archaeologists and rock art researchers. This is regrettable because it is a powerful tool in detecting crucial diagnostic details. In the case of cupules, mortars and natural features resembling them, such details demanding the use of field microscopy are especially:

1. *Impact-modified rock crystals or grains*: all cupules were created by percussion, and in the harder rock types this will lead to the frequent occurrence of fractured, crushed or shattered surface grains, and particularly in quartz grains with typical conchoidal fractures. These unmistakeable signs of impact are rare or absent in any such features other than cupules. Where weathering has not obliterated such details, they provide clear diagnostic evidence.

2. *Abrasion-truncated crystals or grains*: the particles of rock that has been abraded, e.g. as a metate or quern stone, are inevitably truncated at the surface. Unless

Figure 21. Specially adapted binocular microscope in use to examine cupules on quartzite at Inca Huasi site, Mizque valley, Bolivia.

they have been lost to granular surface exfoliation, these grains or crystals provide solid evidence of grinding or abrasive action (Bednarik 2000).
3. *Striations*: grains or crystals truncated by abrasion may bear microscopic striae dating from the last use of the surface. Where these are orientated in similar directions, the use of the surface as a metate, in a to-and-fro movement, is indicated, whereas random orientation implies use as a quern stone.
4. *Microerosional indices*: Where mineral crystals, such as the quartz grains of sandstones or quartzites, have been either truncated by abrasion or fractured by percussion, the newly formed edges of the new surfaces correspond in age to the last use of the feature. These edges then begin to form micro-wanes, i.e. they become rounded with time. Such rounded edges provide therefore a metrical index of the age of the feature, and where the wane development process can be calibrated against time, they facilitate absolute age estimation of the cupule or mortar. This is the basis of the principal method of microerosion analysis (Bednarik 1992).

The availability of such significant analytical features indicates the importance of microscopic examination of cupules and any other phenomena these have been confused with. It is hoped that this paper can help prompting archaeologists to consult specialists of rock markings (rather than general geologists) when facing such issues, and particularly when needing to discriminate between cupules and other rock markings.

REFERENCES

ALVAREZ, S. H. and D. W. PERI 1987. Acorns: the stuff of life. *News from Native California* 1(4): 10–14.

AMPUERO, B. G. 1993. *Arte rupestre en El Valle de El Encanto*. Editoral Museo Arqueológico de La Serena, La Serena.

AMPUERO, B. G. and M. RIVERA 1964. Excavaciones en la Quebrada de El Encanto, Departamento de Ovalle. *Arqueológico de Chile Central y Areas Vecinas*, Santiago.

AMPUERO, B. G. and M. RIVERA 1971. *Las manifestaciones rupestres y arqueológicas del Valle de El Encanto*. Publicaciones del Museo Arqueológico de La Serena, Boletín 14, La Serena.

ANATI, E. 2001. *Gobustan, Azerbaijan*. Edizioni del Centro, Capo di Ponte.

BAYLY, I. A. E. 1999. Review of how indigenous people managed for water in desert regions of Australia. *Journal of the Royal Society of Western Australia* 82: 17–25.

BEDNARIK, R. G. 1990. Annual AURA Meeting 1989. *AURA Newsletter* 7(1): 2–3.

BEDNARIK, R. G. 1992. A new method to date petroglyphs. *Archaeometry* 34(2): 279–291.

BEDNARIK, R. G. 1994. The discrimination of rock markings. *Rock Art Research* 11: 23–44.

BEDNARIK, R. G. 2000. Age estimates for the petroglyph sequence of Inca Huasi, Mizque, Bolivia. *Andean Past* 6: 277–287.

BEDNARIK, R. G. 2007. *Rock art science: the scientific study of palaeoart* (2nd edn; 1st edn 2001). Aryan Books International, New Delhi.

BEDNARIK, R. G., G. ANDREWS, S. CAMERON and E. BEDNARIK 2007. Petroglyphs of Meenamatta, the Blue Tier mountains, Tasmania. *Rock Art Research* 24: 161–170.

BRANAGAN, D. F. and H. C. CAIRNS 1993a. Marks on sandstone surfaces – Sydney region, Australia: cultural origin and meanings? *Journal and Proceedings, Royal Society of New South Wales* 126: 125–133.

BRANAGAN, D. F. and H. C. CAIRNS 1993b. Tesselated pavements in the Sydney region, New South Wales. *Journal and Proceedings, Royal Society of New South Wales* 126: 63–72.

BUBBERMAN, F. C. 1977. Slijpgroeven. In *Encyclopedie van Suriname*, pp. 566–567. Amsterdam.

CAIRNS, H. C. and D. F. BRANAGAN 1992. Artificial patterns on rock surfaces in the Sydney region, New South Wales: evidence for Aboriginal time charts and sky maps? In J. McDonald and I. P. Haskovec (eds), *State of the art: regional rock art studies in Australia and Melanesia*, pp. 25–31. Occasional AURA Publication 6, Australian Rock Art Research Association Inc., Melbourne.

CALVERT, A. F. 1897. *My four tours in Western Australia*. Heinemann, London.

CAMPBELL, A., J. CLOTTES and D. COULSON 2007. Modern use of rock paintings sites in Kenya and Uganda. *International Newsletter on Rock Art* 49: 19–25.

CARNEGIE, D. W. 1898. *Spinifex and sand*. Arthur Peason, London.

CLEGG, J. 2007. Science and rock art research of the world. In P. Chenna Reddy (ed.), *Exploring the mind of ancient man (Festschrift to Robert G. Bednarik)*, pp. 52–60. Research India Press, New Delhi.

CLEGG, J. 2008. Snames. *Rock Art Research* 25: 211–

CONCA, J. L. and G. R. ROSSMAN 1985. Core softening in cavernously weathered tonalite. *Journal of Geology* 93(1): 59–73.

COOKE, R., A. WARREN and A. GOUDIE 1993. *Desert geomorphology*. UCL Press, London.

CREMEENS, D. L., R. G. DARMOD and S. E. GEORGE 2005. Upper slope landforms and age of bedrock exposures in the St. Francois Mountains, Missouri: a comparison to relict periglacial features in the Appalachian Plateau of West Virginia. *Geomorphology* 70(1–2): 71–84.

DE SERRES, P. M. T. 1835. *Essai sur les caverns à ossemens et sur les causes qui les y ont accumulés*. Loosjes, Haarlem.

DRAGOVICH, D. 1969. The origin of cavernous surfaces (tafoni) in granitic rocks of southern South Australia. *Zeitschrift für Geomorphologie* 13(2): 163–181.

ELSTON, E. D. 1917–1918. Potholes — their variety, origin and significance. *Scientific Monthly* 5: 554–567; and 6: 37–53.

GAJARDO-TOVAR, R. 1958–59. Investigaciones acerca de las piedras con tacitas en la zona central de Chile. *Anales de Arqueología y Etnología* 14(5): 163–204.

GALLARDO IBÁÑEZ, F. 1999. El Norte Verde y su prehistoria. La tierra donde el desierto florece. In *Chile antes de Chile: prehistoria*, pp. 32–43. Museo Chileno de Arte Precolombino, Santiago.

GILBERT, R. 2000. The Devil Lake pothole (Ontario): evidence of subglacial fluvial processes. *Géographie physique et Quaternaire* 54(2): 245–250.

GILES, E. 1889. *Australia twice traversed*. Sampson Low, Marston, Searle & Rivington, London.

HELMS, R. 1896. Anthropology [Elder Scientific Expedition]. *Transactions of the Royal Society of South Australia* 16: 237–332.

HOWARD, K. A. 2004. Ancestral Colorado River potholes high above Hoover Dam. Paper presented to the Annual Denver Meeting of the Geological Society of America, 10 November 2004, Paper No. 22-8.

IRRIBAREN, C. J. 1949. *Paradero indígena del Estero de Las Peñas*. Publicaciones del Museo Arqueológico de La Serena, Boletín 4, La Serena.

IRRIBAREN, C. J. 1954. *Los petroglifos de la Estancia Zorrilla y Las Peñas en el Departemento de Ovalle y un teoría de vinculación cronológica*. Revista Universitaria 34, Santiago.

JENNINGS, J. N. 1985. Cave and karst terminology. In P. G. Matthews (ed.), *Australian Karst Index 1985*, pp. 14.1–13. Australian Speleological Federation, Broadway.

JUTSON, J. T. 1934. *The physiography (geomorphology) or Western Australia*. Bulletin 95, Geological Survey of Western Australia, Perth.

KAYSER, E. 1912. *Lehrbuch der Geologie*, Teil I (4th edn). Stuttgart.

KLEIN, O. 1972. Cultura Ovalle. Complejo rupestre 'Cabezas-Tiara'. Petroglifos y pictografias del Valle del Encanto, Provincia de Coquimbo, Chile. *Scientia* 141: 5–123.

LANGE, F. W. 1996. *Paths to Central American prehistory*. University Press of Colorado. Niwot, Colorado.

LINDSAY, D. 1893. *Journal of the Elder Scientific Exploring Expedition*. Bristow, Adelaide.

LJUNGNER, E. 1927–1930. *Spaltentektonik and Morphologie der schwedischen Skagerrack-Küste*. Parts 1 to 3. Bulletin of the Geological Institution of the University of Upsala, Upsala.

LOWE, D. and T. WALTHAM 1995. *A dictionary of karst and caves: a brief guide to the terminology and concepts of cave and karst science*. Cave Studies Series 6, British Cave Research Association London.

MARTIN, K. 1887. *Westindische Skizzen, Reise-Erinnerungen*. Leiden.

MARTINI, I. P. 1978. Tafoni weathering, with examples from Tuscany, Italy. *Zeitschrift für Geomorphologie* 22(1): 44–67.

MATSUKURA, Y. and Y. TANAKA 2000. Effect of rock hardness and moisture content on tafoni weathering in the granite of Mount Doeg-sung, Korea. *Geografiska Annaler, Series A: Physical Geography* 82(1): 59–67.

MENGHIN, O. F. A. 1957. Las piedras de tacitas como fenómeno mundial. *Publicaciones del Museo Arqueológico y de la Sociedad Arqueológica de La Serena* 9: 3–12.

MIHEVC, A., T. SLABE and S. SEBEL 2004. The morphology of caves. In J. Gunn (ed.), *Encyclopedia of caves and karst science*, pp. 521–124. Fitzroy Dearborn, New York.

MONROE, W. H. (ed.) 1970. *A glossary of karst terminology*. Geological Survey Water-Supply Paper 1899-K. U.S. Geological Survey, U.S. Government Printing Office, Washington, D.C.

PAPANIKOLAOU, S. 2005. *600 'written rocks': channels of primeval knowledge. Prehistoric rock art from the Prefecture of Larissa*. Publications 'ella', Larissa, Greece.

REHBOCK, T. 1917. *Betrachtungen über Abfluss, Stand and Walzenbildung bei fliessenden Gewässern*. Berlin.

REHHOCK, T. 1925. *Die Bekämpfung der Schalenauskolkung bei Wehren durch Zahnschnellen*. Festschrift anlässlich des 100-jährigen Bestehens der Technischen Hochschule Friderician zu Karlsruhe, Karlsruhe.

RICHARDSON, K. and P. A. CARLING 2005. *A typology of sculpted forms in open bedrock channels*. Special Paper 392, Geological Society of America.

SHARLAND, M. S. R. 1957. Symbols of an extinct race. *Walkabout* 23(10): 38, 41–42.

SMITH, B. J. 1978. The origin and geomorphic implications of cliff foot recesses and tafoni on limestone *hamadas* in the Northwest Sahara. *Zeitschrift für Geomorphologie* 22(1): 21–43.

SPRINGER, G. S., S. TOOTH and E. E. WOHL 2005. Dynamics of pothole growth as defined by field data and geometrical description, *Journal of Geophysical Research* 110, F04010, doi:10.1029/2005JF000321.

SPRINGER, G. S., S. TOOTH and E. E. WOHL 2006. Theoretical modeling of stream potholes based upon empirical observations from the Orange River, Republic of South Africa. *Geomorphology* 82: 160–176.

SWINNERTON, A. C. 1927. Observations on some details of wave erosion — wave furrows and shore potholes. *Journal of Geology* 35: 171–179.

TINDALE, N. B. and H. A. LINDSAY 1963. *Aboriginal Australians*. Jacaranda Press, Brisbane.

TWIDALE, C. R. and E. M. CORBIN 1963. Gnammas. *Revue de Géomorphologie dynamique* 14: 1–20.

VAN HOEK, M. 2003. Tacitas or cupules? An attempt at distinguishing cultural depressions at two rock art sites near Ovalle, Chile. *Rupestreweb*, http://rupestreweb.tripod.com/tacitas.html

VORONOI, G. 1907. Nouvelles applications des paramètres continus à la théorie des formes quadratiques. *Journal für die Reine und Angewandte Mathematik* 133: 97–178.

THE TECHNOLOGY OF CUPULE MAKING

Robert G. Bednarik

Abstract. Cupules may seem simple features requiring little technological explanation, until one examines them in their wider context or in scientific detail. The technology of cupule making is considered in an introductory format, leading to a reassessment of the ideas researchers have formed about their significance. Parameters for replication experiments in making cupules are proposed, based on work already undertaken in recent years. The acute need for empirical recording data is identified, leading to a listing of the elements of a scientific system of quantifying cupules in the course of field surveys.

Keywords: Cupule, Replication, Percussion, Hammerstone, Mur-e, Recording standardisation

Introduction

If we exclude what has been written about the distribution of cupules (which is limited and biased), their purported meanings (which is almost universally pure conjecture; see chapter on interpretation in this volume) and futile speculation about their age, we find that the residue of the available literature on this topic is rather limited. This literature has accumulated for much longer than two centuries (consider Abel 1730), and yet it comprises very little in the way of sound scientific information. We have misidentified a host of natural rock markings as cupules and considered them together with authentic ones (see my chapter on discriminating cupules from other markings, this volume); we have invented many idiosyncratic names, cultural roles and attributed cupules to many cultures, usually without evidence. We have speculated about their antiquities and meanings for centuries, and we have without sound data theorised about how they were made. We have created a rich tapestry of cupule mythology, and very little in the way of scientific information.

For instance we have failed to attempt a comprehensive review of the rock types cupules occur on, so we were unable to consider the interdependence of lithology, technology and taphonomy of cupules, which would be a benchmark in their scientific study and a precondition to any valid attempt of etic interpretation. We have severely neglected to secure more ethnographic or emic data relating to them, which of course is an almost universal malaise in the archaeological study of global rock art. We have conducted almost no controlled replication work. Since we failed to develop a standard methodology of surveying cupules empirically, we have no credible statistical and metrical data on cupule morphology, and the published record on the study of work traces in cupules can fairly be described as pitiful. Our endeavours of investigating the gestures involved in the production of cupules are clearly inadequate (de Beaune 2000 being a rare exception), yet without such studies and the introduction of contextual studies our rampant speculations about meanings are mere noise. Archaeologists have even questioned whether cupules should be studied together with other forms of rock art. I contend that rock art science is much better equipped to deal with rock art generally, and with cupules specifically.

Inadequate technological research of cupules (as well as other petroglyphs) has led to numerous assumptions and assertions concerning the way they were made. In particular, many authors have assumed that cupules were produced through indirect percussion, grinding or polishing. For instance, Walsh (1994: 35) contends that some Kimberley cupules are what he terms 'pebraded', i.e. first pecked and then abraded, 'to create a very smooth recess and perimeter'. Although he acknowledges the very great investment of time and energy in making cupules, he goes on to suggest that they were made before the sandstone had fully metamorphosed. This implies that he misunderstood both the technology and the relevant petrography. Taphonomy ensures the preferential survival of cupules on the hardest rocks, which it would be impossible to abrade in the fashion Walsh imagines. The 'abraded' appearance he observed is the result of the pounding action: as the crystals or grains are literally crushed into fine dust particles, the cupule surface and its rim take on a macroscopically polished appearance. But under the binocular microscope, no evidence of abrasion has so far been observed in any genuine cupule anywhere in the world. Not only is the term 'abraded' clearly inappropriate here, the term 'pecked' (Maynard 1977) is so also. There is,

Figure 1. G. Kumar with two replicative cupules near Daraki-Chattan, central India, which were created by Kumar and associates.

as noted, no evidence that cupules were made by pecking (Keyser 2007 notwithstanding).

Until refuting evidence becomes available we may assume that all cupules on hard rock (hardness 4 to 7 on Mohs scale) were created by direct percussion, or pounding, and the type of tools used were those observed in ethnographic petroglyph production as well as in all replication work and relevant excavations to date (Bednarik 1998). Technologically, cupules on very soft rock are perhaps more interesting because in favourable circumstances, good traces of their production have remained intact. The softer the rock is, the greater the chance of detecting such traces, increasing the potential of securing valuable technological data. The softest rock on which cupules have been recorded is moisture-containing limestone in caves (Bednarik 1990), which is of hardness 1 to 1½. At one Australian site, hundreds of cupules have been observed on mudstone (hardness 3) with extensive, perfectly preserved work traces (see my chapter on lithology, this volume). Such instances show that indirect percussion has often been used on soft types of rock, but apparently with tools other than lithics. In particular, cupule-like pits in cave walls are the subject of a study by Yann-Pierre Montelle and myself, examining not only tool traces on limestone, but also the gestures involved in the making of these features. The results of this forensic work will be reported in a future paper.

Replication of cupules

In reviewing the technology of petroglyphs generally, I have briefly considered the replication of cupules I conducted and suggested parameters for standardising such experiments (Bednarik 1998: 30, Fig. 5). Since then, Kumar (see his chapter in the present volume) has undertaken more detailed replicative research (Figure 1) into the production of cupules at Daraki-Chattan, India (Bednarik et al. 2005: 168; Kumar 2007). He recorded the details of the hammerstones used (including their wear) in five experiments, the precise times taken for each cupule and the number of impact strikes counted. The first cupule created under his supervision, in 2002, was worked to a depth of 1.9 mm, using 8490 blows in 72 minutes of actual working time. Cupule 2 required on the first day 8400 blows in 66 minutes and reached a maximum depth of 4.4 mm, after which the maker was exhausted. He continued on a second day for another 120 minutes, achieving a total depth of 7.4 mm (total number of blows not recorded). Three more cupules were made in 2004, taking respectively 6916 blows to reach 2.55 mm depth, 1817 blows to achieve 0.05 mm (abandoned), and 21,730 blows (over 2 days) to reach a maximal depth of 6.7 mm. The experimenters suffered fatigue and physical pain and often had to interrupt their work to rest. Their cupules tend to be larger than those in nearby Daraki-Chattan Cave, illustrating lower striking precision relative to the Palaeolithic cupule makers who, we may safely assume, were also of much greater physical strength (consider traces of skeletal muscle attachments on fossil remains) and endurance (Figure 2). At the time of writing (December 2008), Kumar's continuation of his replication studies sought to determine how to keep the diameter of experimental cupules as small as that of the Lower Palaeolithic specimens.

Figure 2. Replication of cupules by Ramkrishna Prajapati, June 2009, at the location shown in Figure 1. Photograph by G. Kumar.

Kumar's precise observations show dramatically that an incredible physical effort was required

Figure 3. Ethnographically observed production of a cupule, at Pola Bhata, Madhya Pradesh, India, in 2004.

to create the Daraki-Chattan assemblage of more than 540 cupules on this extremely hard, almost unweathered quartzite. Additionally, two significant points must be considered. Firstly, the progress of depth relative to time or number of blows is not a linear relationship; as the cupule becomes deeper, progress slows down. Secondly, the smallness of all Palaeolithic cupules at this site is extraordinary. The modern replicator finds it difficult to match the precision in striking the rock that is so clearly and consistently demonstrated by the Palaeolithic operator. Most of the site's cupules are under 40 mm diameter, yet many are in excess of 6 mm deep. In the most extreme case observed at Daraki-Chattan, a cupule of only 25.5 mm diameter is worked to a depth of 9.2 mm. Kumar's fifth experimental cupule of 6.7 mm depth measured 77.7 mm × 59.0 mm, and had to be struck a staggering 21,730 times. We can reasonably assume that the ancient cupule of 9.2 mm depth required well in excess of 30,000 blows, and these were delivered with a precision that is almost certainly not achievable by a modern human. Thus the actual skill and sheer persistence of the ancient cupule makers is hard to fully appreciate.

It has often been suggested that petroglyphs were made by indirect percussion, and the same has been said about cupules. (Some archaeologists have even claimed that cupules were made by grinding or abrading.) If we assume, conservatively, that on average it took 10,000 blows to create each cupule at Daraki-Chattan, and if these blows had been delivered via an intermediary tool (a chisel or punch), such tools might have been struck, say, 5.4 million times. If we further assume that each chisel had been worn to a slug after being struck, say, 100 times (in reality the number would be much lower before they would need to be discarded), there would have to be at least 54,000 discarded stones with very distinctive bipolar wear at the site (unless someone had removed them intentionally). If each of these discarded chisels had weighed, say, 80 g, I would expect to find over four tonnes of them in the floor deposit. Not a single such implement has been found in the entire excavation, but a good number of mur-e (direct percussion hammerstones) has been excavated (Bednarik et al. 2005). It is also relevant that all petroglyph (including cupule) production observed ethnographically involved direct percussion, or pounding (Figure 3), and not pecking (sensu Maynard 1977); and that those who have conducted controlled petroglyph replication work (Crawford 1964: 44; McCarthy 1967: 19; Sierts 1968; Savvateyev 1977; Bednarik 1991, 1998; Weeks 2001; Kumar 2007) uniformly regard indirect percussion as impracticable or impossible to use effectively.

The production of cupules on extremely hard rock types was therefore a lengthy process demanding great physical power, accuracy and dedication. I note in passing that the deepest cupule measured on very hard rock in India (at Moda Bhata), occurring on pure white quartz, is about 100 mm deep (Bednarik et al. 2005: 181). The number of percussion blows or the amount of time and effort lavished on just this one cupule must be staggering (Figure 4).

Standardisation of experiments

On the other hand, in trying to establish a standardised approach to replicative experiments in petroglyph production, I have nominated 12 mm depth as the standard for cupules, and reported that on well-weathered Gondwana-type sandstone, it takes only about two minutes to create such a cupule (Bednarik 1998: 30). I have worked on

Figure 4. Cupules on crystalline white quartz at Moda Bhata, Rajasthan, India.

such stone in all present major sections of Gondwana (southern Africa, north-western Brazil, northern Australia and India), except in Antarctica. Quartzite is chemically and morphologically very similar to sandstone, except that this sedimentary rock has been metamorphosed (i.e. recrystallised). There is in fact a continuum between the two types of rock, with respective characteristics determined by the degree of metamorphosis. It is obvious that to create a cupule of 12 mm depth on the Daraki-Chattan quartzite would take several days and presumably result in severe RSI (repetitive strain injury). This provides a basic appreciation of the importance of lithology, which is discussed in a separate chapter of this volume.

The study of cupules could be improved significantly by standardising both the descriptive surveys of cupule sites and by adopting specific guidelines for conducting replication experiments. Since my proposal of 1998 remains the only one offered so far, I suggest that it could be adopted to render all such work fully compatible. Accordingly, as a measure of how hard it is to create a cupule on rock of today's weathering condition, one would produce a cupule of the smallest possible size of a depth of 12 mm, using a typical hammerstone (mur-e) of the kind used by traditional cupule makers (Figure 5). This would be a cobble of hard stone, such as quartzite, quartz or granitic stone of roughly 100 to 200 g mass, i.e. about fist size. The stone would not be pre-shaped or trimmed, but there would be a preference for a cobble of slightly elongate shape, perhaps with a somewhat pointed end (Figure 6). The rock would be struck in a rhythm of blows timed to the natural rebound of the tool, the duration of the process would be timed, and perhaps the number of blows would be counted. Thus the diameter of the finished cupule can be measured, but the crucial variable in the experiment is its depth, measured with the help of callipers (it is preferred to use plastic-type callipers rather than metal ones in measuring any dimensions of petroglyphs, so as not to scratch crystal facets or surface features). The depth is measured from the deepest point to a line bridging the cupule rim, perpendicular to that line. The smallness of the cupule diameter is considered to be a function of the accuracy of blows and the skill of the operator.

The results of such experiments will show that the time it takes to make such a standard cupule of 12 mm depth can range from a few seconds (on rock of hardness 1 on Mohs Scale) to several days of actual working time (on rock of hardness 7), i.e. it varies dramatically depending on the rock's hardness, by a factor of up to over one thousand times.

Conversely, the second form of 'standard petroglyph' I have proposed is a groove of 10 cm length and 10 mm depth, to show the times required to create grooves on various lithologies (cf. Figure 5). Little work of this type has been conducted so far.

There is also a great deal of scope for further development of replication experiments with cupules to provide much more comprehensive technological information. This is essential for their systematic study, and needs to become part of general recording procedures. As in any scientific pursuit, there needs to be standardisation of methods, in the case of cupules ranging from replication studies to all aspects of their recording.

Defining cupules scientifically

The principal condition for effectively studying the technology of cupules is the availability of comprehensive empirical descriptions. These are generally lacking at the present time, essentially because no universal recording standard has been proposed. Such a standard would need to facilitate

Figure 5. First recorded replication of a cupule, near Toro Muerto petroglyph site, Mizque, central Bolivia, in 1987 by the author. The linear groove and the cupule were made with the respective hammerstones placed next to each mark.

technological and taphonomic studies of cupules, which should determine its nature and scope. However, limitations of time, resources and competence may impair the comprehensiveness of the recording work possible to any recorder, therefore it seems preferable to introduce two sets of guidelines. I first list the absolute minimum requirements, as I perceive them, and then those I would hope to see met in studies professing to be comprehensive:

Minimum level: petrology, surface condition, rim diameter, maximum depth, ratio of diameter to depth, rim inclination, spatial relationship with other cupules (layout) and other site aspects; for details see corresponding entries for comprehensive level recording.

Figure 6. Typical hammerstones used in direct percussion to produce cupules.

Comprehensive level:
1. Petrology: type of rock, hardness.
2. Weathering condition of adjacent rock surface.
3. Surface condition within cupule (e.g. accretionary deposit, weathering, lichen).
4. General orientation of the cupule.
5. Maximum rim diameter (vertical dimension in case of vertical panel).
6. Rim diameter measured at right angle to the maximum diameter.
7. Maximum depth.
8. Ratio of maximum rim diameter divided by maximum depth.
9. Inclination of a plane formed by the rim, relative to horizontal plane.
10. For cupules on vertical or steeply inclined panels, vertical distance between the deepest point and the projected geometric centre of the rim plane (d^v, expressing the 'sagging' section), see Figure 7.
11. For cupules on vertical or steeply inclined panels, horizontal displacement of deepest point from the geometric centre of the rim plane (presumed to indicate handedness of maker).
12. Definition of overall shape of cupule (e.g. by measuring the diameter at an arbitrarily selected distance from the deepest point).
13. Presence and nature of tool traces in the cupule and on its rim.
14. Any indications that the cupule has been retouched subsequent to a much earlier production.
15. Spatial relationship with other, nearby cupules (e.g. appearance of geometric arrangement, alignment, or random).
16. Presence of other markings (impact, scraping) in the immediate vicinity of the cupule.
17. Exposure of the cupule to precipitation and insolation.
18. General description of the group of cupules.
19. Any indications that the cupules are of similar or different ages.
20. General description of site morphology, archaeology and location.

If possible, a microscopic examination of the cupule floor should also be attempted, and its results recorded. Field microscopy is one of the most important methods in rock art science (Bednarik 2007a: 170–2), and yet it is significantly under-utilised. In the case of cupules it is likely to provide the most important types of empirical information for clarifying the phenomenon's status, especially the following:

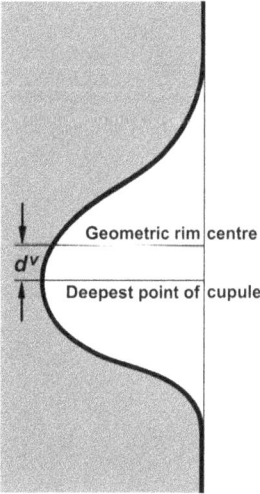

Figure 7. Typical section through the majority of cupules on vertical panels, showing the vertical displacement of the deepest point below the geometrical centre.

a. Presence, nature and condition of impact-damaged crystals or grains (Bednarik 1992).
b. Presence of truncation facets caused by abrasion of crystals or grains (Bednarik 2000).
c. Presence of microscopic striae on abrasion facets (Bednarik 2000).
d. Degree of microerosion on edges of crystal fractures or truncation planes (Bednarik 1992).
e. Weathering state at the microscopic level (Bednarik 2007b).
f. Condition of alveolar erosion patterns (Bednarik 1995).
g. Nature, condition and extent of any accretionary deposit (Bednarik 2007b).

These variables can be decidedly crucial in determining such aspects of cupules as their authenticity, technology and age, but they can also be of great significance to basic recording issues. Most obviously, the specialist will in a recording report look for indications that there are at least remnants of the original surface (i.e. the surface when the cupule was last worked) remaining, which in some cases may well be just a few grains. This information is absolutely essential in determining whether an attempt to apply microerosion analysis is worthwhile. It cannot be recorded without at least careful examination with a magnifying glass (10× or 20×), which is one of numerous reasons why the second-most important implement in a rock art researcher's toolkit (after a colour calibration device, such as the IFRAO Standard Scale) is indeed a good magnifying glass.

It is only through the provision of such detailed and systematic empirical data that the study of cupules generally, and more specifically that of their technology, can expect to attain scientific status. With some very rare exceptions, all information so far provided for cupules is inadequate to initiate a scientific study of this phenomenon. Only the most basic information is usually available, it is unreliable, and distorted by countless epistemological issues, such as preconceived interpretations. On that basis it is clear that the scientific study of cupules remains in its embryonic state, which by extension can be said about most other rock art also. It is up to researchers to change this incipient state of the discipline.

REFERENCES

ABEL, C. 1730. *Teutsche und Sächsische Alterthümer*. Braunschweig.
BEAUNE, S. A. DE 2000. *Pour une archéologie du geste*. CNRS Éditions, Paris.
BEDNARIK, R. G. 1990. The cave petroglyphs of Australia. *Australian Aboriginal Studies* 1990(2): 64–68.
BEDNARIK, R. G. 1991. Standardisation in rock art terminology. In C. Person and B. K. Swartz (eds), *Rock art and posterity: conserving, managing and recording rock art*, pp. 116–118. Occasional AURA Publication 4, Australian Rock Art Research Association, Melbourne.
BEDNARIK, R. G. 1992. A new method to date petroglyphs. *Archaeometry* 34(2): 279–291.
BEDNARIK, R. G. 1995. The age of the Côa valley petroglyphs in Portugal. *Rock Art Research* 12(2): 86–103.
BEDNARIK, R. G. 1998. The technology of petroglyphs. *Rock Art Research* 15: 23–35.
BEDNARIK, R. G. 2000. Age estimates for the petroglyph sequence of Inca Huasi, Mizque, Bolivia. *Andean Past* 6: 277–287.
BEDNARIK, R. G. 2007a. *Rock art science: the scientific study of palaeoart* (2nd edn; 1st edn 2001). Aryan Books International, New Delhi.
BEDNARIK, R. G. 2007b. The science of Dampier rock art — part 1. *Rock Art Research* 24(2): 209–246.
BEDNARIK, R. G., G. KUMAR, A. WATCHMAN and R. G. ROBERTS 2005. Preliminary results of the EIP Project. *Rock Art Research* 22(2): 147–197.
CRAWFORD, I. M. 1964. The engravings of Depuch Island. In W. D. L. Ride and A. Neumann (eds), *Depuch Island*, pp. 23–63. Western Australian Museum Special Publication 2, Perth.
FLOOD, J. 2006. Copying the Dreamtime: anthropic marks in early Aboriginal Australia. *Rock Art Research* 23: 239–246.
KEYSER, J. D. 2007. Direct evidence for the use of indirect percussion in petroglyph manufacture. *International Newsletter on Rock Art* 49: 25–27.
KUMAR, G. 2007. Understanding the creation of early cupules by replication with special reference to Daraki-Chattan in India. Paper presented to the International Cupule Conference, Cochabamba, 17–19 July.
MCCARTHY, F. D. 1967. *Australian Aboriginal rock art* (3rd edn). Australian Museum, Sydney.
MAYNARD, L. 1977. Classification and terminology of Australian rock art. In P. J. Ucko (ed.), *Form in indigenous art: schematisation in the art of Aboriginal Australia and prehistoric Europe*, pp. 385–402. Australian Institute of Aboriginal Studies, Canberra.
SAVVATEYEV, J. A. 1977. *Zalavruga, cast' II. Stojanki*. Nauka, Leningradskoe otdelenie, Leningrad.
SIERTS, W. 1968. How were rock engravings made? *South African Journal of Science* 64: 281–285.
WALSH, G. L. 1994. *Bradshaws: ancient rock paintings of north-west Australia*. The Bradshaw Foundation, Edition Limitee, Carouge-Geneva.
WEEKS, R. 2001. Indirect percussion: fact or fiction. In S. M. Freers and A. Woody (eds), *American Indian Rock Art* 27: 117–121.

UNDERSTANDING THE CREATION OF EARLY CUPULES BY REPLICATION, WITH SPECIAL REFERENCE TO DARAKI-CHATTAN IN INDIA

Giriraj Kumar

Abstract. Daraki-Chattan is the richest known Lower Palaeolithic cupule site, located in the Chambal basin in India. Its two walls bear more than 500 cupules. Most of the first half portion of the southern wall is devoid of cupules on its surface. It must have been exfoliated and fallen below. It means sediments in front of the cave should contain pieces of cupule-bearing slabs and also some of the hammerstones (mur-e) used for their production. It became necessary to understand what sort of hammerstones we could expect from the excavation and how these were used for creation of cupules. Hence we experimented with the round quartzite cobbles obtained from the palaeochannel of the river and tried to replicate the process of cupule creation in 2002 and 2004. It was a successful experiment. The paper presents the experience, results and observations made in this process.

Keywords: Cupule, Replication, Experiment, EIP project, Daraki-Chattan, India

Introduction

Daraki-Chattan is the richest Lower Palaeolithic cupule site currently known, and is located in the Chambal basin in India. It is a small narrow cave in quartzite buttresses of Indragarh Hill, bearing more than 500 cupules on its two vertical walls. Distribution pattern, shape and size of these cupules in Daraki-Chattan were documented by Giriraj Kumar with the help of his son Ramakrishna in 1995 (Kumar 1995: 17–28). Kumar observed that the shape of the cupules in Daraki-Chattan is generally circular, sometimes elongated and rarely angular. The circular cupules are both medium to deep in depth while elongated ones are deeper at their lower portion. Angular cupules are small and have angular periphery and corresponding round base. The cupules bear generally smooth surfaces.

Most of the first half portion of the southern wall is devoid of cupules on its surface. It must have been exfoliated and fallen below. It means sediments in front of the cave should contain pieces of cupule-bearing slabs and also some of the hammerstones used for their production. Both were indeed found during excavations.

Daraki-Chattan and its adjoining region have been intensively studied in 1995 by Kumar (1995: 17–28) and afterwards under the EIP Project, a joint venture by the Rock Art Society of India (RASI) and the Australian Rock Art Research Association (AURA) under the aegis of the International Federation of Rock Art Organisations (IFRAO), with the support from the Archaeological Survey of India, the Indian Council of Historical Research and the Australia-India Council, Canberra. The name EIP Project is a short form of the high-profile multidisciplinary project, 'Early Indian Petroglyphs: Scientific Investigations and Dating by International Commission'. The project commenced in 2001 and is still continuing. The team of Indo-Australian scientists has been working under the direction of Giriraj Kumar and Robert G. Bednarik, the Indian and Australian Directors of the Project. Excavations and explorations at Daraki-Chattan and in the associated region were conducted under the direction of G. Kumar from 2002 to 2006 (Kumar et al. 2005; Kumar 2006). The preliminary results of the EIP Project have been published in 2005 both in India and Australia (Kumar et al. 2005: 13–68; Bednarik et al. 2005: 147–197).

Observations on cupules in Daraki-Chattan in 1995

1. Giriraj Kumar studied and documented 496 cupules on both walls of Daraki-Chattan cave in 1995. Out of these 402 cupules are circular or almost circular, 85 are elongated and 9 are more angular in shape.
2. Almost all the cupules and the bedrock around them bear light-brown patina. Most of them also bear encrustation.
3. The dimension and shape of the cupules, their smooth

Figure 1. Hammerstone obtained from close to bedrock in the eastern part of the trench in Daraki-Chattan, Lower Palaeolithic.

Figure 2. Close-up of the striking end of the hammerstone in Figure 1.

surface and even fracturing of crystals in them indicate that a primitive and stout stone tool with broad and round striking end was used as mur-e for their execution. A few cupules, only 9 out of 496 studied, with conical or angular depth might have been made by the use of an implement with somewhat more pointed striking end.

Why replication of cupule creation?

1. There is no reference of the excavations at the early, more specifically Lower Palaeolithic, cupule site in the world, so also about the replication work for understanding the creation of such early cupules. 'The technology of petroglyphs', a paper by Bednarik (1998: 23–35), presents a preliminary general survey about the state of the knowledge regarding the creation of petroglyphs in general, at a global level. He emphasises the need for replication work with scientific methodology. But it also does not help much to understand our problem, as ours was the first study of its kind on very archaic cupules in the world. Hence we have to follow our own course.

2. We invited Mr S. B Ota, Superintendent Archaeologist, Archaeological Survey of India, Bhopal Circle and Dr R. K. Ganjoo, Reader in Department of Geology, University of Jammu for the study of Daraki-Chattan and river deposits in the Rewa river valley at Indragarh. They visited the site from 8 to 11 June 2002. Ota is an expert in Stone Age archaeology and Ganjoo in Quaternary sedimentology and palaeoclimatic studies. We utilised their visit for discussion on various issues arising from the excavations, study of Daraki-Chattan and the river deposits on the hill and in the river valley at Indragarh. One of the issues was the creation of cupules in the cave. Ota was of the opinion that cupules with smooth surface were produced by rotating a flake as he observed two radiating lines in one of the cupule. Ganjoo also agreed with Ota. But Kumar disagreed with both of them. From the very beginning, he was of the opinion that cupules with smooth surface were produced by direct percussion technique. He was also not convinced with the radiating lines observed by Ota and Ganjoo. They were the result of weathering of the deposited encrustation on the cupule surface. Hence, in order to understand the actual process of cupule creation at Daraki-Chattan Cave and to put an end to the suggestions of unscientific imaginations for cupule creation Kumar decided to replicate cupule creation.

3. As the cave bears more than 500 cupules, many hammerstones (mur-e) must have been used and a sufficient number of them must have been lying buried in the sediments in front of the cave. Hence, we were expecting to find many hammerstones (mur-e) from the excavations, but we were not finding them as expected. Secondly, we were recovering in the excavations hammerstone-like objects, but while observing the battered surfaces under the 10× magnifying glass the crystals appeared in their almost original geometrical shape. The fractured crystals of the battered surface of the hammerstones had been removed by weathering of the cementing material. We found the logical answer to this problem when we observed the ongoing weathering process on the cupules on Chanchalamata hill near Daraki-Chattan, leaving only the cast of the cupules. Therefore, it was necessary for us to understand what kind of the convincing hammerstones (mur-e) we could secure from the excavations and how these might have been used for the creation of cupules.

4. Hence, we tried to replicate the process of cupule creation and did experiment with round quartzite cobbles obtained from the pre-Quaternary palaeochannel of a mighty former river on the eastern side of the Indragarh Hill. Such cobbles had also been used by early humans

Figure 3. Hammerstone obtained from layer 5 in the excavation of Daraki-Chattan, Lower Palaeolithic. Photograph by R. G. Bednarik.

Figure 4. Another early hammerstone obtained from excavation at Daraki-Chattan, Lower Palaeolithic.

as hammerstones as revealed by the excavations at Daraki-Chattan (Figures 1 to 4). It was a major and successful exercise to understand the process of cupule creation in Daraki-Chattan performed in 2002 and 2004.

Replication of cupules

The quartzite rock at Daraki-Chattan is finely crystallised and very hard; hence we cannot produce cupules of the kind in Daraki-Chattan by rotating flakes as suggested by Ota. Even if it could produce such cupules, it must have been a very long labour-some and impractical process of cupule creation.

From the very beginning, as mentioned above, I was convinced that most of the cupules at Daraki-Chattan were created by direct percussion technique with hammerstones (mur-e), as only this method can yield cupules with smooth surfaces observed in Early Stone Age specimens. I decided to experiment on the vertical rock of a rockshelter close to Daraki-Chattan towards its south and produced cupules. In front of it we used to sort out the excavated material on a big flat rock.

12 and 13 June 2002

I brought nine cobbles from Patasi-Ghati because such cobbles were also used as hammerstones as revealed by the excavations at Daraki-Chattan. These cobbles are of hard quartzite rock with nearly 1-mm-thick ochre-yellow rind and very hard purple red core in side. I photographed the rock surface and also the cobbles arranged in three horizontal rows and numbered them from bottom to top, starting from left to right in each row.

Record of the work of Hira Lal Gujar

Cobble No. 6, small in size (9.4 × 9.1 × 3.88 cm) and angular in shape with weathered cortex (rind) was given to Hira Lal Gujar, a right-handed young man. He started work at 8:00 am.

1. 8:00 to 8:25, 25 mins of striking with 110 strokes/min. Rest for 7 mins.
2. 8:32 to 8:52, 20 mins of striking with 125 strokes/min. Rest for 3 mins.
3. 8:55 to 9:00, 5 mins of striking with 120 strokes/min. Rest for 36 mins.
4. 9:36 to 9:41, 5 mins of striking with 120 strokes/min. Rest for 02 mins.
5. 9;43 to 9:50, 7 mins of striking with 120 strokes/min. Rest for 02 mins.
6. 9:52 to 10:02, 10 mins of striking with 120 strokes/min. Rest for 03 mins.

Thus, Hira Lal Gujar worked from 8:00 am to 10:05 am, rested for 53 minutes and actually worked for 72 minutes. He struck the rock 8490 (2750 + 2500 + 600 + 600 + 840 + 1200) times. After two hours of striking Hira Lal produced a small shallow cup mark with smooth surface and measuring 42.0 × 36.6 x 1.9 mm in size. It was recorded as RC.1.

The length of the hammerstone was reduced by 12 mm i.e. from 9.4 cm to 8.2 cm. The angular striking point became flat (31 × 8 mm). Striking also resulted in chipping off the hammer along the striking portion of the cobble. The striking point became smooth because of the fracturing and crushing of the crystals of the cobble.

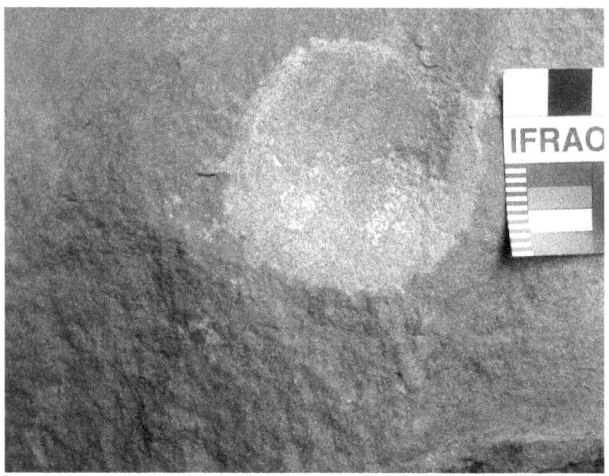

Figure 5. The replicated cupule RC.2 produced by Janaki Lal Gujjar in 2002.

Figure 6. Two cobbles to be used as hammerstones in the replication of cupules in 2004.

Record of the work of Janaki Lal Gujar

Cobble No. 3, a comparatively big and round cobble, flaked off at one portion, hence a triangular stout portion without cortex was available for striking. It was given to another young man, Janaki Lal Gujar, a left-hander. As he was striking directly with the hard purple core with three angular edges merging at the striking point, it was exerting a lot of strength and pressure on the striking surface. His strokes were steady and powerful. He started his work at 8:05 am as follows:

1. 8:05 to 8:23, 18 mins of striking with 135 strokes/min. Rest for 7 mins.
2. 8:30 to 8:51, 21 mins of striking with 130 strokes/min. Rest for 4 mins.
3. 8:55 to 9:00, 5 mins of striking with 120 strokes/min. Rest for 36 mins.
4. 9:36 to 9:44, 8 mins of striking with 120 strokes/min. Rest for 2 mins.
5. 9:46 to 9:50, 4 mins of striking with 120 strokes/min. Rest for 2 mins.
6. 9:52 to 10:02, 10 mins of striking with 120 strokes/min. Rest for 2 mins.

Thus, Janaki Lal Gujar worked from 8:05 am to 10:05 am, rested for 53 minutes and actually worked for 66 minutes. He struck the rock 8400 (2430 + 2730 + 600 + 960 + 480 + 1200) times. His two hours of striking produced a comparatively big and deep cupule with smooth surface, measuring 47 × 58 × 4.4 mm. It was recorded as RC.2.

Janaki Lal started striking at a rate of 135 strokes/min. After 30 minutes the speed of his striking reduced to 120 strokes/min. Being left-handed he did most of the work with the left hand, but sometimes he also used his right hand when he felt tired. The dimensions of the triangular striking end of the hammerstone are 40 × 63 mm. The tool wear occurred along the margin of the struck surface. The big hammerstone produced a big and deep cupule with smooth surface, compared to smaller one, which produced a comparatively smaller and shallow cupule.

Janaki Lal continued working on replication cupule RC.2, now measuring 47 × 58 × 4.4 mm, in the morning on 13 June. Now he took cobble No. 2 as a new hammerstone (mur-e). It measured 10.95 × 9.50 × 4.95 in size and it was half cleaved. This time focusing to strike in the centre became possible with a new hammerstone. Hence, cupule depth increased markedly.

In the beginning we also observed the rim formed of the previously struck surface which ultimately disappeared with the increase in the depth of the cupule. After 60 minutes of striking the new dimensions of the cupule became 54 × 61 × 5 mm. Striking on this cupule went on for the next 60 minutes. The final dimensions of the replicated cupule were 56.4 × 61.0 × 7.4 mm. It was the result of four hours of work over two days on a single cupule (Figure 5).

Hira's strokes were comparatively light to Janaki's. The struck rock being very hard quartzite, the hammer rebounds with equal force with each stroke, and gives a powerful jerk in the shoulder of the worker. Hence, a person working on replication of cupule creation should be of athletic built and considerable physical strength, and have the commitment and patience of Janaki Lal Gujar to produce a big and deep cupule.

Replication of cupules in 2004

To enrich our experience of cupule creation and to record the process more systematically, we resumed the replication of cupule creation on our previous experimental rock panel on the right side of the cave on 19 and 20 June 2004. This time the replication work was done by two urban young men, not by rural ones as in 2002. The main objectives of

Figure 7. Work for replication of a cupule begins in 2004.

Figure 8. Recording of time and strokes in the process of cupule replication.

this exercise were:

1. To determine the duration required creating a cupule.
2. To observe the gradual development in the striking facet of the hammerstone.

Strokes were counted at 15-minute intervals. The diameter and depth of the cupule in the process of its creation were measured, also the dimensions of the developing striking area of the hammerstone at the same time. Both were repeatedly photographed at 15-minute intervals.

We started work by using the pointed stones obtained from excavation as hammerstones, but observed that they are not very suitable for the work because of their weathered cortex. Hence we had to select again the cobbles from Patasi-Ghati for use as hammerstones (Figure 6). Various aspects of this work in 2004 are shown in Figures 7 to 14.

Figure 9. Hammerstone after striking for 15 mins.

Figure 10. Replicated cupule after 15 mins.

Figure 11. Replicated hammerstone after striking for 30 mins.

19 June 2004

Replicated cupule No. RC.3:

Time period in hrs	No. of strokes	Cupule dimensions diameter, depth	Dimensions of the surface of hammerstone
08:00 to 08:15	1826	32.0–32.0 mm, 0.32 mm	22.0 × 37.7 mm, HS-1
08:45 to 09:00	1907	36.0–46.1 mm, 1.80 mm	32.0 × 46.4 mm
09:45 to 10:00	1688	38.8–41.5 mm, 2.00 mm	15.0 × 48.8 mm, HS-2
11:40 to 11:55	1495	38.8–48.5 mm, 2.55 mm	13.0 × 53.0 mm

Observation: chips flaked off on both sides of the striking end of the hammerstone. Two hammerstones were used.

Replicated cupule No. RC.4:

Time period in hrs	No. of strokes	Cupule dimensions diameter, depth	Dimensions of the surface of hammersto
12:35 to 12:50	1817	36.0–36.0 mm, 0.05 mm	40.0 × 46.0 mm, HS-3

Abandoned as it was not on convenient place to work.

Replicated cupule No. RC.5:

Time period in hrs	No. of strokes	Cupule dimensions diameter, depth	Dimensions of the surface of hammerstone
08:05 to 08:20	1570	38.4–32.0 mm, 0.70 mm	43.0 × 21.0 mm, HS-4
08:40 to 08:55	1638	41.0–38.6 mm, 0.80 mm	47.0 × 24.0 mm
10:35 to 10:50	1410 Flaked off	45.5–39.0 mm, 1.00 mm	46.0 × 30.0 mm, HS-5
11:35 to 11:50	1824 Heavily flaked off	43.0–49.0 mm, 2.00 mm	41.1 × 35.6 mm
12:00 to 12:15	1123 Big, heavy flake detached from HS	46.0–64.0 mm, 2.70 mm	35.0 × 44.0 mm, HS-6
12:25 to 12:40	1202 Dia. unchanged	46.0–64.0 mm,	
12:45 to 13:00	1084 Dia. unchanged	46.0–64.0 mm,	
13:15 to 13:30	1443 Dia. unchanged	46.0–64.0 mm, 3.10 mm	HS-7
13:30 to 13:45	1419 Dia. unchanged	46.0–64.0 mm, 3.80 mm	

Work on RC.5 continues on 20 June 2004:

07:30 to 07:45	1488	77.4–58.0 mm, 4.7 mm	28.4 × 55.0 mm
08:15 to 08:30	1285	78.0–62.0 mm, 5.0 mm	31.4 × 56.0 mm
09:00 to 09:15	1255	78.0–62.0 mm, 5.1 mm	31.0 × 57.0 mm, flaked off
12:00 to 12:15	1489	78.0–64.8 mm, 5.7 mm	29.0 × 57.0 mm, flaked off

(HS-7 was used six times of the 15-min duration. Then a new pointed cobble from Patasi Ghati was used as hammerstone No. HS-8.)

12:45 to 13:00	1415	78.0–64.8 mm, 6.0 mm	21.0 × 48.0 mm. HS-8
13:00 to 13:15	1147	................., 6.4 mm	....
13:30 to 13:45	938	77.7–59.0 mm, 6.7 mm	64.0 × 35.0 mm

Only inner portion (57.7 × 46.7 mm) proceeding deep

Figure 12. Another hammerstone used for replication work.

Figure 13. One more hammerstone used at the conclusion of replicating a cupule.

7. After achieving certain diameter and depth, further strokes affect only the inner portion of the cupule, thus the outer diameter generally remains the same while depth gradually increases. It is like cutting through the earlier hammered surface.
8. The hammerstones yielded from the Daraki-Chattan excavation are generally similar to the initial stage of striking of the experimental hammerstones. They were used mostly at more than one point. It means the hammerstones we are getting in the excavation were not used at one point for long, but rather for short durations of direct percussion.

Observations

1. Chips flaked off on both sides of the striking end of the hammerstone (mur-e). The processes of battering of the mur-e surface and chipping on both its sides occur simultaneously.
2. When the hammerstone is struck forcefully, small to big chips chipped off result in elongated battered surface with chipping marks on its both sides, while on striking normally and rhythmically only small chips came out, and chipping remains minimum, thus resulting in the battered round surface facets of the excavated mur-e. In the excavations we found mostly the first kind of mur-e, only one of the second kind that, too, was from the upper levels of the sediments.
3. A broad cupule with irregular periphery means it was created by untrained hands.
4. Medium-size, deep cupules with regular periphery can be produced by trained, skilled and physically strong persons.
5. Creation of deep cupules as in Daraki-Chattan needs many specific hammerstones and use of some specific technique with great patience.
6. Broad deep cupules are executed by use of multiple hammerstones. Heavy hammers are not practically useful for the creation of a cupule.

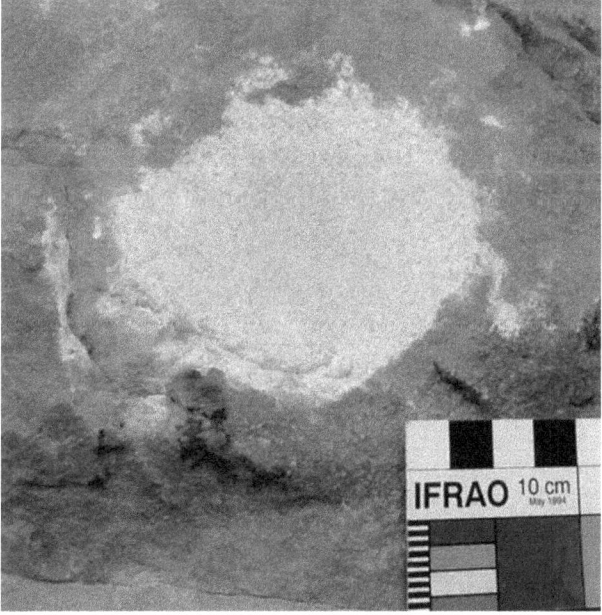

Figure 14. Replicated cupule RC.5 at conclusion of experiment, 2004.

Comments

The replication of cupules helped us understanding that:

1. The creation of cupules on hard quartzite rock is a very long and labour-consuming task. It took the urban workers 240 minutes of actual striking over two days and seven mur-e to produce a cupule of 77.7–59.0 mm diameter and 6.7 mm depth. Janaki Lal Gujar, a shepherd, created a cupule of 56.4–61.0 mm diameter and 7.4 mm depth in 138 minutes of actual striking.
2. However, circular cupules can be created by direct percussion technique by using mur-e of comparatively harder rock as the round quartzite cobbles from Patasi Ghati with very hard purple core.
3. The mur-e must be of suitable size and shape for a firm grip and of suitable weight to be handled comfortably. The weight of mur-e varies according to the strength and capability of its user.
4. The struck rock being very hard, the mur-e rebounds with equal force with each stroke, and gives a powerful jerk in the shoulder of the worker. Hence, the modern person working on replication of cupule creation must have physical strength, commitment and patience, like that of Janaki Lal Gujar, to produce a big and deep cupule.

Acknowledgments

The present work of the replication of cupules is an important part of the EIP project, hence I want to extend my sincere thanks to the authorities of the RASI, AURA, ASI, ICHR and Australia-India Council for their support to carry on this project. I am also thankful to Janaki Lal Gujar, Hira Lal Gujar, Ramakrishna and Mangal Singh for actually performing the task, and to Aniruddh Bhatt and Arakhita Pradhan for recording the strokes. I am also thankful to Mr S. B. Ota and Dr R. K. Ganjoo whose comments persuaded me to embark on the replication of cupules to understand the process scientifically. My heartfelt thanks are also due to Mr Robert G. Bednarik for his suggestions and for reviewing the initial draft of this paper. I am also thankful to Prof. Roy Querejazu Lewis to include the Symposium 7 on replication work with cupules in the International Cupule Conference 2007, Cochabamba, Bolivia, from 17 to 23 July 2007.

REFERENCES

BEDNARIK, R. G. 1998. The technology of petroglyphs. *Rock Art Research* 15: 23–35.

BEDNARIK, R. G., G. KUMAR, A. WATCHMAN and R. G. ROBERTS 2005. Preliminary results of the EIP Project. *Rock Art Research* 22: 147–197.

KUMAR, G. 1995a. Daraki-Chattan: a Palaeolithic cupule site in India. *Purakala* 6(1–2): 17–28.

KUMAR, G. 1995b. Petroglyphs in the rock art of Chambal valley and Aravalli Hills: a new phenomenon. Paper presented in the Symposium 14D, 'News of the World' in the News 95 — International Rock Art Congress, Torino, Italy, 30 August to 6 September.

KUMAR, G. 1996. Daraki-Chattan: a Palaeolithic cupule site in India. *Rock Art Research* 13: 38–45.

KUMAR, G. 2006. A preliminary report of the excavations at Daraki-Chattan 2006. *Purakala* 16: 51–55.

KUMAR, G, R. G. BEDNARIK, A. WATCHMAN and R. G. ROBERTS 2005. The EIP Project in 2005: a progress report. *Purakala* 14–15: 13–68.

KUMAR, G., P. K. BHATT, A. PRADHAN and R. KRISHNA 2006. Discovery of early petroglyphs sites in Chambal valley, Madhya Pradesh. *Purakala* 16: 13–34.

THE INTERPRETATION OF CUPULES

Robert G. Bednarik

Abstract. Cupules have been subjected to interpretation attempts for as long as they have been investigated, and thousands of such attempts have been recorded over the past two centuries. Most of them were presented without any credible supporting evidence and are essentially ethnocentric constructs arrived at by unsophisticated contemplation. They are devoid of any cultural or taphonomic considerations, knowledge of antiquity or technological appreciation, and they are not susceptible to refutation attempts; hence they are not scientifically relevant. Only a minute number of sound ethnographic interpretations are available, and they are always site-specific or culture-specific; therefore no form of generic explanation for cupules can be offered. Such form of interpretation can only be attempted after a massive improvement in the currently very inadequate database we posses of cupules, much of which is distorted by futile interpretation endeavours.

Keywords: Cupule, Meaning, Interpretation, Ethnography, Symbolism, Utilitarian purpose, Belief system

Introduction

In the well over 200 years of research of cupules (Abel 1730), the greatest emphasis has perhaps been placed on the question of their meaning or purpose. By comparison, their scientific properties have been almost completely neglected. Needless to say, before we can address the question of their interpretation we need to secure comprehensive data of their metrical, statistical, distributional and morphological characteristics (see chapter on technology, this volume), and relate these to their lithology and taphonomy before we can say anything relevant about the circumstances of their production, which may in turn permit sound deductions of their purpose. This is the fundamental sequence of research priorities we need to follow.

As we see from the chapter on the ethnography of cupules in this volume, there is almost no sound ethnographic information available globally on the emic significance of cupules. Indeed, that minute data that we do have tell us unambiguously that the correct interpretation could have never been guessed without such information (cf. especially Macintosh 1977). That observation already indicates the futility of trying to invent simplistic explanations.

A list of potential interpretations of cupules

The most commonly mentioned interpretations of cupules found in the literature could be grouped into a number of classes, based on their purported uses.

1. Unspecified or specified cultic or magic rituals

1.1: Components of sacrificial altars (e.g. Anati 1968: 17).
1.2: Human or animal blood sacrifices (e.g. Magni 1901: 91; Tschurtschenthaler 1934a: 63; Schwegler 1992: 14).
1.3: Meeting places of witch covens (e.g. Tschurtschenthaler 1934a: 62; Ricchiardi and Seglie 1987: 54).
1.4: Magical charms protecting dwellings against witchcraft (e.g. Schgör 1970: 332, 1977: 7; Haller 1947: 272).
1.5: Fertility rituals related to rockslides, which are thought to occur widely in Europe, Africa and South America (e.g. Egger 1948: 59).
1.6: Ritual boring relating to the preparation of stone axes (e.g. Egger 1948: 57).
1.7: Snake symbolism (e.g. Pozzi 2000: 30).

2. Utilitarian preparation of substances

2.1: Preparation of paints (Lombry 2008).
2.2: Production of medicines of mineral or organic origins.
2.3: Pounding of pigments of mineral or plant substances.
2.4: Preparation of spices (Pohle 2000: 199) or foods (Lombry 2008).

3. Mnemonic or record-keeping devices

3.1: Measurement of time or as calendars (Innerebner 1937:

46; Parkman 1988).
- 3.2: Commemoration of major events, such as earthquakes (Magni 1901: 90).
- 3.3: Genealogical markers (Rizzi 2007: 93).
- 3.4: Recording of pregnancy months (Haller 1978: 168).
- 3.5: Records of stock animals (Magni 1901: 89; Šebesta and Stenico 1967: 127).
- 3.6: Records of administrators or warriors (Magni 1901: 89; Šebesta and Stenico 1967: 126).
- 3.7: Records of oaths, e.g. concerning land ownership (Gruber 1991: 23).

4. Elements of belief systems

- 4.1: Impressions of hands, feet or knees of saints (Fink 1957: 129; Casagranda and Pasquali 2003: 35, and Note 3).
- 4.2: Use of cupules as receptacles of holy water (Magni 1901: 88; Tschurtschenthaler 1934a: 63).
- 4.3: Use of the resulting mineral powder in amulets or talismans (Rizzi 2007: 110).
- 4.4: Use of cupules in funerary contexts (Magni 1901: 83, 85; Rizzi 2007: 111–114).
- 4.5: Release of a life essence in the form of the resulting mineral powder (Mountford 1976).
- 4.6: Use of the resulting mineral powder to induce pregnancy (Stevenson 1887: 539–540, 1904: 295; Fewkes 1891: 9–10; Barrett 1908: 164–165, 1952: 385–387; Loeb 1926: 247; Gifford and Kroeber 1937: 186; Heizer 1953; Grant 1967: 106; Hedges 1983a, 1983b; Lombry 2008).
- 4.7: To influence wind and weather (Spier 1930: 21; Heizer 1953).
- 4.8: To attract or replace thunder (Parkman 1992: 367).
- 4.9: Use in reported supplication rituals in recent years (Querejazu Lewis 2007).

5. Depiction of heavenly bodies

- 5.1: Depiction of star constellations (Magni 1901; Leonardi 1954; Šebesta and Stenico 1967: 128; Dalmeri 1980: 95–97, 1985; Facchini 1993, 1998; Casagranda and Pasquali 2003: 40; Cairns and Branagan 1991; cf. Cairns and Yidumduma Harney 2003).
- 5.2: Depiction of the Moon or moon phases (Fink 1971: 254; Haller 1978: 172; Pace 1982: 39).
- 5.3: Depiction of the Sun (Pace 1982: 39).
- 5.4: Depiction of observations of supernovae.

6. Depiction of topographic elements

- 6.1: Elements of pre-Historic maps (Anati 1994: 151).
- 6.2: Referents to nearby topographic features, including springs, peaks, rivers and mines (Rizzi 2007: 79).
- 6.3: Aids in orientation (Egger 1948: 57; Malfer 1976).
- 6.4: Markers of land property boundaries (Tschurtschenthaler 1934b; Haller 1972: 242–247; Ricchiardi and Seglie 1987: 64; Gruber 1991: 23).
- 6.5: Purported markers of deposited or hidden goods or treasures (Bednarik 2000).

7. Board games

- 7.1: Use in mancala games (Fu 1989: 179; Bandini-König 1999; Pohle 2000: 199–202).
- 7.2: Use in boa games (Odak 1992).
- 7.3: Games involving the use of marbles or coins (Rizzi 2007: 107).
- 7.4: Use in the board game *huwais* in Arabia (Rice 1994).
- 7.5: Use in the pursuit game *mangura* in the Congo (Lombry 2008).

8. Symbolisms that are no longer recoverable

- 8.1: Indeterminable cabalistic meaning (Magni 1901: 90).
- 8.2: Writing symbols or messages (Šebesta and Stenico 1967: 127; Haller 1972).

9. Receptacles for offerings

- 9.1: For offerings to deities or priests (Rizzi 2007: 97).
- 9.2: For offerings to goblins or lost souls (Magni 1901: 89).
- 9.3: For elves or spirits of nature (Šebesta and Stenico 1967: 127; Dondio 1970: 33–34; Santacroce 1987: 74).
- 9.4: For offerings by the sick (Tschurtschenthaler 1934a: 62).
- 9.5: To deposit supplication coins (Tscholl 1933: 440).
- 9.6: For offerings to flocks of birds to entreat them to spare the fields (Rizzi 2007: 98).
- 9.7: To place food tokens on the thresholds of churches (Wallnöfer 1946: 309; Egger 1948: 64).
- 9.8: For depositing coins or jewellery in cupules on stone crosses (Tschurtschenthaler 1934a: 61–63).

10. Specific symbolisms

- 10.1: Depiction of vulvae, occurring with or without anthropomorphs (Priuli 1983: 48).
- 10.2: To commemorate visit of a location (Mandl 1995: 65).
- 10.3: Production of cupules with coins to convert these into luck charms (Magni 1901: 102).

11. Other purely utilitarian purposes

- 11.1: Use as mortars (Huber 1995: 25).
- 11.2: Use as recess to keep door hinges in place (Huber 1995: 25).
- 11.3: Cooking of food (Magni 1901: 89).

11.4: Use as recess for salt for animals, such as cattle or deer (Fuchs and Huber 1995: 10).

11.5: Receptacles for bird food or to allow butter to melt (Rizzi 1994: 299).

11.6: Illumination or marking of paths with the aid of oil and a wick placed in cupules (e.g. Magni 1901; Bernardini 1975; Schwegler 1992; Pozzi 2000).

11.7: Receptacles of the first berries of the season (Fink 1983: 15; Rizzi 1994: 299).

11.8: Receptacles for smoke or fire signals (Haller 1972: 244).

11.9: Use as lamps (Egger 1948: 63–64; Tschurtschenthaler 1934a: 63; Rizzi 2007: 102–103).

11.10: Production of rock powder for ingestion (geophagy) by humans or animals for medicinal purposes (Trost 1993: 57; cf. Malotki and Weaver 2000: 72; Callahan 2004).

11.11: Receptacles for food and water for chickens (Egger 1948: 68).

11.12: Receptacles for pointed vertical posts in the construction of buildings (Rizzi 1995: Fig. 8, 2001, 2007).

11.13: Supports for the legs of beehives to prevent entry of specific insects (Egger 1948: 68; Rizzi 2007: 104).

11.14: Preparation for splitting of rocks (Dal Ri and Rizzi 1991: 626; Rizzi 2007: 104–105).

11.15: Use to measure quantity of grain (Trost 1993: 57).

11.16: Use as lithophones (Robinson 1958; Conant 1960; Singer 1961; Cooke 1964; Jackson et al. 1965; Montage 1965; Trost 1993: 94; Ouzman 1998: 38; Huwiler 1998: 148; Kumar et al. 2003: Fig. 2; Bednarik et al. 2005: Fig. 42; Bednarik 2008: 74–76).

11.17: Use to indicate local hydrology, as recounted by David Camacho in this volume.

Discussion

The seventy-one potential interpretations of cupules listed above are derived from the literature, some having been suggested frequently, others rarely. Very few can be soundly demonstrated as being valid, based on ethnographic observation, and where this does apply it only refers to specific cases, at specific sites or to specific societies. These cases are listed under the above numbers 4.5, 4.6, 4.7 and 11.16, and number 11.12 appears to be soundly demonstrated archaeologically in a few cases in northern Italy (Figure 1). The five explanations in group 7, that some cupules were used in games, also enjoy various levels of credibility, although not accepted by Rice (1994) for 7.4. However, most of the rest of these many possible interpretations derive from pure speculation. This applies especially to those that seem to be the most popular, such as 5.1 (star constellations), 6.1 (maps) and the various proposed uses in supplication rituals. Moreover, most of these advocated possibilities offer little if any prospects of falsification; they are presented in a scientific vacuum, they

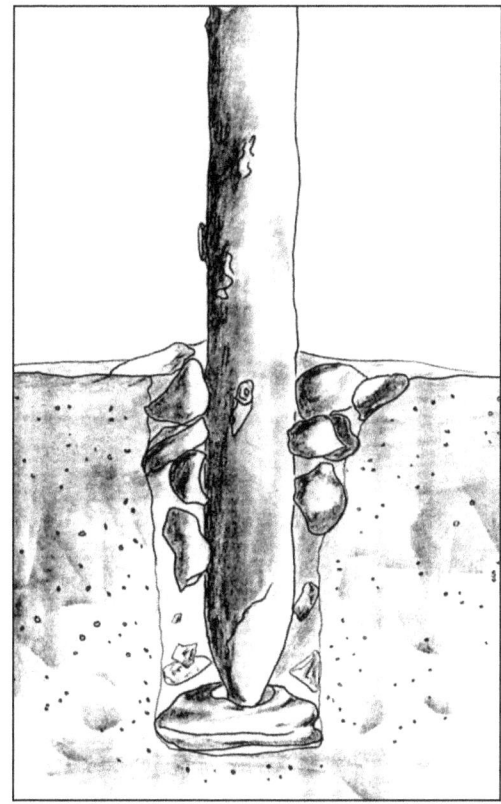

Figure 1. Use of a cupule as receptacle for the pointed end of a vertical wooden post used in the construction of a dwelling, holding the post in position.

cannot be tested.

Therefore the prospects of discovering a generic explanation for cupules (after we have properly identified them, which is yet another problem area), or even just for a significant portion of them, are most discouraging. To begin with, the few solid examples we do have only serve to emphasise this encumbrance: they are applicable only in specific circumstances, and cannot be extrapolated to other cases (Hedges 1983b). Therefore they are of no help in explaining the phenomenon as a whole. Secondly, it is obvious that a great many of the above potential explanations cannot realistically apply to vertical cupules. This applies specifically to those involving the cupules being filled with some material, be it liquid or solid, or most of those invoking some utilitarian purpose. Thirdly, the most popular notions are profoundly ethnocentric, they are the result of perceiving long-gone societies from modern perspectives, or as some kind of 'intermediate' stage in the development towards some cultural 'ideal state' to be reached. This pernicious ethnocentric approach to the past is unambiguously invalid, but it is reflected in many of the interpretation attempts we have seen. To illustrate, consider the popular cases of maps or star charts: the modern investigator, massively burdened by his/her cultural, cognitive and academic baggage, looks over a site and sees its rock art with a perception that is so much conditioned by his/her construct of reality that s/he probably perceives the site quite different from the way the ancient visitor did; ancient artist and modern 'interpreter' would probably be incapable of communicating at a meaningful level — apart from the language barrier.

On top of this incredible encumbrance, there are the 'technical' limitations. In particular, the modern visitor, having determined to 'make sense' of the rock art, tends to ignore that what he sees is in any case — ignoring the profound differences of perception — not the same as what the ancient rock artist saw. Any traditional rock art site is today manifested only as the current outcome of countless taphonomic effects. Most surviving rock art provides little information about the way it appeared to its makers, because much or most of the empirical information that would be required to experience the 'living system' is no longer recoverable, having fallen victim to reduction processes of various types (Bednarik 1994). For instance, the modern visitor may look at a panel of cupules and try to make sense of their arrangement, because his/her culture suggests that arrangements must have meanings, they must be spatially purposeful, there *must* be a way to 'read' them in a way comprehensible to the modern viewer. But if the cupules are the cumulative result of the work of many generations, perhaps even of culturally unconnected societies, how could the arrangement of what has survived have any cohesive meaning? First, it was added to by many different people at different times, perhaps separated by many millennia. Second, most of the empirical traces related to the art production (e.g. paint, shallow engravings, offerings, other work traces etc.) have long disappeared. Therefore we cannot see what was visible to the ancient artists, even if we shared their perception. In this taphonomic regime, simplistic interpretation by a completely uninformed, self-appointed expert is merely an ethnocentric aberration.

The explanation of cupules as patterns of heavenly bodies is particularly popular in China and parts of Europe, but is always offered without any tangible evidence. Star constellations, we can reasonably assume, are random features determined by the projection of three-dimensional arrangements onto a two-dimensional plane as viewed from a particular location, and it is then not surprising that they resemble other random or fortuitous arrangements (indeed, I have witnessed an advocate of this belief surveying a group of potholes, for the purpose of determining their astronomical meaning, unaware that they are purely natural features). However, large groupings of cupules tend to be cumulative, i.e. the marks constituting them were made singly and at greatly different times. That renders such an explanation highly unlikely, if not impossible. In all cases I am aware of, including the sepulchral La Ferrassie block, the resemblance with star constellations is only vague. For the vast majority of cupule constellations, no corresponding star charts have been proposed, and this notion appears to be without empirical basis as well as being unfalsifiable. Moreover, the greater the number of cupules on a single panel, the lesser the resemblance to any star pattern; so when there are several hundred the weakness of the notion becomes clear. But most importantly, it cannot be tested; it is therefore not a scientific proposition.

The explanation of random cupule groups as maps, popular in the Alpine regions of Europe, falls into the same category. It is untestable, has no ethnographic support, and is a priori unlikely unless all cupules and spatially related other features were made at the same time. It is also reminiscent of other endeavours of seeking rock art explanations, in which various patterns are thought to be pre-Historic maps, apparently without justification.

More promising is the notion of the use of cupules in board games. Odak (1992) considers the possibility that cupule patterns at two sites in southern Kenya represent *boa* game boards. Pohle (2000: 199–202) discusses the conceivability of geometrically arranged cupules having been used in the *uluk* and *rama rildok* games of Nepal and accepts that many of the cupule arrangements relate to the latter game (Pohle 2000: Pls 1.1, 14–16, 18.1, 28.2). *Rama rildok* is a mancala game, which Bandini-König (1999) also cites for cupules at Hodar, in the uppermost Indus valley, and Fu (1989: 179) for Chinese sites. Cupules proposed to have been used in board games occur typically in closely packed geometric alignments, i.e. in multiple rows, and on horizontal rock panels. Obviously the ethnographic foundation of this interpretation requires further investigation, but it can be regarded as a possible explanation in certain cases. Mancala (or mankala) games occur widely in Africa and Asia (Murray 1952: 162) and seem to have an ancient history (e.g. Robinson 1959: Pl. 27), apparently extending back to the Neolithic in the Middle East (Rollefson 1992).

Summary

Somewhat better based appears Flood's suggestion that, in central Australia, 'a strong case can be made that cupules are the by-product of increase ceremonies, but the usual caveats must of course be added' (Flood 1997: 149). Mountford's (1976) solid ethnographic account is among the most authoritative we have, and there are similarly sound explanations available from the Southwest of the United States. We therefore have limited ethnographic information that in some of the tens of thousands of cultural traditions that can be said to have existed since the first known cupules were made, they served for purposes related to fertility and to increase rituals (see chapter on the ethnography of cupules, this volume), and we know that many cupules designate lithophones (see chapter on lithophones). However, faced by the immensity of numbers of cupules ever made (very probably many times their surviving number) and of the enormous time span accounting for them (hundreds of millennia), it is obvious that these glimpses are of very limited value in explaining the general phenomenon. For instance, I might consider the sepulchral block with cupules from La Ferrassie, supposedly of the Mousterian (Figure 2). I might note the 'fissure' on it, which several commentators have pointed out, and suggest that it resembles a vulva, flanked on both sides by several cupules. That gels well with the ethnographic observation that some cupules are

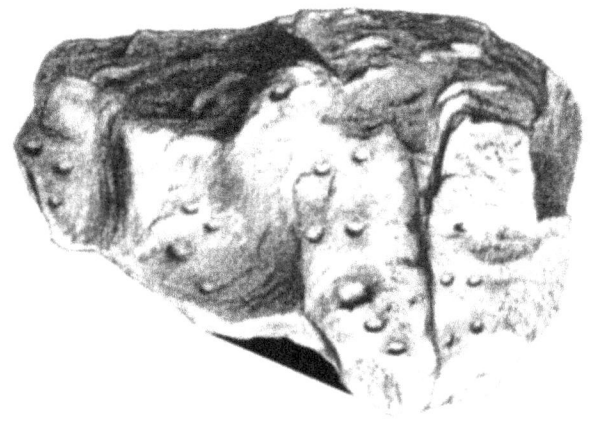

Figure 2. The cupules on the sepulchral limestone block of burial No. 6 in La Ferrassie, France, of a Neanderthal child, either Aurignacian or Mousterian.

Figure 3. Cupules and 'vulvar triangle', Middle Aurignacian, clast No, 16 from La Ferrassie, France.

fertility-related, and even receives good support from the occurrence of cupules in 'vulvar triangles' (Figure 3). But does it justify the application of this interpretation to a specimen that is clearly over 30,000 years old, and either Aurignacian (cf. Bednarik 2007) or Mousterian?

Perhaps that explanation is right (it is certainly more likely so than the various alternative ones we have seen), but scientifically it remains unsatisfactory. It may be more circumspect to regard the snippets of sound explanations we do have as being incidental to some other, less obvious but generic principle. In particular, they raise unanswered questions that imply some unknown cultural dimension in these extremely limited cases we have reasonable explanations for. In all the secure ethnographic interpretations, there is no obvious need for the marks to assume precisely the very specific form of cupules. There is some merit in the assumption that, for lithophonic cupules, impact was focused on a very specific point because it yielded the best sound. However, even this is limited to some specimens, whereas on most lithophones there are numerous markings (Figure 4), all consisting of perfectly formed cupules, i.e. percussion was not just focused in their production, but was highly focused and quite deliberately so.

This, I have noted, is perhaps the most distinguishing characteristic of all cupules: most appear to be as small as technically possible, but made very deeply, relative to rock hardness. Which brings us to the notion that those on the softest rocks are perhaps those most likely to provide the basis of explanatory hypotheses. The harder the rock, the greater the technological limitation imposed on a cupule (see chapter on the relevance of site lithology). It is simply impossible to create a cupule that has a diameter: depth ratio of <1 (i.e. that is deeper than wide) on quartzite, using the means available in pre-History. But it is possible to do so on very soft rock. To me, the most stunning aspect of cupules is that already the earliest examples we have, at such sites as Daraki-Chattan, clearly externalise the principle of smallest diameter and greatest depth achievable. They already seem to be statements of perfection, deliberately made to formalised qualities — an observation I made previously concerning the earliest disc beads we have, also from the Lower Palaeolithic (Bednarik 1997). I found that ostrich eggshell beads of the Acheulian had been made as small as possible, and that the precise central placement of their perforations could only be achieved by a very deliberate process of production. Much the same can be said about the earliest cupules available to us. Having explored the implications of such observations on our concepts of hominin cognition elsewhere, I draw here attention to the idea that the inherent 'mental template' perhaps expressed in cupules appears not to have changed over hundreds of millennia, nor does it seem to vary across the globe. I find it difficult to see this as an artefact of our taxonomy. Therefore, if we are to approach the topic of meaning or purpose of non-utilitarian cupules, we need to consider them as the surviving traces — and probably the *only* surviving traces — of specific behaviour patterns. In some form or fashion, they represent an endeavour of penetrating into rock in a very specific way. This is most evident where they occur on the softest rock types, and where the work traces most clearly express the principle of 'penetrating the rock'. At this stage more should not be said; it is not my purpose here to interpret, and our database

Figure 4. Cupules on a lithophone of gneissic granite, Morajhari, Rajasthan, India.

is quite clearly inadequate for attempting interpretation.

Nevertheless, we can observe profitably that, when we consider that cupules are one of the simplest possible forms of 'rock art', and our profound inability to understand them — even to effectively quantify the surviving corpus so far, or to in any way deal with them comprehensively in the ways of science — we begin to faintly comprehend our academic impotence in dealing with the many far more complex forms of rock art or other palaeoart we have. We glimpse a fleeting proof that, when I emphasise that the *scientific* study of rock art is infinitely more complex than we had imagined, I am quite probably right.

REFERENCES

ABEL, C. 1730. *Teutsche und Sächsische Alterthümer*. Braunschweig.
ANATI, E. 1968. *Arte preistorica in Valtellina*. Centro Camuno di Studi Preistorici, Capo di Ponte (Italy).
ANATI, E. 1994. *Valcamonica rock art: a new history for Europe*. Centro Camuno di Studi Preistorici, Capo di Ponte (Italy).
BANDINI-KÖNIG, D. 1999. *Die Felsbildstation Hodar*. Materialien zur Archäologie der Nordgebiete Pakistans 3, Mainz.
BARRETT, S. A. 1908. The ethnogeography of the Pomo and neighboring Indians. *University of California Publications in American Archaeology and Ethnology* 6(1): 1–332.
BARRETT, S. A. 1952. *Material aspects of Pomo culture*. Bulletin of the Public Museum of the City of Milwaukee 20 (Parts 1 and 2), AMS Press, New York.
BEDNARIK, R. G. 1997. The role of Pleistocene beads in documenting hominid cognition. *Rock Art Research* 14: 27–41.
BEDNARIK, R. G. 2000. Age estimates for the petroglyph sequence of Inca Huasi, Mizque, Bolivia. *Andean Past* 6: 277–287.
BEDNARIK, R. G. 2007. The Late Pleistocene cultural shift in Europe. *Anthropos* 102(2): 347–370.
BEDNARIK, R. G. 2008. Cupules. *Rock Art Research* 25(1): 61–100.
BEDNARIK, R. G., G. KUMAR, A. WATCHMAN and R. G. ROBERTS 2005. Preliminary results of the EIP Project. *Rock Art Research* 22(2): 147–197.
BERNARDINI, E. 1975. *Arte millenaria sulle rocce alpine*. Milano.
CAIRNS, H. C. and D. F. BRANAGAN 1992. Artificial patterns on rock surfaces in the Sydney region, New South Wales: evidence for Aboriginal time charts and sky maps? In J. McDonald and I. P. Haskovec (eds), *State of the art: regional rock art studies in Australia and Melanesia*, pp. 25–31. Occasional AURA Publication 6, Australian Rock Art Research Association Inc., Melbourne.
CAIRNS, H. and B. YIDUMDUMA HARNEY 2003. *Dark sparklers*. Self-published, Merimbula (Australia).
CALLAHAN, K. L. 2004. Pica, geophagy, and rock-art in the eastern United States. In C. Diaz-Granados and J. R. Duncan (eds), *The rock-art of eastern North America. Capturing images and insight*, pp. 65-74. University of Alabama Press, Tuscaloosa.
CASAGRANDA, W. and T. PASQUALI 2003. Le coppelle dei Casteleri di Lona. In T. Pasquali (ed.), *I Casteleri di Lona e il Dos del Castel di Lases*, Comune di Lona-Lases (Italy).
CONANT, F. 1960. Rocks that ring: their ritual setting in Nigeria. *Transactions of the New York Academy of Sciences*, Series 2, 23(2): 155–162.
COOKE, C. K. 1964. Rock gongs and grindstones: Plumtree area, southern Rhodesia. *South African Archaeological Bulletin* 19: 70.
DALMERI, G. 1980. Serso (rinvenimento di masso a coppelle). *Preistoria Alpina* 16: 95–97.
DALMERI, G. 1985. Fornaco (Trento). *Preistoria Alpina* 21: 57–52.
DAL RI, L. and G. RIZZI 1991. Il colle di Albanbühel in Val d'Isarco (Bolzano). *Rassegna di archeologia 10/1991–1992; Congresso: L'Età del Bronzo in Italia nei secoli dal XVI al XIV a.C.*, p. 626. Editore all'Insegna del Giglio, Florence.
DONDIO, W. 1970. Schalensteine auf St. Verena. *Der Schlern* 44: 33–34.
EGGER, A. 1948. Schalensteine, eine volkskundliche Studie. *Schlern-Schriften* 53: 57–75.
FACCHINI, F. 1993. L'osservazione astronomica nei castellieri preistorici del Trentino. *Natura Alpina* 44(4).
FACCHINI, F. 1998. 3000 anni fa. Testimoni le stelle. In *Castello Roccabruna a Fornace*. Associazione 'Amici della Storia', Pergine.
FEWKES, J. W. (ed.) 1891. *A journal of American ethnology and archaeology*. Houghton, Mifflin, New York.
FINK, H. 1957. *Eisacktaler Sagen, Bräuche und Ausdrücke*. Innsbruck.
FINK, H. 1971. Schalensteine um Brixen. *Der Schlern* 45: 254–255.
FINK, H. 1983. *Verzaubertes Land. Volkskult und Ahnenbrauch*. Verlag A. Weger, Brixen.
FLOOD, J. 1997. *Rock art of the Dreamtime: images of ancient Australia*. Angus and Robertson, Sydney.
FU, C. Z. 1989. *The rock arts of China* (in Chinese). The Jiang Photographic Art Press, Beijing.
FUCHS, G. and A. HUBER 1995. Der Schalenstein auf der Schöneben (Gem. St. Peter am Kammersberg, BH Murau, Steiermark). *Mitteilungen der Anisa* 16: 8–18.
GIFFORD, E. W. and A. L. KROEBER 1937. Culture element distributions: IV. Pomo. *University of California Publications in American Archaeology and Ethnology* 37: 117–254.
GRANT, C. 1967. *Rock art of the American Indian*. Promontory Press, New York.
GRUBER, K. 1991. Bischofkofel, Prälatenstein und Welscher Ring. *Der Schlern* 65: 23.
HALLER, F. 1947. Schalensteine in Südtirol. *Der Schlern* 21: 268–272.
HALLER, F. 1972. Die Sonnenkultstätte am Pfitscher Sattel nördlich von Meran. *Der Schlern* 46: 242–247.
HALLER, F. 1978. *Die Welt der Felsbilder in Südtirol. Schalen und Zeichensteine*. Munich.
HEDGES, K. 1983a. A re-examination of Pomo baby rocks. *American Indian Rock Art* 9: 10–21.
HEDGES, K. 1983b. The Cloverdale petroglyphs. *Rock Art Papers* 1: 57–64.
HEIZER, R. F. 1953. Sacred rain-rocks of northern California. University of California Archaeological Survey, Report 22. *Reports of the University of California Archaeological Survey* 20: 33–38.
HUBER, A. 1995. Die Fussabdrücke am Schalenstein auf der Schöneben. *Mitteilungen der Anisa* 16: 52–62.
HUWILER, K. 1998. *Zeichen und Felsen*. Freemedia, Germany.
INNEREBNER, G. 1937. Der Jobenbühel, eine zeitweise Kultstätte der Urzeit. *Der Schlern* 11: 46.
JACKSON, G., J. S. GARTLAN and M. POSNANSKY 1965. Rock gongs and associated rock paintings on Lolui Island, Lake Victoria, Uganda: a preliminary note. *Man* 5: 38–40.
KUMAR, G., R. G. BEDNARIK, A. WATCHMAN, R, G. ROBERTS, E. LAWSON and C. PATTERSON 2003. 2002 progress report of the EIP Project. *Rock Art Research* 20: 70–71.
LEONARDI, P. 1954. Vorgeschichtliche Felszeichnungen im Etschtal

bei Castelfeder. *Der Schlern* 28: 3.

LOEB, E. M. 1926. Pomo folkways. *University of California Publications in American Archaeology and Ethnology* 19(2): 149–405.

LOMBRY, G. E. 2008. Congolese uses of cupules. *Rock Art Research* 25: 207–208.

MACINTOSH, N. W. G. 1977. Beswick Creek Cave two decades later: A reappraisal. In P. J. Ucko (ed.), *Form in indigenous art*, pp. 191–197. Australian Institute of Aboriginal Studies, Canberra.

MAGNI, A. 1901. Pietre cuppelliformi nuovamente scoperte nei dintorni di Como. In *Rivista archeologica della provincia di Como*, Vols 43–44, pp. 19–139. Como.

MALFER, V. 1976. Christliche Wegzeichen. *Der Schlern* 50: 52.

MALOTKI, E. and D. E. WEAVER Jr. 2002. *Stone chisel and yucca brush. Colorado Plateau rock art*. Kiva Publishing, Walnut, CA.

MANDL, F. 1995. Näpfchen, Schälchen und Schalen in der ostalpinen Felsritzbildwelt. *Mitteilungen der Anisa* 16: 63–66.

MONTAGE, J. 1965. What is a gong? *Man* 5: 18–21.

MOUNTFORD, C. P. 1976. *Nomads of the Australian desert*. Rigby, Adelaide.

MURRAY, H. J. R. 1952. *A history of board-games other than chess*. Clarendon, Oxford.

ODAK, O. 1992. Cup-marks patterns as an interpretation strategy in some southern Kenyan petroglyphs. In M. Lorblanchet (ed.), *Rock art of the Old World: papers presented in Symposium A of the AURA Congress, Darwin (Australia) 1988*, pp. 49–60. IGNCA Rock Art Series 1, Indira Gandhi National Centre for the Arts, New Delhi.

OUZMAN, S. 1998. Towards a mindscape of landscape: rock art as expression of world-understanding. In C. Chippindale and P. S. C. Taçon (eds), *The archaeology of rock art*, pp. 30–41. Cambridge University Press, Cambridge.

PACE, D. 1982. Aspetti petroglifici nel promontorio Grosino di Giroldo. *Sibrium* 16: 5–16.

PARKMAN, E. B. 1988. The Hupa calendar stones at Takimitlding and Medilding, north-western California. *Rock Art Research* 5: 72–74.

PARKMAN, E. B. 1992. Toward a Proto-Hokan ideology. In S. Goldsmith, S. Garvie, D. Selin and J. Smith (eds), *Ancient images, ancient thought: the archaeology of ideology*, pp. 365–370. Proceedings of the 23rd Annual Chacmool Conference, University of Calgary, Calgary.

POHLE, P. 2000. *Historisch-geographische Untersuchungen im tibetanischen Himalaya*. Giessener Geographische Schriften 76/1and 76/2, Institut für Geographie der Justus-Liebig-Universität, Gießen.

POZZI, A. 2000. Incisioni rupestri a S. Maria Rezzonico a Cremia. *Rivista Archeologica dell'Antica Provincia e Diocesi di Como*, Vol. 180. Società Archeologica Comens, Como.

PRIULI, A. 1983. *Le incisioni rupestri dell'altipiano dei Sette Comuni*. Quaderni di cultura Alpina. Priuli & Verlucca Ed., Milano.

QUEREJAZU LEWIS, R. 2007. Cupules in Bolivia. Paper presented at the International Cupule Conference, Cochabamba, 18 July (in press).

RICCHIARDI, P. and D. SEGLIE 1987. Caratteri generali e tipologia delle incisioni rupestri nelle Alpi Occidentali. In *Arte rupestre nelle Alpi Occidentali dalla Valle Po alla Valchiusella*, pp. 35–40. Torino.

RICE, M. 1994. *The archaeology of the Arabian Gulf, c. 5000–323 BC*. Routledge, New York.

RIZZI, G. 1994. Coppelle un fenomeno multiforme? — Considerazioni su alcuni dati dall'arca altoatesina. *Ladinia* 18: 299–322. Istitut Ladin 'Micurà De Rü – San Martin de Tor', Presel, Bolzano.

RIZZI, G. 1995. Schalensteine, ein vielfältiges Phänomen? Überlegungen zum Forschungsstand in Südtirol. *Mitteilungen der Anisa* 16: 78–97.

RIZZI, G. 2001. The dating of cup-holes in South Tyrol. *Preistoria Alpina* 33: 78–97.

RIZZI, G. (ed.) 2007. *Schweigende Felsen. Das Phänomen der Schalensteine im Brixner Talkessel*. Geschictsverein Brixen, Sudmedia Verlag, Vahrn (Italy).

ROBINSON, K. R. 1958. Venerated rock gongs and the presence of rock slides in southern Rhodesia. *South African Archaeological Bulletin* 13(50): 75–77.

ROBINSON, K. R. 1959. *Khami ruins: report on excavations undertaken for the commission for the preservation of natural and historical monuments and relics, Southern Rhodesia, 1947–1955*. Cambridge University Press, Cambridge.

ROLLEFSON, G. O. 1992. A Neolithic game board from 'Ain Ghazal, Jordan. *Bulletin of the American Schools of Oriental Research* 286: 1–5.

SANTACROCE, A. 1987. Incisioni rupestri nella valle di Susa. In *Arte rupestre nelle Alpi Occidentali dalla Valle Po alla Valchiusella*. Torino.

SCHGÖR, J. 1970. Steinzeichen. *Der Schlern* 44: 332.

SCHWEGLER, U. 1992. *Schalen- und Zeichensteine der Schweiz*. Antiqua 22, Gesellschaft für Ur- und Frühgeschichte, Basle.

ŠEBESTA, C. and S. STENICO 1967. Introduzione ad un catasto della coppellazione e segnatura nel Trentino. *Studi Trentini di Scienze Storiche* 16(2): 107–128.

SINGER, R. 1961. Incised boulders. *South African Archaeological Bulletin* 16: 27.

SPIER, L. 1930. Klamath ethnography. *University of California Publications in American Archaeology and Ethnologie* 30: 1–338.

STEVENSON, M. C. 1904. The Zuni Indians: their mythology, esoteric fraternities, and ceremonies. *Twenty-third Annual Report of the Bureau of American Ethnology*, pp. 3–634. Washington

STEVENSON, T. E. 1887. The religious life of the Zuni child. *Fifth Annual Report of the Bureau of American Ethnology*, pp. 533–555. Washington.

TROST, F. 1993. *Ethnoarchäologie in Südwest-Burkina Faso. I. Das Fundmaterial*. Akademische Druck-u. Verlagsanstalt, Graz.

TSCHOLL, J. 1933. Zum Rätsel der Schalensteine. *Der Schlern* 14: 440–442.

TSCHURTSCHENTHALER, P. 1934a. Der Hexenstein bei Terenten im Pustertal. *Der Schlern* 15: 61–63.

TSCHURTSCHENTHALER, P. 1934b. Der Palmstein im Brunecker Feld and andere Palmsteine. *Der Schlern* 15: 164–167.

WALLNÖFER, L. 1946. Schalensteine in Südtirol — Schalensteine im Vinschgau. *Der Schlern* 20: 237–238, 309–312, 344.

CIRCULAR CONCAVITIES IN THE ROCK ART OF THE CACHIYACU RIVER BASIN, LORETO, PERU

Gori Tumi Echevarría López
Translated by Penny Berliner

Abstract. Employing an analysis of multiple variables, the author presents one of the most important petroglyph groups of the archaeological site Chayahuita, which is characterised by, among other features, the presence of concavities (cupules) of high-quality technique and form. Chayahuita is a highly complex site, with at least three large groups of petroglyphs displaying differentiated figurations. The study yielded information important to the process of identifying the internal context of this group of petroglyphs and establishes a base for later comparative studies.

Keywords: Petroglyph, Cupule, Multivariate analysis, Chayahuita site, Cachiyacu River, Peru

Introduction

This report presents the study of a group of concave circular petroglyphs (cupules) discovered in the basin of the Cachiyacu River, in the Peruvian Amazon, at an archaeological site named 'Chayahuita'. This evidence is part of a broad group of engraved images that includes numerous and varied figurations constituting an extraordinary and highly complex site of rock art.

Since this is a defined archaeological study, the argument of this text will basically consist of a multivariable analysis of the group of images where the figurations of concavities were inscribed, including an examination of their appearance and an analytical reflection of their archaeological context. The result of this study clearly demonstrates the singularity and value of this Amazon cultural material, which we are just beginning to understand in detail.

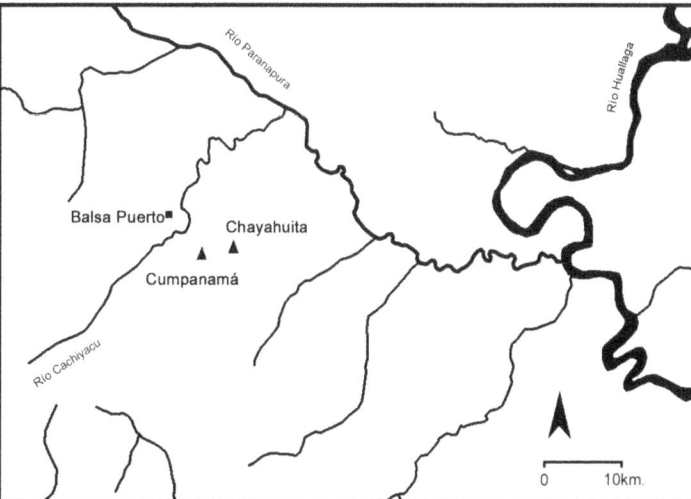

Figure 1. Location of the study area and the archaeological sites mentioned in the text.

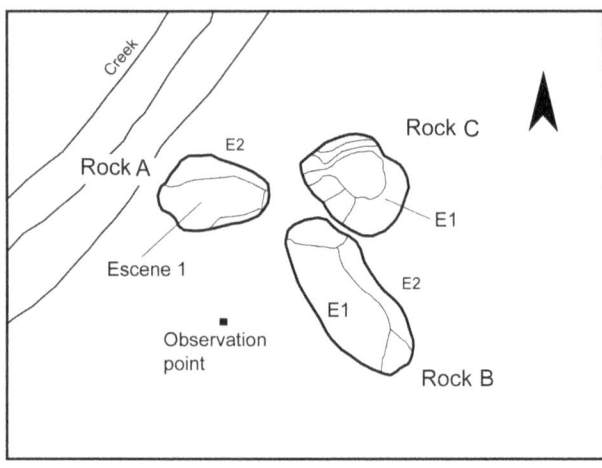

Figure 2. Sketch of the site.

The archaeological site Chayahuita

This archaeological site is found in the lower basin of the Cachiyacu River, corresponding to the basin of the Huallaga River in the eastern slope of the Amazon of north-central Peru. It is located in what could be considered a fluvial low 'yunga' characterised by primary tropical forest and a semi-abrupt geography with low hills and small water-collecting gulches (Figure 1).

Located at the entrance of a small gulch in the confluence of a creek and mountainous hills, the site consists of a group of three smooth sandstone rocks located in radial form on a small plateau on the left side of the aforementioned creek (Figures 2 and 3). Although there are petroglyphs on the three big rocks, most of the motifs were found among the biggest opening of the radial disposition oriented in general form toward the southwest. The three rocks were partially covered with loose earth, leaves, branches and roots and over the base a thin layer of humus hid part of the surface and some motifs. Although the entire site was protected from solar radiation by the shade of the trees, the rocks are exposed to consistent natural erosion due to their location in a zone of high atmospheric humidity, with frequent rains, dense vegetal cover and associate fauna.

The intervention of the site was carried out as part of an archaeological evaluation in which the author participated in the year 2002, having conducted a systematic registration during several days of encampment in the zone. The evaluation concluded, to the extent that visual exploration was possible, that the site is an archaeological deposit of rock art whose value is exceptional for the quantity, variety, and quality of its petroglyphs, one that requires immediate safeguarding and protection.

The investigation

The 2002 campaign (Echevarría 2006) provided us with a primary classification of the representational motifs by culturally significant groups, organised in a temporal internal sequence of three phases of development of petroglyphs at the site. The three groups, 'non-schematic naturalistic', 'schematic geometric' and 'schematic geometric naturalistic', were arranged in this order after a general multivariable evaluation that included an artefact analysis of the intrinsic characteristics of the petroglyphs, an analysis of their overlapping, and an analysis of their location based on a visual perspective (Table 1).

One of the groups isolated presents a set of highly distinctive representations with multiple characteristics that highlight the execution technique, form, scale, style of representation

Group	Basic characteristics
Schematic geometric naturalistic	Pure geometric forms and geometric and naturalistic outlines, use of concavities (cupules) of high quality
Schematic geometric	Square geometric forms in horizontal arrangement
Non-schematic naturalistic	Ovoid forms not outlined, naturalistic features

Table 1. Main tendencies, distinguished by groups with cultural implications, determined in the site Chayahuita.

Figure 3. Site view to the south-west, from the summit of rock C.

Figure 4. Side view of rock A.

and location; that is, almost all of the significant features under consideration in this analysis. This group proved to be highly unique, as well as the latest of the series, that is, 'schematic geometric naturalistic'.

This group was also important in that it displayed a completely original element in terms of form in respect to the other motifs of the group, which is the most important visual characteristic of the group: its circular concavities (cupules). These concavities were included in very complex outlined designs without parallel in the other groups.

Although the results of the initial registration were significant, no deep analysis in any of the specific groups could be carried out. Thus, the main considerations have a normative value in highlighting archaeological material that is extremely complex and difficult to access. The present analysis aims to supplement the previous results by examining in greater detail the group with these remarkable concavities.

The concavities and their artistic context

As stated, the group in which the concavities were found is called 'schematic geometric naturalistic', a name that describes the main figurative tendency of this group. This group is characterised mainly by its strongly geometric content and by the presence of highly standardised images of naturalistic forms, zoomorphic or anthropomorphous.

In contrast with the other groups comprising numerous petroglyphs, this group displays a limited number of motifs, distributed in the three main groups and on the three rocks at the site with petroglyphs. The number of motifs and their presentation in the groups can be summarised in the following way:

Rock A, group 1: 10 motifs; group 2: 1 motif (or theme).
Rock B, group 1: 3 motifs (unconfirmed count)
Rock C, group 2: 1 motif

According to the count, the total group included at least 15

Figure 5. Partial view of the 'scene 1' of rock A.

motifs, which vary by location and distribution and stand out because of a strong stylistic connection. Although the group was basically characterised by the presence of these motifs with concavities, several other features make this group even more singular. In the following analysis, we will try to define the context of this group of representations.

Location

Of the three rocks with motifs corresponding to this group, only rock A presents a defined arrangement of motifs in respect to its location on the base, which enables us to use it as a basis of comparison to define where the motifs are located. On rock B, the motifs were organised in random fashion; likewise in rock C, but in a spot not observable from the base point used to describe the location of the petroglyphs. Locations are defined according to the main visual perspective, arbitrarily situated southwest of the main opening of the disposition of the rocks.

Rock A displays an ascending horizontal linear arrangement of motifs across the most exposed face (M2, M3, M4, M5, M6 and M7), listing in general direction toward the right within the limits of the most prominent group, which is always the one at the front of the opening (Figure 4). Other motifs generally alternate above the main line of images (M2, M3, M4 and M5) that form a particular group, which is superimposed over previous images and composes another, much more complex group (Figure 5).

Other similar motifs exist, but they are located in parts of rock A that are not visibly accessible, such as the summit or back face of the rock. This group 2 is clearly less populated but it includes at least one motif (M1) (Figure 6) that is associated with this group. In the case of the rock C, only one motif has been documented, and it is in combination with another motif belonging to another group. However, this is located at the end of the surface of the rock that cannot be seen unless one climbs up to it.

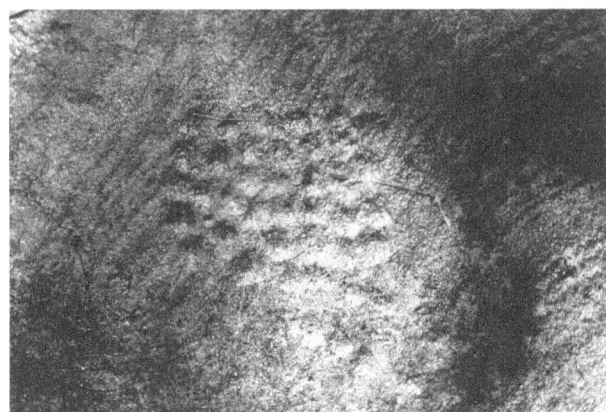

Figure 6. Motif 1.

Rock B (Figure 7), which is amply covered by motifs of the other two groups, also displays motifs of this group (schematic geometric naturalistic), although only three have been reliably documented. They are located in random form over the main group of this rock, clearly superimposed over previous motifs to form a densely populated group, and the most complex in the entire site.

It is clear that, with the exception of rock A, the location of motifs on the other rocks followed a varied pattern in their own bases. However, except for the uniform linear location of the main motifs on this rock, several other motifs of this group were situated in the upper half of this group, apparently following an alternate pattern. The other motifs in their own groups do not seem to have been placed by any defined organisation, so, lacking better information, the general group is defined by random placement in the groups, although always oriented toward the largest space generated by the disposition of the rocks.

Scale

Scale is clearly an important feature of the group. The majority of the simple motifs and all of the compound motifs display a scale that is relatively uniform in respect to their representation, regardless of the base on which they are found. Although in a few cases there is a strong disproportion between motifs of the preceding groups, this material stands out for its remarkable uniformity of form and dimensions.

Motif	Average scale (cm)		
	10-20	20-40	40-90
1	-	X	-
2	-	X	-
3	X	-	-
4	-	-	X
5	-	X	-
6	-	X	-
7	-	X	-
8	-	-	X
9	-	X	-
10	-	X	-
11	-	X	-
12	X	-	-
13	-	X	-
14	-	X	-
15	-	X	-

Table 2. Variation in average lengths of motifs.

Although the length between the compound motifs fluctuates strongly, between approximately 25 and 90 cm (see Table 2),

Figure 7. Side view of rock B.

Figure 8. Naturalistic motif of the 'scene 1', rock B.

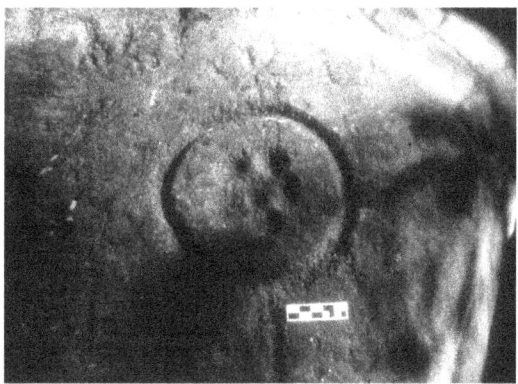

Figure 9. Motif 5.

Figure 10. Motif 7.

there is an above-average tendency between 30 and 40 cm, with jumps, up to the largest motif (M4), at 90 cm. Among the simpler motifs (compositions with independent circular concavities), the variation is minimal, fluctuating between approximately 10 and 15 cm.

Despite the fluctuation of limits, the dimensions are rather standard and contrast with the motifs of the other groups that can form, from extended complex units (more than a metre long) to simple motifs of few centimetres; that is, there is no apparent organisation by size, although some of the motifs display a uniform scale of representation (Figure 8).

Technique

The execution technique of the motifs is also a remarkable feature of the group. Although it is clear that the motifs were achieved through deep percussion, not the light percussion generally used at the site, this technique was carefully executed to obtain a high degree of uniformity in the relief of the surface of the stone, at least on the most representational motifs on rock A that highlighted the technological pattern displayed. An additional detail of technique encountered in most of the motifs, whether grooves or concavities, is a variation of depth fluctuating between 1 cm and 1.5 cm on average, except for a few lighter motifs that do not fall within the model.

As is visible in the images, the majority of the motifs were achieved by the use of lines, grooves or concavities, either individually or in various combinations. Only a few motifs utilised area percussion in conjunction with grooves or light lines, although these, when present, are overwhelmingly so, indicating that there was a non-random selection employed to execute the petroglyphs.

Form

An important variation of the group is the clear distinction of images on the basis of their form, between pure geometric and geometric naturalistic. The most outstanding forms in the horizontal series of rock A (M2, M4, M5, M6 and M7) (see Figures 4 and 5) exemplify the tendency toward variation and are key to associating the motifs inside the group.

The forms within the group of pure geometric motifs include singular motifs or compound units formed by circular clusters of concavities with a central concavity (point) (example M3); as well as highly complex motifs made up of lines and singular motifs in combination (M2, M4 and M10). The basic forms are always simple (pure) geometric outlines like circles (M3, M5, M7, M12 and M14) (Figures 9 and 10), quadrangles (M4) (Figure 11) or triangles (M2).

Within this subdivision, all of the simple forms are present as basic forms, that is, without big alterations, a distinctive feature being the inclusion of simple motifs inside closed forms (M5, M14), or the termination of lines in 'circular clusters of concavities', which is the 'simplest' form

Figure 11. Motif 4.

Figure 12. Motif 13.

Although the description highlights the remarkable difference between the two larger 'representational tendencies' of this group, a coherent relationship clearly exists in terms of form identification within it, as can be seen in motifs 4 and 6 (Figures 11 and 13), which are found on the group 1 of the rock A. In terms of form, there is no doubt that both motifs are clearly related.

Although this relationship is convincing, an asymmetrical relation exists in terms of the quantitative variation in the series of forms by sub-variations, which obviously generates a representative conflict. Unlike the important geometric variation in the pure forms, the geometric naturalistic form generates a uniform series that stands out from the group. Statistically, this tendency must be considered an internal sub-variation of form, parallel to the pure geometric (see Table 3).

Motifs	Basic forms			
	Pure geometric			Geom. naturalistic
	Triangular	Circular	Square	Square
1	-	-	X	-
2	X	-	-	-
3	-	X	-	-
4	-	-	-	X
5	-	X	-	-
6	-	-	-	X
7	-	X	-	-
8	-	-	-	X
9	-	-	-	X
10	-	-	-	X
11	-	-	-	-
12	-	X	-	-
13	-	-	-	X
14	-	X	-	-
15	-	-	-	X

Table 3. Variation of form by motif.

Style

Although all the motifs present in this group maintain a general regularity in respect to the approach to form, a considerable number of associated stylistic features characterise the few variants that exist. These features include a deliberate selection of technical attributes and details of form that create a separation by style, which confirms the group subdivision noticed in the preceding analysis.

In the variation by technique, there are defined features like hammered linear grooves, which are universal in the fabric of all compound motifs. Area percussion is used solely for the naturalistic motifs, and specifically for the description of their corporal trunk (M9, M13, M15) (Figures 12 and 13), but is included in an extraordinary manner inside the conformation of motif 4 (Figure 11). Only one motif (M8) displayed area percussion throughout the entire body.

Another interesting aspect of the design, which can be included as a trait within the representational style of the group, is that all of the motifs displayed a symmetrical arrangement in their construction and a disposition oriented to the arrangement of this symmetry.

of the group. Except for the circular forms (all compound), the forms of motifs 2 and 4, although geometric, do not form closed pure forms but linear figurations arranged in a geometric manner.

In the case of geometric naturalistic motifs, the internal variation is minimal. These always form square designs: four opposed and parallel linear members always displaying linear or quadrangular bodies (percussion area) with additional naturalistic details (Figure 12). The concept of form is clearly schematic although some motifs include variations in the regular 'tendency' of form, whether these are the incorporation of arms pointing down (M10) or the 'naturalisation' of the general design of the motif (M15) (Figure 13).

Motif 2 is a remarkable example of this arrangement, since it displays a defined orientation with a symmetrical base of two opposite diagonal lines and a single vertical line towards the top. All of the other complex motifs, especially the naturalistic, follow this arrangement: two lines below, an upper line in the centre, and two lines above; the symmetry only becomes complicated vertically.

An additional feature of the style are the endings of the lines in the compound motifs, which 'close' in simple motifs (circular groupings of concavities for the case of pure geometric motifs) or in three short lines with two sub-variations for the naturalistic compound motifs: crosses of 90 degrees, or three diagonal lines (Figure 13). This last ending without doubt describes fingers for the naturalistic motifs.

Contrary to the details of fingers, and only in the naturalistic motifs, the clusters of circular concavities appear in a variety of positions (in addition to isolated), complementing both group sub-variations of motifs; the more remarkable being linear endings in the geometric motifs and as internal complement in circular motifs (M5 and M14) (Figure 9).

An additional feature in the naturalist composition is the incorporation of a vertical apex complementing the pair of parallel lines of the base in the geometric square outline of these motifs. This line, which can be interpreted as a tail, is seen in the majority of the motifs of this type (M4, M10, M13 and M15) (Figures 11, 12, 13); evidently a complementary descriptive image has been introduced.

Additional complementary elements not common (that appear exclusively in one motif) are parallel lines that close off the opening of motif 4 (Figure 11), the horizontal line that unites the lower interior fingers of motif 13, forming two opposing quadrangles with internal concavities (Figure 12), and the concentricity of circles (M7) (Figure 10); although the latter is a characteristic implicit in the organisation of the composition of concavities.

The tabulated series of features used in the analysis can be seen in Table 4. It is clear from a quantitative perspective that the features of stylistic form, like geometric perspective, symmetry, and the use of circular concavities define the stylistic personality of the group, while the addition of naturalistic features defines the internal tendency of the naturalistic representative group.

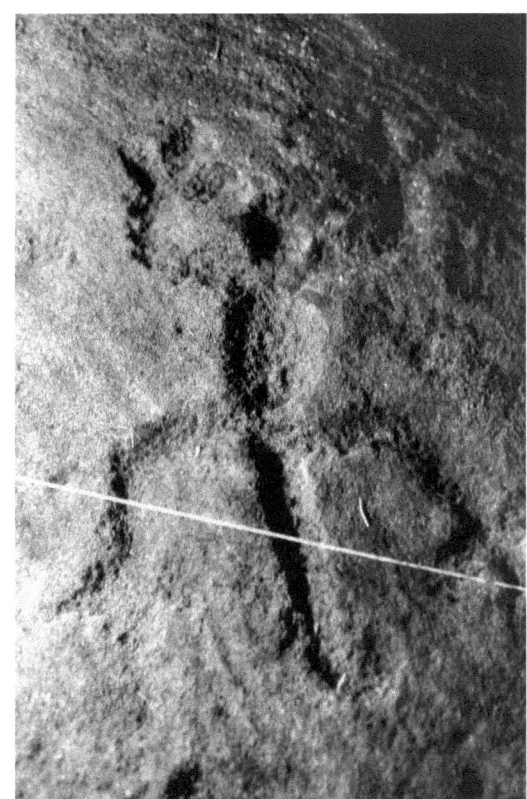

Figure 13. Motif 15.

Archaeological context

Based on the analysis of this group's motifs, an identity of form and style with two principal variations is evident, one that describes pure geometric schemes and one that describes geometric schemes of natural forms. It is clear that both stylistic sub-variations are strongly connected,

		Motifs														
		1	2	3	4	5	6	7	8	9	10	11	12	13	14	15
Techniques	Lineal percussion	X	X	X	X	X	X	X	X	X	X	-	X	X	X	X
	Area percussion				X				X	X			X		X	
	Concavity	X	X	X	X	X	X	X			X	X	X		X	
Stylistic	Geometric description	X	X	X	X	X	X	X	X	X	X	X	X	X	X	X
	Symmetric perspective	X	X	X	X	X	X	X	X	X	-	X	X	X	X	X
	Circular concavities (cupules)	X	X	X	X	X	X	X	X	-	X	X	X	X	X	-
	Circular endings	-	X	-	X	-	X	-	-	-	-	-	X	-	-	-
	Line 'fingers' ending	-	-	-	-	-	X	-	X	X			X			X
	Head				X		X		X	X	X			X		X
	Tail				X						X			X		X

Table 4. Variation of stylistic attributes present in the motifs examined.

Figure 14. General view of the 'scene 1' of the site Cumpanama.

and there is not sufficient reason to establish a separate subdivision. Both tendencies must be considered as contemporaneous and developed together in all of the groups at the site.

The sequence determined by the previous study of this site, which placed the group as the latest representations, is correct; a variety of evidence indicates a superposition of motifs belonging to different groups, making clear the later relationship of the motifs of the group 'schematic geometric naturalistic' in all of the groups; which is further confirmed by the analysis of location. It seems evident that the motifs were made first on rock A according to non-random selection and later on other rocks in the final stage of petroglyph production at the site.

Although we recognise that the two early groups determined in the first technical examination of the evidence must be revised, it is clear that a coherent relationship exists between the development of petroglyphs at the site in its early phases, until the appearance of the group of later representations. Thus, there is no significant relationship between the appearance of the group 'schematic geometric naturalistic' and the preceding groups ('non-schematic naturalistic' and 'geometric schematic'), according to this analysis, except for their belonging to the archaeological site.

For now, lacking better information, it must be recognised that the 'schematic geometric naturalistic' group made a sudden appearance in the history of the site's rock art without any significant antecedent of technique, form or style. This means that there is no comparative evidence sufficiently concrete to establish a relationship of continuity, or even a representational antecedent of cultural value in the petroglyphs of prior groups. This assertion obviously does not deny that certain minor figurative parallels do exist.

The group is unique, and although characterised by its decidedly geometric design, it stands out more for the presence of the concavities, which 'appear' in the register as circular clusters around a central concavity. This arrangement, and in essence the concavity itself, demonstrate an outstanding quality of form and technique that make the figurative composition of the compound motifs impressive; this highly formalised characteristic is unparalleled in known Peruvian rock art of any time, and even less so in the rock art of the Amazon, where there are several outstanding examples.

I think that the introduction of the group 'schematic geometric naturalistic', with these motifs, signified the arrival to the area of a strong cultural influence that was recorded graphically in these rock groups. Based on an examination of all archaeological evidence, particularly of rock art, I offer the preliminary conclusion that this group constitutes an 'intrusive context' in the local artistic development, as suggested by this evidence. That is, it appeared 'breaking' the traditional representational scheme of the site.

Although this conclusion is contextually important by itself, the lack of comparative parallels in the area makes a cultural correlation of extended or regional archaeological value difficult. The closest site, Cumpanamá (Figures 14 and 15), located at least 5 km away, does not present levels of relevant correlation in the variables of attributes used in the particular analysis of the group; despite the fact that, like the previous local groups, there are some similar features of stylistic form (cf. Echevarría 2006). This basically isolates this evidence.

Up to now, the state of the question is clear and one must accept, without extenuating circumstances, that this group and its motifs composed of concavities and lines, as well as the extraordinary motifs engraved at Cumpanamá, has no context of established correlation. Thus, the archaeological context remains undefined. There is no cultural association and the chronology is based on an extremely ambiguous general correlation; likewise, the three groups of Chayahuita would correspond to the 'incised and punctuate horizon style' period, posterior to 1000 C.E. (see Echevarría 2006).

It is evident that this chronology is insufficient; nevertheless, until more sites can be identified and more investigations realised, it will not be possible to improve this scheme. In any event, it is possible to adjust the sequence for now, by proposing at least two contextually extended chronological phases defined for the site Chayahuita: Phase 1, comprised by the groups non-schematic naturalist and geometric schematic; and Phase 2, comprised by the group schematic geometric naturalistic. Both phases are clearly differentiated (Table 5).

That the group 'schematic geometric naturalistic' (the later group) corresponds to an intrusive context in the site suggests the impact of a strong representative tradition, especially considering the extremely high consistency in the outlined geometric figuration. It is possible, if we assume that Cumpanamá corresponds also to a foreign

Figure 15. 'Scene 1' of Cumpanamá, detail.

introduction inspired in the art of initial periods (before Common Era) that we are in the presence of two strong horizontal representative traditions impacting the local figurative traditions.

Conclusions

First of all, this report should be considered, from a purely methodological perspective, as a specific advance in the examination of the rock art of the site Chayahuita, which was initiated when the entire complex of representations was studied in 2002 (Echevarría 2002). The focus of this

Group	Phases	Characteristics	Context
Schematic geometric naturalistic	2	Geometric outlines, high-quality concavities (cupules)	Intrusive
Schematic geometric	1	Sinuous naturalistic forms, and geometric figurations in linear disposition	Local
Non-schematic naturalistic			

Table 5. Phases of groups of representations in the site.

study emphasises the cultural archaeology of the 'geometric schematic naturalistic' group and its extraordinary figurations of circular concavities.

This analysis confirms the originally established distinction of groups, successfully complementing the characteristics of the later group, emphasising its extension and principal attributes in addition to establishing with greater precision its relative sequence and its archaeological context within the site. Based on its result, the site of Chayahuita, specifically its group of representations, is probably the best body of comparative information of the rock art of the basin of the Cachiyacu River and this part of the Peruvian Amazon.

The petroglyphs of the Chayahuita site constitute one of the most notable examples of rock art of the Cachiyacu River basin found to date, and doubtless the sustained and systematic examination of this rock art evidence, added to conventional archaeological evidence, will bring recognition of the great cultural value of these sites and its definitive introduction within the context of both the cultural history development of Peru and the Amazon.

REFERENCES

Echevarría López, G. T. 2002. Diario de campo. Registro arqueológico en Balsa Puerto. Sitios arqueológicos Chayahuita y Cumpanamá. Unpubl. MS, Alto Amazonas, Loreto, Peru.

Echevarría López, G. T. 2006. Petrograbados en la cuenca del río Cachiyacu. Una aproximación arqueológica en contexto industrial. *Rupestreweb*, ISSN: 1900-1495 *http://rupestreweb2.tripod.com.cachiyacu.html*

PASHASH (PERU) CUPULES AND SIGNIFICANT FIGURATIONS

Alberto Bueno Mendoza
Translated by Penny Berliner

Abstract. This paper presents an initial approach to the study of the cupules of 'Pashash', a complex Andean culture of Peru. We will begin with a general description of the site and the characteristics of its cupules and other petroglyphs, emphasising the social relationships inferred by these figurations, based on their Andean interpretive value.

Keywords: Petroglyph, Cupule, Archaeology, Terminology, Interpretation

Introduction

For archaeology, rock art constitutes true graphic text that is self-informative, because it emerges from the social-cultural context of the place where people settle and live. Empirical forms of knowledge are gleaned from the feelings and intuitions captured and made graphic in these petroglyphs.

Pallasca is the northernmost high Andean province of the Chavín region, belonging to the western slope of the Andes in northern Peru. By agreement between the University of Texas (U.S.A.) and the Instituto Nacional de Cultura (Peru), we executed the 'Pashash Project for Archaeological Research' (1971–1975) within its territory. In the centre of the archaeological zone called 'Pashash', we found a rocky outcrop with the group of cupules and figurations that are the subject of this paper. The archaeological site is located one kilometre south of the city of Cabana, the political capital of the province of Pallasca, at 3225 metres above sea level (Figure 1).

Archaeological context

The archaeological zone of Pashash includes a square kilometre that extends along a smooth slope with rocky outcrops covered with bushes, grasses and other vegetation. There are two natural rocky outcrops.

On the first and higher one, known as 'Cerro la Capilla', a series of constructions were discovered on top of a large

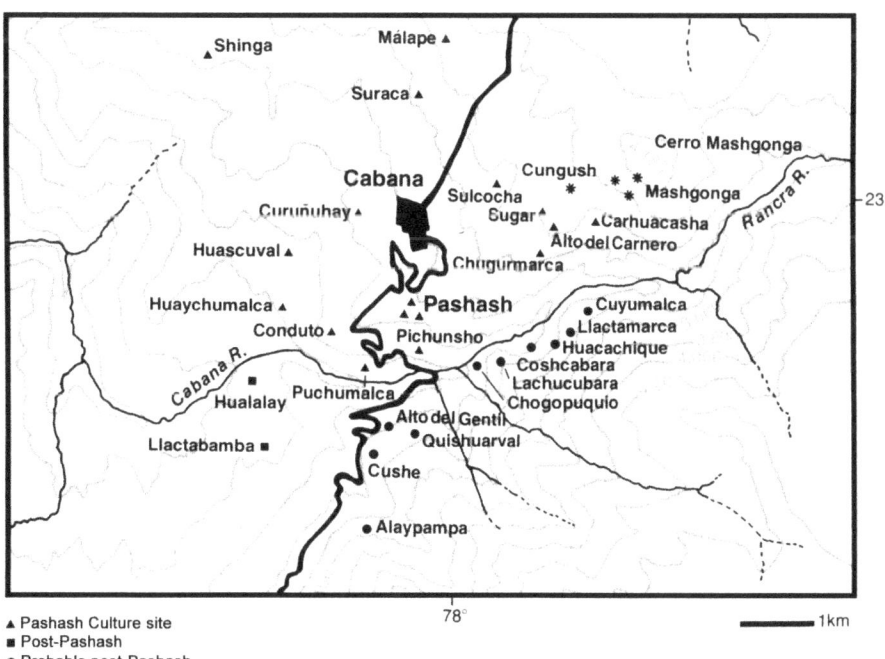

Figure 1. Map of the Pashash site and the Cabana town area. Province of Pallasca, Peru.

Figure 2. Segment of cupules made by percussion, lower stone.

perimeter wall embellished with a cornice of flat stones on its upper third, surrounding it. In the subsoil of the constructions, a tomb with offerings such as polychrome ceramics, metal forms of copper dipped in gold, and stone sculptures in the shape of pedestal glasses etc., were excavated.

The architecture of Pashash, consisting of rectangular buildings and a volumetric elevation of 35 × 10 × 15 metres, has been defined as funerary mausoleums with interior chambers at the end of short galleries, its sole entrance located on the north side.

The ceremonial and cult architecture ('Cerro la Capilla' and three funerary mausoleums) is surrounded by the

Figure 3. Several petroglyphs of geometric design, second lower stone.

foundations of simple constructions (houses) that form a permanent urban centre whose radiocarbon dates indicate a chronological sequence between 500 B.C.E. and 500 C.E. The association of the petroglyphs with this architectonical context suggest that they also date from that period.

The second natural rocky outcrop exposes two horizontal flat stones that emerge from the bedrock. On the front surface are petroglyphs different in morphology from the figurative imagery. This sector with petroglyph rocks is located at the centre of the archaeological zone, equidistant to the mortuary mausoleums and Cerro la Capilla, contextual vectors associated with the important funeral depositions of the site.

Terminology and technical problems

The terminology that rock art researchers apply to cupules differs according to where they are studied: 'cupules' (U.S.A., Eurasia etc.); '*cúpulas*' (Bolivia, Colombia); '*escultura lapidaria*' (Argentina); '*piedra-tacita*' (Chile); '*hoyos*', '*pocitos*' and '*copillas*' (Peru).

In this report we will use the term 'cupule', which is becoming the prevalent usage of choice. We formalise this identification in acknowledgement of the need to be precise and focus on the concept of the cupule.

The author's inferred techniques of the petroglyphs are: percussion and rubbing, which impact the stone surfaces, hollowing out and deepening the concavities; and, finally, polish to achieve a smooth finish of the small depressions, according to the perspective of what the executors wanted to achieve.

The cupules and other petroglyphs of Pashash

The rocks with petroglyphs are natural rocky outcrops of granite, whose exposed surfaces support the designs and display the graphics. The site is a natural superposition of the two stones used.

The upper stone includes a segment with the cupules whose right side is delimited by an incised groove with sloping slides (Figure 2), perfectly worked. As can be seen, the surface of the rock has undergone breakage due to natural factors. In the interstices grow reddish and blackish lichens that colour the surface.

The entire surface of the lower stone displays petroglyphs (Figure 3), separated by channel-like grooves that divide four segments of figurations with geometric outlines, lines in zigzag, spirals (Figure 4), geometric forms, concentric holes etc., which are in context with the profuse decoration of the archaeological ceramics already known from this site (Grieder 1978).

Interpretive reflections

On the upper stone, the arrangement of the cupules is circular, becoming more concentrated from outside to inside; that is, toward the interior of the decorated space. The second (lower) engraved stone displays a concentration of incised sculpted motifs with more variety, giving form to linear-geometric motifs that may expand our information about the relation between the figurations and ideology.

The cupules may be seen as virtual receptacles collecting life when it rains; the petroglyphs fill and drain through the grooves (like a terrestrial river), and in this movement the generative realities of nature may be heralded.

The petroglyph site ('cognitive figurations' and cupules) was the fixed and central point around which mortuary rituals may have been performed; the multiple holes could represent the transit toward the sojourn of the dead. The central location of the site of the cupules and other petroglyphs, with its proximity and contiguousness to the mausoleums, would have been similar in relation to the night and stars: stimulus to public rituals, a social-psychological ceremony. Ritual connects man with the transcendental forces and prepares him to avoid death by being converted into a living symbol. This is credible if we consider that the inside of the mausoleums, the mortuary chamber, symbolises the eternal home, where one returns to life and to one's beginning (regeneration), because death is the door through which the cycle of the life, in the Andes, passes to infinity (*ukupacha/hananpacha*).

Figure 4. Petroglyph made by percussion showing a geometrical spiral design, second lower stone.

REFERENCE

GRIEDER, T. 1978. *The art and the archaeology of Pashas.* University of Texas Press, Austin and London.

THE AMBIGUITY OF DEPRESSIONS IN ROCK ART

Maarten van Hoek

Abstract. This essay discusses three types of depressions that I observed at two rock art panels occurring at two distant rock art sites. The first type involves one (probably) natural oval depression on a petroglyph panel at Checta, Peru. The other two types of (definitely anthropic) depressions occur together on a large rock panel near Bluff, Utah, U.S.A., and comprise an excess of both 'atypical' cupules and abraded grooves. The author argues that the two much differing depressions at the Bluff Site may share the same concept, while the depression at Checta may demonstrate that a natural depression may acquire a cultural meaning.

Keywords: Petroglyph, Cupule, Definition, 'Atypical' cupule, Checta, Bluff site

Introduction

Both North and South America are well known for their wealth of fascinating rock art comprising numerous petroglyphs, pictograms and geoglyphs. However, one of the simplest, yet most enigmatic petroglyph forms seems to be underestimated and even neglected in many rock art studies. It is the cupule, a small, hemispherical depression ground or pounded into rock surfaces, used for non-utilitarian purposes. For that reason I welcomed the initiative by Prof. Roy Querejazu Lewis to organise an international conference about cupules, which was held in Cochabamba, Bolivia, in July 2007.

The study of cupules is problematic for several reasons. They occur in so many differing chronological and cultural contexts that it is impossible to attribute one single meaning to them. Moreover, often natural depressions occur on rock art panels, which are occasionally mistaken for anthropic cupules. To complicate things further, it proves that there is no consensus about the status of the cupule. Terms used to describe an anthropic depression often refer to both utilitarian and non-utilitarian depressions. Then there are more or less circular but definitely anthropic depressions that deviate from the 'conventional' cupule because they display excessive, 'non-standard' size and 'atypical' shape. When I use the term 'atypical' in this essay it refers to depressions that in my view deviate strongly from the 'standard' appearance of the cupule; thus my term 'atypical' is a taxonomic egofact. Consequently, it will be necessary to use a definition of a 'standard' cupule.

Checta, Peru

Checta is a well-known public rock art site situated about 65 km NE of Lima, Peru. The site is situated about 100 m above and south of the floodplain of the river Chillon. A large area of angular blocks of volcanic stone litters a small terrace (average altitude about 1150 m) on a steep mountain slope (Figure 1). About 450 blocks of stone bear

Figure 1. The rock art site at Checta, Peru, showing a petroglyph rock in the foreground, looking SW. Photograph by Maarten van Hoek, July 2004.

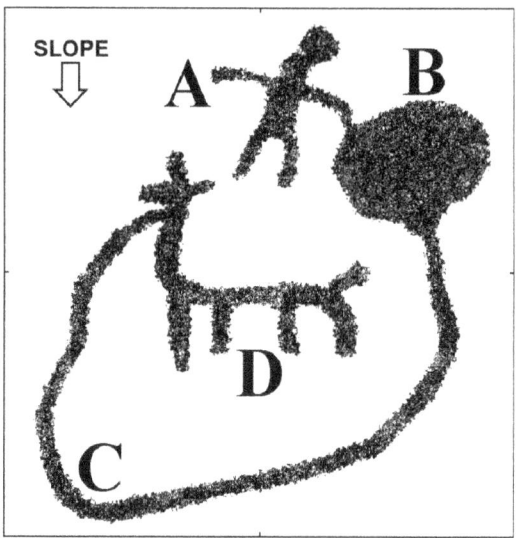

Figure 2. Petroglyph from Checta, Peru. See the text for explanation. 20 cm frame shown. Drawing by Maarten van Hoek, based on Figure 3.

Figure 3. Petroglyph from Checta, Peru. 20 cm frame shown. Photo by Maarten van Hoek, July 2004.

up to 4750 petroglyphs. Biomorphs are relatively scarce: 4.7 % represent zoomorphs (223 examples) and about 1.2 % depict anthropomorphs (a little more than 50 examples). The other petroglyphs are mainly 'geometric' designs and other marks. Importantly, at least six boulders have been reported to bear altogether hundreds of definitely anthropic cupules (Guffroy 1980–81; 1999).

The petroglyphs discussed here are found on an almost vertical panel of a small boulder (36 cm in height by 25 cm in width). The stone is partially buried and seems to be part of one of the anthropic circular structures that are found distributed within the boulder field. The shallow grooves of the petroglyphs are all lightly pecked and rather weathered. The ensemble constitutes four major elements (Figure 2):

A: a simple but rather small anthropomorphous figure with outstretched 'arms' and no further anatomical details.
B: an oval area situated only 1.5 cm from the right-hand edge of the stone, measuring 4 cm by 6 cm.
C: a long sinuous line that connects the oval area with the neck of a zoomorph.
D: a simple matchstick-like zoomorph (probably a llama).

What cannot be seen from my drawing, however, is that the oval area is actually a depression (Figure 3) measuring about 3 cm in depth. Two questions immediately pop up. Firstly, is the depression natural or cultural? And secondly, is the depression part of the anthropic imagery? Unfortunately, its origin could not be scientifically established at the time of inspection, but from naked-eye inspection I am reasonably confident that the depression is natural. Importantly, however, one of the 'arms' of the anthropomorph touches the depression, and, more meaningfully, it seems to be connected, via a band of light pecking *inside* the depression, with the groove that runs towards the 'llama'. Thus, part of the depression has definitely been worked on and has been incorporated into a more complex design, whether on purpose or not. However, in view of the thousands and thousands of true cupules found all over the world and the several instances of natural holes being incorporated into rock art imagery, it may be safely assumed that holes in a rock surface (whether natural or cultural of origin) were important in many cultures. Caves and holes in rock surfaces often are regarded as entrances to the spirit world. The inclusion of the oval natural depression on the Checta panel may therefore well be deliberate. So, it does not matter whether the Checta depression is of natural or cultural origin, it is certain that the whole ensemble, *including* the depression, is a cultural manifestation. In case of the Checta cupule it is evident that the depression unambiguously acquired a cultural context because of the band of pecking inside the depression. But even when there would not have been such a pecked line inside the depression, it still might have formed part of the design. For that reason the depression should always be included into illustrations, simultaneously mentioning its ambiguous nature in the text or caption. For that reason I regret that distinct circular depressions are often omitted from illustrations, like the examples on *Piedra* 13 and *Piedra* 42 at Yonán, Peru (Núñez Jiménez 1986: Figs 342 and 356). At *Piedra* 13, a groove seems to avoid the cupule-like depression, which may be a clue as to the greater cultural antiquity of the depression, if anthropic.

Cupules

Guffroy (1999: 123) calls the smaller circular cupules on the *other* six stones at Checta *tacitas* or *cúpulas*. This labelling presents the first general problem regarding cupules, since the term *tacita* is used indiscriminately for *both* utilitarian and non-utilitarian depressions in Spanish literature. Too many different Spanish terms are used to indicate cupules. So far I could find: '*hoquedades*' (Van Hoek 1997: 37), '*cazoletas*' (Van Hoek 2003a: 75), '*pequeños hoyos hemisféricos de planta circular y fondo cóncavo - también conocidos como "coviñas" y "fosettes"*' (Costas and Novoa 1993: 23), '*pocitos*' and '*pequeñas cavidades*' (Mountjoy 2001: 58). Querejazu Lewis (1998: 48) distinguishes between '*cúpulas*' — true cupules, and '*morteros*' — grinding hollows. Other Bolivian researchers have used the word '*cúpulas*' as well, but make a distinction between '*cúpulas auténticas*' — true cupules, and '*cúpulas utilitarias*' — grinding hollows, the latter also known as '*batanes*' or '*moledores*' (Methfessel and Methfessel 1998: 36). It gets even more confusing when other scholars use terms like '*tacitas*' (Klein 1972; Guffroy 1999: 123; Núñez Jiménez 1986: 66: Mostny and Niemeyer 1983: 33), '*huequillos*', '*huecos*' and '*hoyuelos*' (Núñez Jiménez 1986: 66 and Fig. 1194), '*cráteres*' (Mostny and Niemeyer 1983: 12), '*pozuelos*' and '*tacitas cupulares*' (Ampuero 1993), in some cases making no distinction between utilitarian and non-utilitarian anthropic depressions. Klein (1972: 103) even suggested that cupule-like depressions at the most elaborately '*Piedra Tacita*' at El Encanto, Chile, are unfinished '*tacitas*', but for several reasons I have refuted this idea and postulated that the majority of the small anthropic depressions at El Encanto are a different cultural manifestation entirely and must be regarded as true cupules (Van Hoek 2003b). To bring the Spanish terminology more in line with the English term *cupule*, and to avoid confusing utilitarian and non-utilitarian anthropic depressions, I would like to suggest to use the terminology used by Querejazu Lewis and use the term '*cúpula*' to indicate all non-utilitarian anthropic depressions, and '*mortero*' to indicate the utilitarian anthropic depressions like grinding hollows. In order to distinguish between 'true' cupules and 'atypical' cupules, this essay, first and foremost, needs an unfailing definition of the true cupule. The standard definition is 'a hemispherical percussion petroglyph, which may occur on a horizontal or vertical surface (Bednarik et al. 2003, in Bednarik 2008: 70), although, of course, cupules also occur on sloping surfaces. There are several properties that a true cupule must have: origin, shape, size and function. These properties will be briefly discussed.

Property 1: origin

First of all, a true cupule must be a *cultural* (or *anthropic*) depression. This statement, however, needs some refinement. Although by definition a true cupule has never been formed by natural forces only, it is possible and even likely that the presence of natural depressions have triggered the execution of anthropic cultural depressions. Therefore, when recording depressions in rock art studies, I would like to recommend to always make a clear distinction between three categories of rock hollows: natural depressions, cultural depressions and natural depressions that to some degree, but unmistakably have been culturally modified. As we have demonstrated with the depression from Checta, the third type may have been accomplished by the (partial) re-working (and possibly deepening) of a natural depression, or by purposefully incorporating a natural depression (whether re-worked or not) into a more complex rock art design in which case the natural depression acquires a cultural meaning.

Property 2: dimensions

A true cupule is a hemispherical *depression* by definition and therefore must have certain dimensions regarding diameter and depth. Generally it is said that true cupules average 5 cm in diameter and 3 to 5 cm in depth, but there are also smaller and shallower cupules of around 2 cm, as well as larger ones measuring up to 10 cm. In addition, weathering processes often make it very difficult to recognise true cupules. However, not every anthropic depression will be regarded to be a true cupule. For instance, a large circular depression, measuring about 9.5 cm in diameter, with only 4 mm in depth in its centre, should not be admitted as a true cupule. This means that many circular marks with a negligible depth or no depth at all must be rejected as true cupules. It moreover is the context that determines whether the depression is a cupule. For instance, an anthropic depression larger than 10 cm among a large number of true cupules *might* as well be regarded to be a true cupule, especially when occurring on a vertical or steeply sloping surface.

Property 3: shape

It proves that shape is also a defining characteristic. A true cupule is a *hemispherical* (hence *circular*) depression by definition. Also slightly oval depressions may be regarded as cupules, but clearly oval cupules could be classified as 'atypical' cupules. Yet, the property of shape must be regarded in its context. For instance, if a rock surface would feature a large number of *only* kidney-shaped, anthropic depressions, there will be very few rock art researchers (if any) who would classify those depressions as true cupules. On the other hand, when one kidney-shaped depression occurs among a number of true cupules, there is a good chance that it will be classified as a kidney-shaped cupule.

Property 4: function

It is often stated that cupules are *non-utilitarian* by definition (for instance Taçon et al. 1997: 943) and were not intended for secular practices. However, Bednarik argues that 'there is no obvious or self-evident separation between some of the[se] economic features and non-utilitarian cupules ...' (2008: 69). The meaning of the cupule is probably wholly ritual, symbolic and/or religious, but Bednarik rightly reasons that 'A cupule could only be entirely non-utilitarian (symbolic) if no practical consideration were involved in its production' (2008: 69). So, although the distinction between utilitarian and non-utilitarian dimensions is often hard to determine, cupules are definitely not to be confused with grinding hollows that are often much larger (they may range from 5 cm to over 30 cm in diameter), though not necessarily deeper than cupules. Grinding hollows are abrasion-formed depressions (of natural or cultural origin) and are often very smooth as they are used for processing or grinding food, dyes or other materials. Another distinction is that true cupules may appear on horizontal, steeply sloping *and* vertical rock panels and even on ceilings (Bednarik 2008: 71), whereas grinding hollows almost exclusively are found on rock surfaces that are horizontal or nearly so. The Checta depression is found on an almost vertical surface, shows internal pecking, and could be regarded as an 'atypical' cupule (if natural, by association).

In conclusion, circular, anthropic depressions may be labelled as *true* cupules, or, alternatively, as *typical, standard, conventional* or *normal* cupules. However, some cupules may be 'oversized', distinctly oval shaped or do not have the maximum depth in their very centre (however, see Bednarik 2008: 71 and Fig. 20). In this paper I refer to cupules having irregular, non-hemispherical shapes and/or deviant sizes as 'atypical' cupules, stressing again that this is a taxonomic egofact.

Figure 4. The Bluff Site, Southeastern Utah, U.S.A., looking N towards the sandstone cliffs. Photograph by Maarten van Hoek, July 2005.

The Bluff Site, U.S.A.

The Colorado Plateau in the Southwest of the U.S.A is home to thousands of pre-Historic rock art sites. A very large part of the imagery on the Plateau is ascribed to the Anasazi, a pre-Historic people that inhabited the area from 1000 B.C.E. to 1850 C.E. Although several sites occasionally feature rock depressions of probable Anasazi origin, cupules are hardly ever mentioned, let alone described, in rock art literature. A large rock art site near the village of Bluff in south-eastern Utah will demonstrate this. Location details of the Bluff Site will not be given here as the site is too easily accessible and the local and national authorities prefer not to reveal the precise location to avoid further damage to this important site.

The Bluff Site (Figure 4) is formed by a complex of vertical sandstone cliffs that overlook a dry river valley. The main rock wall faces SW and is just NE of an enormous sand dune that in places blocks the view from some of the rock art panels. The base of the cliff is at about 1625 m O.D. and its average height is estimated to be about 60 m. Several petroglyphs are in a typically inaccessible position and probably have been made with the aid of ladders, scaffolding or ropes. The site has both true *and* 'atypical' cupules on *vertical* cliff faces. The 'atypical' cupules at this site are labelled as such because they are larger than standard cupules, often are not hemispherical but rather oval shaped (in relation to either their vertical or horizontal axis) and frequently have their deepest point well below the geometrical centre of the depression. However, it has been confirmed by replication that this latter characteristic is related to the biomechanics of cupule making, especially on vertical surfaces (Bednarik 2008: 71 and Fig. 20). Moreover, the 'atypical' cupules at the Bluff Site clearly show rather crude peck marks, which indicates that they have definitely not been used to grind something.

The petroglyphs of the Bluff Site are found in an area of about 500 metres, which includes at least ten different and well-separated (groups of) rock art panels. One large section (labelled panel 4 by me) features many faint petroglyphs, mainly of the Basketmaker Anasazi Period (dating based on Castleton 1987: 209), including several anthropomorphs in the San Juan anthropomorphous style ascribed to the Basketmaker II period (dating based on Schaafsma 2001: 109), similar to impressive examples at Butler Wash, a well-known site on the nearby San Juan River. More importantly, panel 4 is dominated by a large number of anthropic depressions that are not mentioned in the only work known to me describing the site (Castleton 1987: 209). Besides panel 4, at least five other panels feature anthropic depressions. Panel 1 (the major panel, at the SE end of the complex, which is densely packed with figurative imagery) has a group of 12 very superficial, paired depressions, a horizontal row of possibly up to 14 true cupules very close to ground level, and a closely packed cluster of at least 35 small anthropic depressions capped by a groove. Panel 3C has at least two 'atypical' cupules, while panel 3E has three, possibly four 'atypical' cupules in a random position. Panel

Figure 5. *'Atypical' cupules and other petroglyphs on Panel 4, the Bluff Site, Southeastern Utah, U.S.A.. The cupules at the bottom part are found on a more recently exposed part of the cliff, which is clearly less patinated. The largest cupule (near the centre) measures approximately 11 in width by 18 cm in height. Photograph by Duke Hayduk, Bluff, Utah, November 2005.*

3F has at least one 'atypical' cupule. Panel 10, further west, has possibly seven 'atypical' cupules.

One of the many (tourist) attractions in the Bluff area is the rock art site of Butler Wash on the San Juan River. As access overland is very difficult, the site can only be reached by a guided boat trip. The site is well known for its imposing row of large petroglyphs depicting 'heroic' anthropomorphs that are characterised by drooping hands and feet and 'strange' extensions from the ears and heads. We also noticed recent Navajo petroglyphs and a small number of 'atypical' cupules. Also conspicuous at Butler Wash are many abraded grooves.

The day before our visit to Butler Wash, Vaughn Hadenfeldt of Bluff, knowing our interest in cupules, told us that there was another site near Bluff with cupules. This knowledge, combined with the experiences at Butler Wash, became the main reason for us to visit the Bluff Site.
To our surprise, many of the anthropic depressions at the Bluff Site turned out to be identical to the Butler Wash 'atypical' cupules. However, there were some major differences. First, there is the number of cupules. Butler

Figure 6. *Close-up of one of the 'atypical' cupules on Panel 4, the Bluff Site, Southeastern Utah, U.S.A., showing crude peck marks. Photograph by Duke Hayduk, Bluff, Utah, November 2005.*

Wash features altogether 12 'atypical' cupules, whereas the Bluff Site has more than 125 such cupules, the majority concentrated on panel 4, which has more than 110 examples. Several 'atypical' cupules at the centre of panel 4 are found on a lower area of the vertical cliff that apparently once was covered with talus debris; the surface has a less patinated appearance (Figure 5). It is possible that the talus debris, especially at the eastern part of panel 4, covers further cupules.

Second, the distribution of the cupules across the panel differs. At Butler Wash vertical, linear rows predominated, but at panel 4 of the Bluff Site, most of the 'atypical' cupules were distributed randomly across the rock surface. Although the 'atypical' cupules are similar in size and shape to the Butler Wash cupules, some are less deep and more superficially executed; especially the larger examples that, moreover, often clearly show deep peck marks (Figure 6). However, several examples do not show any or hardly any peck marks (Figures 7 and 8). It seems that they have been rubbed; possibly at a later stage.

Associated features

The ('atypical') cupules at the Bluff Site are

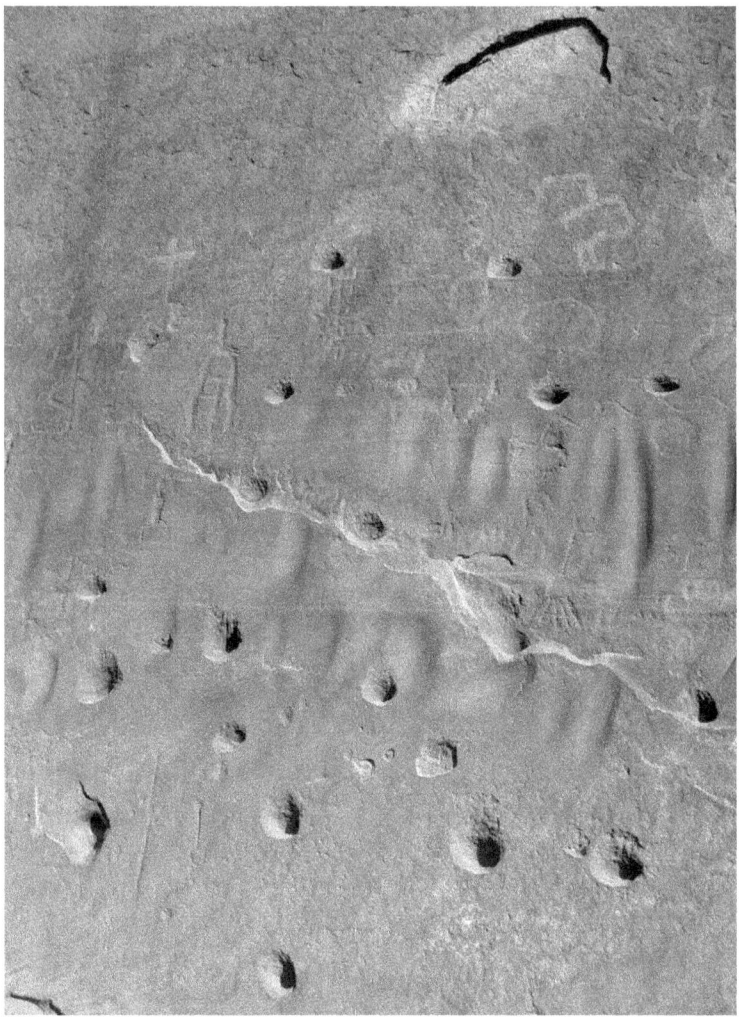

Figure 7. 'Atypical' cupules and other petroglyphs on Panel 4, the Bluff Site, Southeastern Utah, U.S.A.. A close-up of the cupule in the left-hand bottom corner of the photo can be seen in Figure 8. Photograph by Duke Hayduk, Bluff, Utah, October 2005.

found together with (but not associated with) anthropomorphs, zoomorphs, phytomorphs and geometric designs. However, panel 4 is not only exceptional for its concentration of 'atypical' cupules, but also noted for its large number of vertically orientated, abraded grooves. Unlike Butler Wash, where those abraded grooves are found in two major concentrations *outside* the petroglyph areas, the abraded grooves at panel 4 are found 'randomly' positioned among cupules and other petroglyphs, yet many arranged in horizontal groups (Figure 9). Although not so deep as the examples at Butler Wash, they are easily recognisable. Some are more than 30 cm in length and 10 cm wide. Like at Butler Wash, the 'atypical' cupules and abraded grooves have the same degree of patination as the surrounding natural rock surface and (most of) the figurative art.

There is another association of the panel 4 cupules that may be significant. A short distance west of it is a large cliff area that features dark coloured, vertical stripes caused by run-off water of a waterfall that pours down from the cliff during the wet season. The large concentration of 'atypical' cupules may be explained by the location of the panel close to that temporary waterfall.

Meaning

Since they are found at vertical cliff faces and clearly show large peck marks, it is certain that the 'atypical' cupules at the Bluff Site are anthropic and non-utilitarian. Importantly, because of their size and shape, these depressions differ from true cupules. Still, their execution must have been important, although, because no ethnographic records are available for this site, it can only be guessed at what their function and/or meaning has been. Yet, other rock art sites may offer a clue, especially when anthropic depressions are found at *specific* spots on figurative imagery. For instance, another rock art site in south-eastern Utah features a zoomorph with five anthropic depressions, obviously executed at a much later time, specifically at the head, heart area and extremities, thus possibly acquiring power from the animal image (Malotki and Weaver 2000: 72).

However, the 'random' and unrelated positions of the Bluff Site 'atypical' cupules indicate that other rationales must have been the cause for these cupules. Notably the presence of the large number of abraded grooves might give a clue. Especially at panel 4 of the Bluff Site, there clearly is an *excess* of such polished depressions. In contrast, these abraded grooves are lacking at the major panel of the Bluff Site, located only 250 m to the SE, which is far more densely engraved with figurative imagery. It appears that the abraded grooves were not used to sharpen the instruments with which the petroglyphs on the same panel were made (although this can never be ruled out). This seems to be confirmed by the fact that many other major petroglyph panels on the Colorado Plateau (and beyond) seem to lack these abraded grooves (or they have not been reported at those sites, like there is no record known to me of the abraded grooves at Butler Wash). Also, there would exist more abraded grooves at other sites where these features do occur. This generally is not the case. For instance, at the Potash Road rock art complex near Moab, Utah, I noticed only two true cupules and one simple abraded groove close together on one of the huge vertical faces that are full with figurative art.

Even though the reason to execute 'atypical' cupules and abraded grooves at the Bluff Site will remain obscure, it is possible and even likely that the execution had more to do with the site and/or the rock itself, than with the figurative rock art. This seems to be confirmed by rituals among the Zuni Indians, who still live in western New

Mexico, U.S.A. Zuni women and men wishing to have a female child used to visit a 'Mother Rock' where pregnant women removed grains of sandstone for an offering to be left at the site (Stevenson 1904: 294, Pl. 12; quoted in Cole 1990: 41).

> An illustration of Mother Rock shows a surface that is densely pockmarked with abstract imagery, including small pits [cupules], larger holes or niches, and grooves. Vulva-like symbols have been formed by using pits and incised lines.

Several distant rock art sites may offer similar explanations in which the depression is not the intended product of the action. The first three examples are ethnographically supported. A large boulder near Nantaguna springs in the Northern Territory of Australia bears in a recess around sixteen horizontal cupules. They are the result of a ritual conducted to cause a specific bird to lay more eggs. This is accomplished through the mineral powder rising into the air as the cupules are pounded (Flood 2006: 244; Bednarik 2008: 72). A similar ritual involved the collection of the 'fertilising" dust created by Pomo women pounding cupules on specific boulders in California (Bednarik 2008: 73). Cupules on a

Figure 8. Close-up of one of the 'atypical' cupules on Panel 4, the Bluff Site, Southeastern Utah, U.S.A., showing the smooth (rubbed?) interior. Photograph by Duke Hayduk, Bluff, Utah, October 2005.

Figure 9. Horizontal rows of vertically orientated abraded grooves and other marks on a vertical sandstone cliff at Panel 4, the Bluff Site, Southeastern Utah, U.S.A.. Photograph by Duke Hayduk, Bluff, Utah, October 2005.

lithophone (rock gong) at Pola Bhata in India were witnessed by Robert Bednarik to be used and explained to him in 2004 (Bednarik 2008: 73–4).

Besides a relatively small number of cupules, many of the temples in Egypt, like Medinet Habu, Luxor and Karnak, feature thousands and thousands of abraded grooves, identical to those in Utah. Several examples clearly superimpose the art of the ancient Egyptians and in some cases even destroy petroglyphs added by later peoples onto the walls of these temples. Although these abraded grooves may have been produced as a sort of 'gestural art' to record a visit to a site in analogy with ethnographically recorded instances in Australia (Flood 2006: 240–1), these abraded grooves most probably have also been made to derive the power of these ancient temples.

Similar abraded grooves occur elsewhere in Africa and for instance have been reported by Simonis et al. (1998) from at least three of the five so-called Niola Doa petroglyph panels in the Ennedi plateau in eastern Chad (1370 km SW of Luxor). At least seven such polished grooves can be seen in their illustration of panel 3 (1998: Figs 2 and 3), while another seven examples appear on panel 2 illustrated by Simonis et al. (1994: Fig. 4). Coulson and Campbell illustrate Panel 1 at Niola Doa and this panel features at least four abraded grooves. Importantly, Coulson and Campbell argue that 'at a later period, vertical grooves were ground between the figures; such grooves appear throughout Africa and even on Egyptian temple walls where women rub them to increase their fertility (Coulson and Campbell 2001: Fig. 15). All examples at Niola Doa have been executed in a vertical position, like most of the Egyptian and Utah examples. Perhaps the resulting stone powder from the Egyptian temple walls was taken home, or even occasionally swallowed.

On the north coast of Rapa Nui (Easter Island) is a low eminence of irregular lava called 'Ava 'o Kiri. On this outcrop are three petroglyph panels with altogether six large petroglyphs: a fish-within-fish; a tail-of-fish (not an unfinished fish) and a complete 'tuna fish' associated with two 'fish-hooks'; all executed in outline. There are also some scattered, possibly cultural cupules, as well as a few faint and indeterminate markings. Importantly, at the foot of the knoll and out of sight of the fish petroglyphs is a horizontal outcrop. It is covered with some cupules and more than 30 flat and oblong depressions that also occur at other sites at Rapa Nui and that are referred to by Lee as tool sharpening depressions (1992: Fig. 4.29). Those tools could have been adzes. Despite the fact that petroglyphs of 'adzes' only appear at two sites on Rapa Nui, Lee emphasises the importance of the adze as a tool, but also states that the object could also have had religious and ceremonial connotations as a sacred symbol of the forest god, Tane (Lee 1992: 115).

The execution of an extremely small number of figurative images on top of the eminence does not justify the presence of so many oblong depressions as it is very unlikely that these adzes were used to actually produce those petroglyphs. Therefore, I suggested (Van Hoek 2000: 14–6) that the lower outcrop was specially selected by the islanders to sharpen specific tools like the aforementioned adzes or just rub the stone with some kind of object because of the importance of the place, also acknowledged by the execution of a special sequence of fish engravings. Perhaps it was thought that spirits supposed to reside in the rock could be appeased (Lee 1992: 124) or supernatural potency (called *mana* in the Polynesian culture) derived by sharpening their tools or rubbing the rock surface or by executing cupules at specific spots. The people of Rapa Nui possibly thought that, in general, touching the stone at 'Ava 'o Kiri and other sites on the island in a specific way would imbue their tools and/or themselves with supernatural potency. Could this idea also explain the execution of 'atypical' cupules and abraded grooves at the Bluff Site? Might the non-visual explain many of the 'atypical' cupules and abraded grooves?

Interestingly, Ouzman postulated a similar idea (2001: 245). He describes some animal petroglyphs from southern Africa that were carefully and repeatedly rubbed with the fingers or pieces of hide *at specific spots*. Ouzman argues that 'rubbing them [those spots] allowed people to access the potency they embodied' (ibid. 247). Although in the first instance the manufacturing of cupules does not actually represent instances of rubbing (though tool sharpening activities do), their execution may still have had the same purpose. Ouzman notably argues that 'Such cutting and hammering of the rock also functioned more generally as a means of piercing the rock so that potency could flow from the Spirit World into the Ordinary World' (ibid. 248) and into the person or even the group that manufactured those openings. This concept would explain the random placement of such cupules on the rock. If the purpose of those rituals were to release potency from the Spirit World, it would not really matter where those depressions were placed.

Ouzman offers a further explanation. Apart from possibly representing passages between the 'Spirit World' and the 'Ordinary World', the execution of those cupules could fulfil the desire to *possess* pieces of such potent places (ibid. 248). When rock art panels have been flaked, this could point to the desire to possess a part of a potent site (ibid. 250).

But the execution of cupules hardly ever produces flakes suitable to take away. Therefore, to overcome this problem, another method might have been invented. The manufacturing of cupules often produces a fine stone powder that can easily be swallowed by a person without causing harm. It is known that animals, like elephants and giraffes, and even groups of people and/or individuals occasionally consume certain types of clay during severe shortages of food (Callahan 2000) Consuming stone powder from certain rock surfaces has also been reported from other areas. It is suggested that the deliberately executed holes at the aforementioned zoomorph in south-eastern Utah may have been motivated by the idea of utilising the power inherent in the animal fragments to obtain favourable outcomes for hunting or ritual-related activities similar to those depicted on the rock art panel. In fact, rock flour from the petroglyphs may actually have been ingested by the ritual participants, an act referred to as geophagy, that is, the 'consumption of earth' (Malotki and Weaver 2000: 72). Also in Europe, cupule-powder is said to have been used as or in medicine (Evers 1996: 83; Schwegler 1992: 29; see also Callahan 2000 for a full report). In this respect it is worth mentioning that Ouzman (2001: 251) tentatively and carefully suggests that the ingestion of rock powder might also have been a possible way for selected people in southern Africa to inherit the potency of a rock or rock art site.

Thus the execution of ('atypical') cupules and abraded grooves at certain panels at the Bluff Site (and elsewhere in the world) may have been intended to create visible passages to the spirit world and possibly simultaneously to produce a powder that could be ingested (or flakes that could be taken) in order to absorb metaphorically *and* literally the potency of the place. Also the execution itself may have had ritual significance.

It may therefore be concluded that the majority of the cupules and abraded grooves at the Bluff Site that are found together with figurative petroglyphs probably express an intimate relation with the rock and/or the place where they are found rather than with the figurative imagery itself. Such rock, site or place-related cupules and abraded grooves may represent a means of contacting and accessing the spiritual world hidden 'behind' the rock surface. An additional reason to produce cupules and abraded grooves might have been the desire to acquire (or even ingest) powder or pieces of those sacred places, possibly also as mnemonic devices. A mnemonic device is a memory aid. For instance, ethnographic records confirm that abraded grooves at the Yiwarlarlay rock shelter in the Northern Territory of Australia were cut into the rock to record that a specific person visited the site, or as Flood states 'That mark means I was here' (2006: 240). Similarly, items (like stone flakes from a specific site like the Berlin Wall) could be taken home to remind the visitor that, by looking at the device, he or she could say 'I once was there'. In this way tourists have adversely damaged the megaliths of Stonehenge by chipping off stone flakes probably as mnemonic devices.

Acknowledgments

First of all I would like to thank Prof. Roy Querejazu Lewis, who was so kind to read, in my absence, this essay (originally submitted as two separate, more comprehensive papers) to the audience at the International Cupule Conference, held in Cochabamba, Bolivia, in July 2007. I also appreciate the ever-constructive comments offered by Robert G. Bednarik after having read the draft text of the paper, but I note that he is not responsible for any shortcomings. I am also most grateful to Duke and Sarah Hayduk of Bluff, Utah, for taking a large number of extra photographs of the Bluff Site for me. I am also indebted to Vaughn Hadenfeldt of Bluff, for informing me about the cupules at the Bluff Site. Last but not least, I thank my wife Elles for her assistance during all the field trips in Utah and Peru.

REFERENCES

AMPUERO, B. G. 1993. *Arte rupestre en El Valle de El Encanto*. Editoral Museo Arqueológico de La Serena, La Serena.

BEDNARIK, R. G. 2008. Cupules. *Rock Art Research* 25-1: 61-100. Melbourne.

BEDNARIK, R. G., G. KUMAR, A. MUZZOLINI, D. SEGLIE, Y. A. SHER and M. CONSENS. 2003. Rock Art Glossary: a multiregional dictionary. IFRAO Brepols Series 2, Brepols, Turnhout.

CALLAHAN, K. L. 2000. *Pica, geophagy, and rock art: Ingestion of rock powder and clay by humans and its implications for the production of some rock art on a global basis*. In http://www.geocities.com/athens/acropolis/5579/pica.html

CASTLETON, K. B. 1987. *Petroglyphs and pictographs of Utah. Volume two: The south, central, west and northwest*. Utah Museum of Natural History, Salt Lake City.

COLE, S. J. *Legacy on stone. Rock art of the Colorado Plateau and Four Corners Region*. Johnson Books, Boulder, CO.

COSTAS GOBERNA, F. J. and P. NOVOA 1993. *Los grabados rupestres de Galicia*. Monografías 6, La Coruña.

EVERS, D. 1996. *De magie der beelden. Prehistorische Scandinavische rotstekeningen*. Dutch edition of *Magie der Bilder*. 1995. Pulsa-Verlag, Warmsroth.

FLOOD, J. 2006. Copying the dreamtime: Anthropic marks in early Aboriginal Australia. *Rock Art Research* 23-1: 239-246. melbourne.

GUFFROY, J. 1980–81. Les pétroglyphes de Checta: éléments interprétatifs. *Bulletin de la Société des Américanistes*; t. LXVII: 69–96. Paris.

GUFFROY, J. 1999. *El arte rupestre del antiguo Peru*. IFEA, Lima.

KLEIN, O. 1972. Cultura ovalle. Complejo rupestre 'Cabezas-Tiara'. Petroglifos y pictografías del Valle del Encanto, Provincia de Coquimbo, Chile. *Scientia* 141: 5–123.

MALOTKI, E. and D. E. WEAVER Jr. 2002. *Stone chisel and yucca brush. Colorado Plateau rock art*. Kiva Publishing, Walnut, CA.

METHFESSEL, C. and L. METHFESSEL 1998. Cúpulas en rocas de Tarija y regiones vecinas. Primera aproximación. *SIARB Boletín* 12: 36–47.

MOSTNY, G. G. and F. H. NIEMEYER 1983. *Arte rupestre Chileno*. Serie El Patrimonio Cultural Chileno, Collección Historia del Arte Chileno. Publicación del Departemento de Extensión Cultural del Ministerio de Educación.

MOUNTJOY, J. B. 2001a. Ritos de renovación en los petroglifos de Jalisco. Arqueología de occidente. *Arqueología Mexicana* 8(47): 56–63.

NÚÑEZ JIMÉNEZ, A. 1986. *Petroglifos del Peru. Panorama mundial del arte rupestre*. 2da. Ed. PNUD-UNESCO – Proyecto Regional de Patrimonio Cultural y Desarrollo.

OUZMAN, S. 2001. Seeing is deceiving: rock-art and the non-visual. *World Archaeology* 33(2): 237–256.

QUEREJAZU LEWIS, R. 1998. Tradiciones de Cúpulas en el Departamento de Cochabamba. *SIARB Boletín* 12: 48–58.

SCHAAFSMA, P. *Indian Rock Art of the Southwest*. University of New Mexico Press, Albuquerque.

SCHWEGLER, U. 1992. *Schalen- und Zeichensteine der Schweiz*. Antiqua 22, Basel.

SIMONIS, R., G. FALESHINI and G. NEGRO 1994. Niola Doa, 'il luogo delle fanciull' (Enedi, Ciad). *Sahara*, 6: 51-62.

SIMONIS, R., A. CAMPBELL and D. COULSON 1998. A Niola Doa 'lost site' revisited (Enedi, Ciad). *Sahara*, 10: 126-129.

STEVENSON, M. C. 1904. The Zuni Indians: Their mythology, Esoteric fraternities, and ceremonies. In: *Twenty-third Annual Report of the Bureau of American Ethnology*, U.S. Government

Printing Office, Washington, D.C.

TAÇON, P. S. C., R. FULLAGAR, S. OUZMAN and K. MULVANEY 1997. Cupule engravings from Jinmium-Granilpi (northern Australia) and beyond: exploration of a widespread and enigmatic class of rock markings. *Antiquity* 71(274): 942–965.

VAN HOEK, M. 1997. El arte neolítico en las Islas Británicas: Un fascinante legado cultural. En: Arte Rupestre Mundial. El mensaje pétreo de nuestros antepasados. *Arqueologia sin fronteras*, pp. 36–42. Arqueohistoria S.L., Madrid.

VAN HOEK, M. 2000a. Fish petroglyphs at 'Ava 'o Kiri, Rapa Nui. An approximation of a remarkable rock art site at Easter Island. *Rapa Nui Journal* 14: 13–17.

VAN HOEK, M. 2003a. El círculo, el ciervo y la trampa: grabados de cuadrúpedos en rocas con combinaciones circulares en Europa. *Brigantum* 14: 75–88.

VAN HOEK, M. 2003b. Tacitas or cupules? An attempt at distinguishing cultural depressions at two rock art sites near Ovalle, Chile. Rupestreweb, *http://rupestreweb.tripod.com/tacitas.html*.

CUPULES IN BOLIVIA

Roy Querejazu Lewis

Abstract. This paper presents the results of cupule fieldwork by the author in Bolivia, taking into account the spiritual idiosyncrasy of Andean populations, past and present. This is why, themes such as possible function and symbolism of cupules are covered, but, taking into consideration that interpretational hypotheses may not be scientific. Nevertheless, questions such as why, when and by whom cupules were made are considered important by the author, even if we do not have precise answers. The paper also includes the results of recent ethnological research concerning cupules, mostly related to the re-use of cupules; and the didactic effects of the International Cupule Conference. This includes the differentiation of cupules, the results of anthropic activity, and potholes, the results of kinetic geological phenomena.

Keywords: Cupule, Symbolic function, Ethnography, Sorcery, Mizque valley, Pothole, Kalatrancani, Bolivia

1. Introduction

Cupules are one of the commonest forms of rock art throughout the world. This phenomenon also occurs in Bolivia, especially in the Department of Cochabamba, where the First International Cupule Conference took place (in the city of Cochabamba) in July 2007. As I mentioned in the Conference Programme, cupules exist in a variety of geographical and environmental areas with a wide diversity of possible functions and symbolisms, belonging to almost all pre-Historic cultural periods. Some are even in use nowadays. In spite of this, they have received very little attention from rock art researchers in general (Querejazu 2007: 6–7).

From a Bolivian perspective, the first International Cupule Conference had the merit of having accomplished its objectives, which were centred on attention to the academic aspect, which scientifically was needed for cupules, the didactic aspect, contributing to the formation of young future researchers, and the initiation of future work with local indigenous communities in tourism and conservation projects.

In the present paper I will cover some of the teachings this Conference has left us, which have changed in a great way the view we had on cupules in Bolivia. In the first place, this First International Cupule Conference has proved that a small academic gathering concentrated on a specific subject can be highly productive in benefiting rock art research and conservation. Personally, I have benefited from two aspects related to the understanding of cupules: the discrimination of natural potholes (non-anthropic)

and cupules, and the taphonomy of cupules. Both themes were presented by Robert G. Bednarik, and, of course, in the case of Bolivian cupules, both are interrelated. Taphonomic logic leads to understanding better the effects of weathering and other influences on cupules.

In this paper I will cover the themes I presented at the Conference, but from a different perspective, that is, taking into account the teachings the Conference provided to me and the corrections I have made of some aspects of cupule understanding in Bolivia. In this sense, I shall cover the following themes: the possible function and symbolism of cupules, the re-use of cupule sites, and misunderstanding natural potholes (the case of Tarata).

2. Possible function and symbolism of cupules

Cupules were made for some reason. They meant something to their producers. This meaning could be manifested in the cupule itself, as a result of a repetitive percussion action, or in the use or re-use it was subject to. This leads us to the symbolism they may have had for their producers and/or the function they may have provided.

I am conscious that in this analysis I am entering a speculative and subjective area, which some rock art scholars prefer to avoid or simply are not interested in. As the assumptions presented cannot be proved or disproved, it does not fit within scientific rules. Nevertheless, cupules were made for some reason, and while observing them, one cannot avoid asking, why?

If we ask why, and expect a coherent answer, then we must ask other questions, and such inquiries lead us to ask when and by whom, and perhaps the answers to these last two questions lead us to scientific ground. They are more technical, less spiritual. But is rock art not part of the remains of spiritual activity? This is why I insist in asking myself, why?

While trying to answer 'why', other considerations come into scene, such as the location of the site and the disposition of the remains of anthropic activity on the rock surface. The site containing the rocks with the cupules could be below a high mountain peak (the case of Kalatrancani and the Tunari mountain peak in Cochabamba), or it could be associated with a spectacular agricultural landscape (the case of La Choza in the Tarija valley); or a cupule may be situated below or adjacent to a rock painting panel (the case of Incamachay in Chuquisca or Pultuma in Oruro), or the rock containing the cupules could be situated on the edge of a hill with the community houses below (the case of Lakatambo in Mizque), or a cupule may be part of a figurative schematic figure (the case of cupules forming the head of schematic zoomorphic figures in Almacigar in Santa Cruz).

I do not know why these cupules were made in each case, but I suppose that in each one of them, the motivation was different, and yet, the shape of the cupules remained the same. This leads us to the definition or classification of a cupule. Must cupules always have the same circular shape? This subject has been covered by Maarten van Hoek (see his paper in this volume). What about the oval shaped cupules in Tarija, for example, on Roca Cabildo. Van Hoek mentions 'kidney-shaped depressions'.

Nevertheless, van Hoek defines true cupules as 'circular, non utilitarian, anthropic depressions' (van Hoek 2008). Robert Bednarik in his *Rock Art Glossary* (2003) defines cupules as 'a hemispherical percussion petroglyph, which may occur on a horizontal or vertical surface'. In this paper I shall concentrate on cupules that respond to the two previous definitions.

In respect to the functionality of cupules, in my paper 'Tradiciones de Cúpulas en el Departamento de Cochabamba' (1998a) I classified them as:

- The pre-Hispanic ritual function of cupules.
- The contemporaneous ritual function of cupules.

In that paper I had also mentioned the utilitarian function of some depressions, but those are mortars, which do not fit in our definition of cupules.

3. Pre-Hispanic ritual function of cupules

An important area for analysing the possible ritual function of cupules in pre-Hispanic times is below the Tunari summit, on the lower slopes, just above the valley of Cochabamba (Bolivia). In an area not larger than 10 km along the mountain range there are eight known concentrations of petroglyphs. Seven of them contain cupules, and some of them contain several sites. For example, at Kalatrancani, during the International Cupule Conference excursions, with Robert Bednarik we discovered two more important rocks with cupules (Roca Fortunato 1 and 2), and he alone discovered another three rocks, each one of them being considered as a site.

Each one of the eight petroglyph concentrations presents a variety of rock art manifestations. Of the seven areas with cupules, four present grooves, which are connected with cupules, all seven areas have incised lines, in most cases superimposed on cupules, and three have polished surfaces as in Inca Huasi Uyuchama in Mizque. One of these areas (Buena Vista) has circuitous and serpent-shaped grooves. At another site, where there is only one rock (Llave Chico), there are cupules disposed as a telephone dial or a feline footprint, with one large cupule at the centre and six smaller cupules around the larger one. At Combuyo, one of the fifteen rocks also has an abstract non-figurative figure and a pair of arrow-like engravings, besides two squares with straight lines that connect the angles. At Kalatrancani, Roca Fortunato presents a huge number of cupules (originally it must have had more than 1000 cupules), grooves connecting a few of them, and an important and significative occurrence of incised lines. This important site also features quartzite and quartz artefacts that were used for the petroglyph production.

The cupules of the seven areas present a variety of sizes. The smallest ones (at Pairumani) are only 1.5 cm in diameter and about 3 mm in depth. The largest cupule is 13 cm in diameter (rock No. 3 at Buena Vista). Nevertheless, the average size of the cupules in the whole area is between 4 and 5 cm in diameter and between 3 and 4 mm in depth.

The rocks of the region seem to belong to some kind of metamorphic rock (R. G. Bednarik, pers. comm., December 2008) and form part of the geological landscape of the Tunari mountain chain. I presume that human activity on these rocks must have taken place in agricultural and pottery periods, probably starting in the Formative Period in the first millennium B.C.E. and continuing up to Inca times in the late fifteenth century. This presumption is based on the possible relation to water and fertility, both concepts linked to sedentary cultures and agriculture in the Andes.

In what concerns the possible ritual pre-Hispanic function of cupules, of the eight areas just mentioned, the most important one is Kalatrancani (Figure 1), which exhibits the largest quantity of rocks with cupules connected with grooves that descend towards or are connected with natural crevices, that descend to the surrounding soil. On the highest point of several of these rocks, cupules (generally larger than the other cupules on the same rock) are situated, from which sinuous grooves descend towards the mentioned natural crevices. These top cupules are situated on relatively horizontal surfaces, in which some liquid element can be contained. An example of these larger cupules that can retain water is the top cupule on Rock No. 1 in Kalatrancani, from which descends the longest of the grooves. This cupule has 12 cm in diameter, while the average of the remaining cupules on the same rock have 5 cm in diameter. The overflow of water or any other liquid descends along the grooves.

The fact of replicating possible past offerings by pouring water on these top cupules and rendering evident the relation between them and the descending grooves allows us to postulate the possibility that these cupules might have had a pre-Hispanic ritual function related with the Tunari mountain summit. It seems that these cupules on the higher part of the rocks in Kalatrancani, that retained water (or some other liquid element) until the cupule was filled and then started to overflow the liquid along the grooves towards the lower natural crevices, and then to the surrounding ground, were used in rites destined to 'fecundate' symbolically the surrounding soil of the rocks that contained the cupules, grooves and natural crevices. These rites would have been seemingly related to the Tunari sacred mountain, were the meteorological phenomena took place (and continue to do so) that yielded water that descended along the ravines and then fertilised the valley soils and provided water to domestic animals and the local population. In consequence, these symbolic offerings might have been dedicated to the Tunari, so that the Sacred Mountain would reciprocate the offerings, making water descend, which was necessary for the survival and prosperity of the local populations living in the Cochabamba valley below the mountain (Querejazu 1992: 52–3).

Figure 1. Cupule, groove and other cupules in Kalatrancani (Pre-Hispanic ritual function of cupules).

It is important to mention that reciprocity relations are an integral and essential part of Andean cultures since pre-Hispanic times. It is also crucial in this hypothesis to be conscious of the fact that rocks with cupules only seem to occur in an area of about ten kilometres, in view of the Tunari peak. Further to the east and further to the west, rocks do not contain cupules. If this hypothesis were correct, the importance water had for the local communities would suggest a relative chronology pertaining to the Andean Formative Period (covering the first millennium B.C.E. and the first half of the first millennium C.E.) up to agricultural and pottery societies that developed before the Inca Period. According to Robert Bednarik, at least some of the petroglyphs at Kalatrancani 3 pertain to the Inca period (fifteenth and sixteenth centuries C.E.), based on his microerosion analyses.

In the River Mizque Basin, near Omereque, there is another site with cupules related to a possible pre-Hispanic ritual function. The site is called Pukara Cupúlas. It is at 1750 m above sea level on the top of a hill that is an archaeological site containing pottery remains of various pre-Hispanic cultures. It has cupules that form four circles situated on a horizontal (slightly inclined) sandstone rock surface on the border of a natural reservoir surrounded by other rocks, giving the pond a rectangular shape. The natural dam measures approximately 8 m long by about 3 m high. In its eastern side it must have had a system of flood-gates for water control.

Two of the mentioned circles (including the largest one) have 18 cupules (some are hardly perceivable), another has 16 cupules, and the smallest one six cupules. There are other cupules that are randomly situated. The cupules vary between 3.1 cm and 5 cm in diameter, with depths varying between 1.4 and 1.7 cm. Two grooves are also present. They have also been made with percussion strokes, and are related to one of the circles. One of the grooves cuts perpendicularly the mentioned circle, and the other one joins three cupules. There also is a mortar (polished inside) with a small outlet groove (oriented towards the south) that leads to a natural crevice that descends to the surrounding soil of the rock towards the south and the south-west. The mortar has a 35 cm diameter and 20 cm depth. Close to the cupules there also are polished surfaces.

Seemingly, the cupules would correspond to the occupation period of the area by different agricultural and pottery cultures from 300 to 1400 C.E. (Cespedes, pers. comm., April 1998). This chronological hypothesis tends to be

Figure 2. Percussion strokes on top of Pre-Hispanic paintings in Kelkata Río Tambillo (Pre-Hispanic ritual function of cupules).

confirmed by the fact that although the cupules have an ancient appearance, the evident weathering is due above all to the type of sandstone, which is very frail. Likewise, the cement between the sand grains has not retreated much, a phenomenon that frequently occurs in quite ancient rock surfaces, and on the other hand, the percussion strokes in the cupules can be seen, which in some cases of very ancient cupules has been erased by weathering.

The pre-Hispanic ritual function of the cupules of this site has its importance in the re-use of these rock manifestations in pre-Hispanic times. A re-use that originated in the functional and ritual character the site seems to have had. The information obtained at the site suggests that the different cupules (including the cupule circles), the grooves, and mortar had a relation with the natural dam.

We suggest that the natural reservoir (including another smaller one adjoining the larger one) served to store water and for its later use in various life activities. On the other hand, the cupules, grooves and mortar may have been utilised in ceremonies or rites, using some liquid element with the purpose of propitiating the existence of water in this arid terrain. In other words, the orientation, location and disposition of the different reservoirs, natural and anthropic, suggest an intentional relationship between them, induced by the inhabitants of the time.

On the other hand, it is interesting to mention that on the top of another rock at about six metres towards the north from the large natural reservoir, there are various natural concavities of geological origin. These round concavities are very similar to anthropic cupules. Nevertheless, they do not seem to form part of the possible ritual ensemble just mentioned (Querejazu 1998b).

A third site, where percussion strokes have produced concavities similar to the classical cupules is Kelkata-Río Tambillo, situated in the Yanakaka Cordillera. It is a vertical panel oriented towards the east (70°) of a large rock at 3703 m above sea level. The panel has abstract rock paintings in different red hues and lines in black. Superposed on the rock paintings there are circular percussion concavities of about 4 cm diameter. They are not traditional cupules. The process that produced them seems to be different from 'normal' cupules. They have the appearance of not being finished (Figure 2).

They seem to be the result of one or various rites and that had a specific function. It is obvious that the makers did not have in mind the production of cupules as we conceive them. Likewise, these percussion strokes must have had a certain meaning. Many of them are superimposed on pre-Hispanic rock paintings. On the other hand, two periods of time in the execution of the strokes seem to be evident. Some of the cupules have a darker patina while others are light coloured.

These pre-Hispanic irregular concavities seem to be the result of an activity destined to obliterate the rock paintings. It seems to be an iconoclast activity, the imposition of a culture, an ideology, or a creed over another. In this sense, apart from the purpose of this activity (either iconoclastic, that is to say, the destruction of ancient rock paintings, or the imposition of a new cultural tradition), the fact is that these circular concentrations of percussion strokes remain. Be it one way or another, they seem to represent (as a result of the possible destruction action) a certain symbolism perhaps related to a new culture or creed that occupied this Andean – Amazonian region.

4. Contemporaneous ritual function of rocks with cupules

The most explicit case in Bolivia is Lakatambo, in the proximity of the town of Mizque. Lakatambo is an archaeological site situated on the lowest of three hill terraces in the Mizque valley. The site contains pottery shards and stone remains of foundations, walls and silos. The site was occupied by the Lakatambo culture that occupied the area in the Late Intermediate Period (1100

Figure 3. Rock No. 1 in Lakatambo where a variety of offerings took place (contemporaneous ritual function of rocks with cupules).

– 1438 C.E.), and later, possibly also, by the Inca conquest of the region.

On the western side of the terrace, on the limits of the archaeological material remains, stands out a large rock, denominated by us as rock No. 1. It is one of several rocks in the area bearing cupules (Figure 3). Because of its location (on the border of the ancient town), size (about 1.85 m high and 1.60 m width in both directions), shape (seen from the east it resembles a puma face) and colour (covered by black and orange lichens), it may have had an important supernatural significance for the local population in pre-Hispanic times.

On the relatively horizontal top of the rock, there are cupules and incised thin grooves, which descend towards the eastern side. When we visited the rock in September 1987, the cupules had no offerings at all. Then, in a later visit, in April 1990, in a natural triangular crevice on the top we found a quartz stone of 10 cm long, with a good quantity of masticated coca leafs beside it. The quartz stone and the masticated coca leaves ('*acullicos*') had been placed in the natural crevice as an offering. One of the cupules also contained small stones with masticated coca leaves stuck on them (Figure 4).

In November 1991, the offerings in the natural crevice and in the cupule remained the same. In July 1994, we found a broken small movable pre-Hispanic mortar (not exceeding 22 cm) placed at a distance of one metre form the rock. These mortars were used for grinding grains, and therefore, this offering may have had a symbolic relation with agriculture, crops, rain or fertility. Curiously, the mortar was not there on previous visits.

All this tends to suggest that the motivation behind all these offerings was the drought that then affected the region during more than five years. The offerings of stones (a common offering in the Andes), including the white quartzite stone and the masticated coca leafs, seemingly were placed with the purpose of propitiating rain.

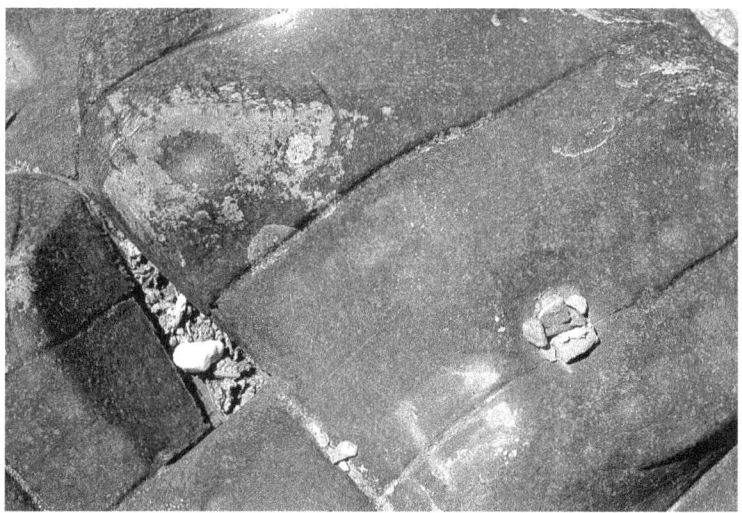

Figure 4. Natural crevice and cupule with masticated coca leaf offerings on Rock No. 1 in Lakatambo (contemporaneous ritual function of rocks with cupules).

According to the annual precipitation diagram prepared by CEDEAGRO, a non-government organisation dealing with agricultural projects in the region, as from 1989 the Mizque zone had a constant decrease in the level of annual precipitation, which coincides exactly with the time the stone and coca offerings were placed on rock No. 1 of Lakatambo. These offerings must have occurred early in 1990, because in April 1990, the coca '*acullicos*' were still fresh. Besides, January or February (beginning of 1990) correspond to the maximum intensity of the rainy season. Between 1991 and 1997, no more offerings were carried out to the best of our knowledge (Querejazu 2001: 152–4).

On the other hand, research carried out on this remarkable rock bearing cupules, among other special characteristics (mentioned above), has shown that it is considered as sacred, and therefore, venerated and worshiped, not only by the local community, but also by people that come from far away, as far as the town of Quillacollo, at about 170 km distance.

According to Augusto Meneces who lives in Sauces, below the terraces of Lakatambo, a person from Quillacollo called José Fernández, married with a woman from Mizque, had carried out the last offerings consisting of liquor bottles and beer cans. On the other hand, the local people in the community of Lakatambo prefer not to speak openly about this matter. The use the rock is subject to remains as an intimate part of their identity and cultural traditions, and they do not share these traditions with outsiders.

Nevertheless, in conversations with Marino Meneces (son of Augusto), I managed to obtain another name related to the offerings, which is Elias Piedra. It is interesting to note that 'piedra', the surname of Elias, means 'stone'. Now, Elias Piedra is also from Quillacollo. The son-in-law of Elias Piedra is Benito, who lives in the region.

According to Gabriel Alvarez, a syndicate leader of the nearby community Poqho,

> in Lakatambo a goat shepherd while passing by in a dark night, heard a very strong noise that frightened the goats. He had to give up his route and he left the place. They say that in these places where they make offerings, they expect a retribution in gold (Alfredo Vallejos, pers. comm., Tunas Qaqa, 22 April 2005).

The next day, Augusto Meneces, told us that the son-in-law, Benito, a sorcerer, 'has relations with Santiago, he talks with him. If he asks a favour from him, from the rock, he can heal, he makes the favour. He cures down here in his house, he is a *curandero*'. Santiago, in Andean mythology, is a Catholic saint, related with thunder and rain.

> When it does not rain, we must ask to the stone, as if it were a saint. We have believed a little, as if it were a saint. The stone must not be touched, molested. When we approach the stone, the wind comes, as a tornado, the bad wind. You must not bother the stone. You must make a *coa*, with a llama foetus, an offering. We must invite as if it were a saint.
> Only the *curanderos* make offerings. The señora Manuela in San Pedro, beside Lakatambo, is one. We only ask the stone, let us expect that this year there will be.

In those days (in 2005), a graffiti appeared on rock No. 1 that reads 'Ronald Delgadillo Fuentes'.

> They say that it is the name of the rock. The son of Feliciano Fernández, called César, from Lakatambo, has said that the stone is always powerful, potent. Everything can be asked from the saint, because the money abounds in the stone (Augusto Meneces, pers. comm., Sauces, 23 April 2005).

The next day, 24 April 2005, we found down (small chest feathers, probably of a partridge), apparently stuck as an offering on the northern vertical side of the rock. On the base of the rock was a stone containing fossils, also placed as an offering, whereas the bottles and cans had been removed. Only some glass pieces and cans remained at about five meters from the rock.

This was the first time that in Bolivia feathers were found as the result of an offering in a site containing rock art. Feathers have formed an important part of the spiritual and supernatural world of the indigenous ethnic groups in South America, especially for the Amazonian people. Nevertheless, the use of feathers in the Andes has had a variety of functions, and the fact of finding a feather offering in Lakatambo constitutes a new research area concerning the re-use of rock art sites.

According to Rafael Karsten (1926: 75–101) feathers were used when native people established relation with the spiritual world. Feathers had a magical power connected to the spirit of the animal, while this spirit was concentrated in the feathers. It is also worth mentioning that it was only men who used feathers as ornaments (with a spiritual connotation). Karsten had the advantage to carry out his fieldwork when the indigenous people in South America had still conserved a lot of their traditions and beliefs. Feathers, according to him, were essentially means of enchanting or exorcising.

Was this the case of the feathers stuck on rock No. 1 in Lakatambo? We do not know, but feathers were apparently used in some sort of ritual. It is also very significant that only small chest feathers were used, and also that a stone with fossils was placed at the base of the rock.

Although, perhaps not related with these offerings, during our April visit to the site we found scratches on rock number one. Some of them had been produced by goats that climbed the rock (and left their manure), but others were clearly long anthropic incised lines. On a couple of smaller rocks nearby, scratched drawings of skeletons were found.

We returned to Mizque in July 2005 as part of an AEARC research field trip, in which Gori Tumi Echevarría, Raquel Velasco, Rodolfo Rodríguez, Pamela Rodríguez, Hugo

Santa Cruz, Mirta Pedraza, Juan Miguel Fajardo, Ximena Albornoz, Andrea Ríos and Mariel Ríos participated. On the 22nd we secured another conversation with Augusto Meneces. This time he said that the person that carried out the '*challa*' (offering with liquors and beer) was called Benedicto. Augusto continued saying that they tried to hit him, saying that he was a sorcerer, 'he only asks for himself'. The San Pedro community 'threw him away'. 'He comes from Quillacollo to ask for himself a power that is given. If at least he would help by healing'. Then they told him 'you are *macumbiando* the stone, you will both make people die. That is why they killed him' (Augusto Meneces, pers. comm., Sauces, 22 July 2005).

'*Macumbiando*' was a way of expressing *macumba*, the Brazilian rite of sorcery. The next day (23 July) we climbed the Lakatambo terrace once again in order to visit rock No. 1. The incised lines remained, but of course the fragile little feathers were gone. This time we found that rock No. 2 also had incised lines around the cupules, as well as recently polished surfaces and percussion marks. Near rock No. 1, towards the north, there was another rock with incised words related to the Catholic religion. The creator apparently was the same person who drew the skeletons. It was apparent that he had an obsession with death and religious punishment. A gloomy skeleton was also drawn on the same rock. He chose rocks almost covered by black lichens as a support for his manifestations.

As it seems, it was not the result of an act of vandalism. Marino Meneces, the son of Augusto Meneces (who now is an expert in cupules of the region, having discovered another rock with cupules) told us that he knew the young man who made the lines and the drawings, and wrote the words. His name is Daniel Arias, a very introvert lad from Mizque. 'He thinks he is a sinner, and sees Sweet Jesus', said Marino.

5. Possible symbolism of cupules

There are cupules or groups of cupules that do not present signs of having had a ritual or offering function. Nevertheless, the task of doing them, especially when they were very numerous, must have had a certain importance for the artificers; perhaps a cultural or traditional importance. If they were not used for something, either a utilitarian or a ritual purpose, the cupules must still have meant something. In other words, they must have had a certain symbolism that, of course, we ignore.

Cupules of this kind might be those that do not show any signs of a ritual or utilitarian use. They could have a certain geometric disposition (forming lines or circles) or they could be placed at random, or they could be situated on a vertical surface where they could not retain any liquid element.

In a previous paper I have suggested that cupules in sites such as Inca Huasi-Uyuchama, Uyuchama 2, Lakatambo, possibly Llave Chico, and some others below the Tunari summit (Querejazu 1998a: 52–53), might have had a certain symbolism. In most of the cases just mentioned, the verification of such a supposition seems impossible. In my research in this area I am conscious that what cannot be tested is not scientific. But, nevertheless, there are two cases of cupules in Bolivia that I esteem worth considering as pertaining to the subject I am dealing with, which is the possible symbolism of cupules. The first case belongs to a possible pre-Hispanic symbolism. The second case, to a relatively recent attribution of a symbolism of a rock containing cupules.

The first case corresponds to circles that are formed by 18 cupules. On the second terrace of Lakatambo there are two rocks, separated by about 200 m, with 18 cupules forming a circle. On the third terrace, about 80 m higher up, there is another flat rock bearing a circle on its upper horizontal surface. It therefore seems that the repetition of 18 cupules was intentional. If it was so, why? All I can say is that the eighteen cupules forming a circle must have meant something to the makers. In other words, the arrangement had a certain symbolism for them.

I do not intend to enter in a speculative debate about the meaning of eighteen cupules forming a circle. For example I could quote Dick Edgar Ibarra Grasso suggesting that the central circle in the Inca Ceremonial Rock in Samaipata, containing nine carved triangular depressions and nine square depressions (giving a total of 18), and counting the spaces between each concavity, with a total of 36, could correspond to the days of the round year (Ibarra Grasso 1982: 357). All I am saying is that the repetitive existence of 18 cupules must have meant something, and that their production could have been intentional — especially if we take into account the circles in Pukara Cupúlas that I mentioned previously.

At Pukara Cúpulas, near the town of Omereque, more than 70 km from Lakatambo, there are four circles formed by cupules. Two of these circles (including the largest one) apparently have 18 cupules (some are hardly perceivable). The third circle has 16 cupules and the remaining one six cupules. There are also other cupules occurring randomly.

The second case of symbolism corresponds to the relatively recent attribution of a symbolism of a rock featuring cupules. Just on the border of the first terrace at Lakatambo, there is a loose rock on top of another, fixed one, full of cupules on its upper horizontal surface. It seems that the local community brought this rock containing the cupules from nearby, for it does not match the bedrock of the site. Just beside this rock, two Christian crosses had been placed. The crosses and the rock with the cupules overlook the indigenous communities of Lakatambo and San Pedro (Figures 5 and 6).

In pre-Hispanic times, in the Andes, mountains and hills above native villages were considered as guardians. In fact, the Aymara speakers, who are culturally very much interrelated with the Quechuas, call these high Andean sanctuaries '*achachilas*'. According to Hans van den Berg they were also considered as the spirits of the ancestors that remain close to their community, 'watch over the life of their descendants, share their sufferings and grief, and give them their blessings. The population pays them for all this, venerating them with prayers and offerings'.

The site I am describing would correspond to the second kind of '*achachilas*', which are those 'identified with the hills that surround the communities; these are spirit protectors of the local communities: this way each community also has its own *achachila*' (van den Berg 1985: 11).

When the Spaniards arrived, the Catholic missionaries found it very difficult to eradicate these 'pagan' beliefs. So as part of their Idolatry Eradication Policy (that emanated form the Second Council in Lima in 1567) they started to place the Christian cross on these '*achachilas*', which were considered as sacred for the native population. As a result, one can now see in the Altiplano of Bolivia, on top of small hills, Christian crosses and small chapels as a result of the imposition of the new creed arrived from Europe. These Christian symbols occupy the place of the '*achachilas*' (they are placed on the same hills) and accomplish a similar function as guardians of the villagers below.

We consider this case as unique, for it combines the Christian cross, with all the symbolism it has, with a rock containing more than two hundred cupules, which must have had a certain symbolism for the local indigenous people. The Christian cross, symbol of the new religion arrived during the Colonial period, and the rock with the cupules, symbol of the native and pre-Hispanic beliefs, intermix their supernatural forces to the benefit of the local population living below.

Figure 5. Catholic cross with rock containing cupules on top of the local communities of Lakatambo and San Pedro (possible symbolism of cupules).

superficial holes were known. Our insufficient scientific knowledge about the formation of geological rock markings induced us to consider all these holes on rock surfaces as cupules (anthropic). The same occurred with the local

6. Potholes and cupules

The First International Cupule Conference has been of great importance for rock art research in Bolivia. In the first place, it is worth mentioning that a good part of the audience was composed of young AEARC members and tourism students from the Major University of San Simon in Cochabamba. These young scholars had the opportunity to learn from international experts. And, at the same time, rock art researchers from South America, especially from Bolivia, had the invaluable experience of learning more about cupules and natural cupule-like features in rocks.

This was also my case, I must recognise. For many years, in two sites of Karakara, where Osvaldo Sánchez, the community spokesman, lives, deep holes together with other anthropic

Figure 6. Slab containing cupules close to the Catholic cross (possible symbolism of cupules).

population, although their perception was not directed to the way these holes were formed, but to their significance as the product of 'ancient peoples — their ancestors'.

Then, some five years ago, another discovery of 'cupules and rock carvings' was made known by a German archaeologist. The site was called Chutu Kollu. This induced us to expand the exploration of the area, and together with Hugo Santa Cruz and Ana María Urquidi we discovered two other sites with similar holes and rock carvings. These sites, Punku Kocha (Mendez Mamata) and Rocas Río Milloma had similar characteristics. The holes and carvings were situated in rocks that formed part of ravines and small waterfalls. They were, in fact, remarkable because of their well-formed conical holes, as well as smooth rock carvings, that made us think about their possible function, in the sense that their artificers intended to direct water symbolically towards the agricultural fields further down. At all these sites there are agricultural fields nearby. Yes, my interpretation of these different sites was that they were made in pre-Hispanic times (although some holes seemed older than others) as part of rituals intended to produce rain and water for the agricultural fields.

This conception I had was presented as part of one of my dissertations at the International Cupule Conference, and together with other AEARC members we decided to include these sites in the conference excursions. I am of the opinion that during the last 20 years, when responsible and dedicated rock art research started in Bolivia, we have advanced enormously in SIARB (Bolivian Rock Art Research Society) and in AEARC (Cochabamba Rock Art Research Association), but, as in any scientific field, we still have much more to learn.

While the main group of the conference excursion continued to Mizque, with Robert and Elfriede Bednarik we remained a couple of days more in Tarata in order to dedicate more time examining these holes in the rocks of the area. All the deep conical holes at the waterfalls turned out to be 'natural, cupule like features' called 'potholes' (Bednarik 2007a: 273–5).

In fact, their often conical shape may have made it extremely difficult, if not impossible, to introduce a hand and arm and hammer the bottom of the hole. Robert Bednarik described the potholes in Rocas Río Milloma as potholes (Figure 7), some absolutely conical, with accretions that have been formed of mineral components containing manganese and iron. These holes were formed on the basis of a slight natural depression in the river course, which began to retain running water, forming eddies that dragged small quartzite clasts and sand. Being harder than the schistose bedrock, these abrasives began polishing the surface circularly, result eventually in deep conical holes. Some of these potholes have an irregular, non-conical bottom, horizontal or even convex, that is to say, they have not been polished into a conical shape. According to Robert Bednarik, this is due to 'the centrifugal force of the abrasive material' (Bednarik

Figure 7. Potholes or natural concavities in Rocas Río Milloma (potholes).

2008: 63).

The potholes of the region were formed during the Pleistocene and Holocene. Some of them could have gone through an erosion process for as much as 20,000 years. Later on, during the Holocene, they inspired the execution of anthropic cupules, which in some sites are found next to potholes (Bednarik, pers. comm., Tarata region, 21 July 2007).

The knowledge acquired during this positive experience has prepared us to differentiate in a proper way what is natural from what is anthropic. A variety of natural rock markings have geological and biological origins (Bednarik 1994). During our research experience in Bolivia we have been more acquainted with the second variety, which are plant and animal markings. The Tarata experience has provided us with more light concerning kinetic markings, especially, 'clastic movement marks' (Bednarik 2007b: 24).

Based on the academic and field experience of this First International Cupule Conference we consider that small events of this kind, focused on one important subject of rock art, produce far more scientific knowledge than other larger congresses, where many subjects are covered, and where one does not have the opportunity to attend all of what is of interest. The experience we had in Cochabamba with this event has been unique and most enriching, not only for the new researchers that are emerging, but also for understanding the cupule phenomenon as a whole, that is, from different approaches. A cupule is not just a little concavity made by humans; there is much more to it.

REFERENCES

BEDNARIK, R. G. 1994. The discrimination of rock markings. *Rock Art Research* 11: 23–44.

BEDNARIK, R. G. (ed.) 2003. *Rock art glossary – a multilingual dictionary*. IFRAO – Brepols, Turnhout.

BEDNARIK, R. G. 2007a. The First International Cupule Conference: a report. *Rock Art Research* 24: 273–275.

BEDNARIK, R. G. 2007. *Rock art science: the scientific study of paleoart* (second edition). Aryan Books International, New Delhi.

BEDNARIK, R. G. 2008. Cupules. *Rock Art Research* 25: 61–100.

KARSTEN, R. 1926. *The civilization of the South American Indians*. Kegan Paul, Trench, Trubner & Co. Alfred A. Knopf, London and New York.

IBARRA GRASSO, D. E. 1982. *America en la Prehistoria Mundial*. Tipográfica Editora Argentina, Buenos Aires.

QUEREJAZU LEWIS, R. 1992. El Tunari: montaña sagrada. In R. Querejazu Lewis (ed.), *Arte rupestre Colonial y Republicano de Bolivia y paises vecinos*, pp. 52–66. Contribuciones al Estudio del Arte Rupestre Sudamericano 3, SIARB, La Paz.

QUEREJAZU LEWIS, R. 1998a. Tradiciones de cúpulas en el Departamento de Cochabamba. *SIARB Boletín* 12: 48–58.

QUEREJAZU LEWIS, R. 1998b. Cúpulas Rituales en Pukara. In: Suarez R., Ana María and Ortuño C., Lorena (Editors), *Dimensiones*, No. 1. Colegio de Arquitectos de Cochabamba, Cochabamba, pp. 70–74.

QUEREJAZU LEWIS, R. 2001. *El Arte Rupestre de la Cuenca del Río Mizque*. Universidad Mayor de San Simón. Prefectura del Departamento de Cochabamba. Sociedad de Investigación del Arte Rupestre de Bolivia (SIARB).

QUEREJAZU LEWIS, R. (ed.) 2007. *International Cupule Conference Programme*. Asociación de Estudios del Arte Rupestre de Cochabamba (AEARC) — Fundación Simón I. Patiño. Centro Pedagógico y Cultural Simón I. Patiño, Cochabamba.

VAN DEN BERG, H. 1985. *Diccionario religioso Aymara*. Semillas. CETA-IDEA. Iquitos.

VAN HOEK, M. 2008. Atypical cupules and lancet — Shaped depressions in rock art. Unpubl. MS, 10 p.

A SHORT ETHNOGRAPHY OF CUPULES

Robert G. Bednarik

Abstract. Globally we have quite limited ethnographic information about petroglyphs, about their emic meaning or purpose. Such information is even more limited for cupules, amounting to just a few fragmentary and very isolated accounts. The currently known examples are cited, their scientific veracity is discussed, and it is demonstrated through them that the endeavours of archaeologists to determine the meanings or significance of cupules are generally misguided. Such etic interpretation is impossible, and where it is attempted it is scientifically irrelevant, except for the cognitive scientist in studying the cognition of the interpreter.

Keywords: Cupule, Ethnography, Interpretation, Central Australia, California, India, Africa, Nepal

Most of the thousands of publications about cupules comprise some commentary on their meaning or cultural role — their significance to those who made or used them. Almost invariably, these speculations lack any scientific veracity; they are simply notions of the observers who completely lack any emic access to meaning, and in most cases have no idea of the ages of the rock art, or its provenience or cultural affiliation. Here we find a mother lode of archaeological humbug still awaiting detailed mining. Let us be quite blunt on this point: archaeology has not presented a scientifically based, or even plausible, explanation or interpretation of the rather unusual behaviour pattern manifested in cupules. That behaviour is documented in most of the world's rock art regions, and in some of them over enormous time spans. Cupules were still made in the early 20th century, in a very few places, and yet the ethnographically sound information collected about them is extremely sparse.

The most commonly mentioned archaeological interpretations of cupules could be grouped into a number of classes, based on these purported uses (but see more detailed discussion in the chapter on interpretation, this volume):

1. The preparation of paints.
2. Unspecified or specified cultic or magic rituals.
3. The pounding of medicines (mineral or plant), pigments or spices.
4. The placement of offerings ('*Opferschalen*'), including human blood and semen.
5. The depiction of star constellations.
6. The map-like depiction of topographic elements of nearby landscapes.
7. Board games.
8. A symbolism that is no longer recoverable.

Four of these explanations could at best only account for horizontal cupules and can therefore be excluded for all others, or at least vertical ones. Moreover, they are proposed without the facility of falsification, i.e. no evidence for them is presented, they are simply guesses. The explanation as patterns of heavenly bodies is particularly popular in China and parts of Europe, and is also offered without any tangible evidence. Star constellations, we can reasonably assume, are entirely random features, and it is then not surprising that they resemble other random or fortuitous arrangements. Large groupings of cupules tend to be cumulative, i.e. the marks constituting them were made singly and at greatly different times. That renders this explanation highly unlikely, and in all cases I am aware of, the resemblance with star constellations is only vague. For the vast majority of cupule constellations, no corresponding star charts have been proposed, and this notion appears to be without empirical basis as well as being unfalsifiable. It therefore is not a scientific proposition.

The explanation of random cupule groups as maps, popular in the Alpine regions of Europe, falls into the same category. It is untestable, has no ethnographic support, and is a priori unlikely unless all cupules were made at the same time. It is also reminiscent of other endeavours in seeking rock art explanations, in which various patterns are thought to be pre-Historic maps, apparently without justification. For instance, it has been proposed that the spatial configurations of French caves resemble the local topography surrounding those caves, and the Pleistocene animals depicted refer to their former distribution in the vicinity of the site. Such attempts to interpret the sites and their rock art lack any empirical basis.

I am only aware of a few sound ethnographic explanations

Figure 1. The Tukalili increase site near Nantaguna springs, Northern Territory, Australia. The precise emic significance of the cupules has been recorded (1940 photograph by Charles P. Mountford).

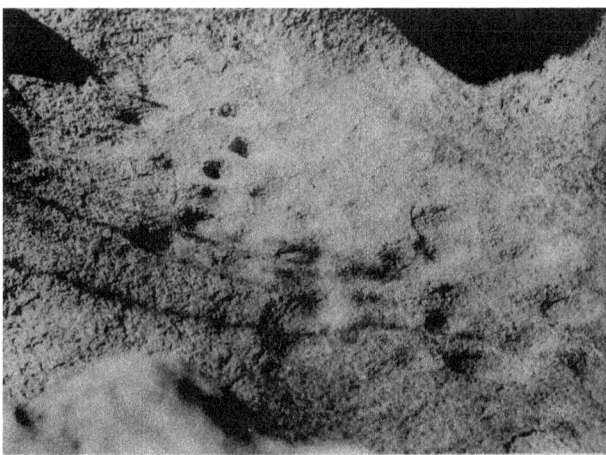

Figure 2. The cupules of the Tunalili increase site (photograph by C. P. Mountford).

of cupules in the world literature, of which one or two are probably 'derived' interpretations, and another two are of little help in formulating anything approaching a generic explanation. Only Mountford's (1976) observation of 1940 and perhaps a few American examples meet the strict requirements of a scientific interpretation, and it is limited to a very small number of cupule locations. The first case concerns the story of the death of Tukalili, the cockatoo-woman, a creation myth collected in the Northern Territory of Australia (Figures 1 and 2). Her totemic body, a large boulder near Nantaguna springs, bears in a recess around sixteen horizontal cupules. They are the result of *pulkarin* rituals conducted to cause the pink cockatoo (*Cacatua leadbeateri*) to lay more eggs (Figure 3). This is accomplished through the mineral powder rising into the air as the cupules are pounded. The dust represents the *kuranita* of the rock and, as it is thus released, it fertilises the female cockatoos. *Kuranita* (life essence) can rise like a mist into the air from any 'increase site', impregnating a specific plant, animal or natural force the site is associated with, through its release by an appropriate ceremony. It then increases the supply or strength of that entity, which can range from a plague of head lice to bring down on one's enemies to the supply of an edible tree gum. It has also been suggested (Taçon et al. 1997: 947) that some cupule sites near the Mann River in eastern Arnhem Land are related to Green Plum Dreaming ceremonies but there is no evidence that this was their original use.

In Mountford's example the cupules are clearly not the intended result of the exercise; the fertilising dust is the crucial element (Figure 4). The cupules are an incidental but the only surviving consequence of the ritual activity in question, and what we need to be most aware of is that this authentic interpretation of cupules could never be determined archaeologically. This example is not just one of the very few scientific explanations of any cupules in the world, it also shows the general impotence of archaeology in explaining archaeological phenomena. Without the

*Figure 3. The pink cockatoo (*Cacatua leadbeateri*).*

Figure 4. Stone powder from increase site being used for body decoration.

Figure 5. Renewal/reuse of a cupule on a lithophone or rock gong, Pola Bhata, Madhya Pradesh, India, in 2004.

recorded ethnographic observation, an archaeologist could never expect to formulate the authentic explanation. All correct interpretations of the residue that archaeologists chose to call archaeological remains are just as remote and unfathomable (i.e. emic) as is the interpretation of the cupules at Tukalili's site.

A second ethnographic explanation of cupules on a limited number of specific rocks comes from California and was recorded early in the 20th century by Barrett (1908: 164–165, 1952: 385–387; see also Loeb 1926: 247; Gifford and Kroeber 1937: 186; Heizer 1953; Grant 1967: 106; Hedges 1983a, 1983b). Specific boulders bearing collections of cupules were visited by Pomo women to conduct fertility ceremonies. These rituals, intended to lead to conception, involved the collection of the 'fertilising' dust created in pounding the cupules. The rock is either steatite or chlorite schist, the powder was made into a paste which was usually applied to the woman's skin, or, in one case recorded, was inserted into her vagina to achieve pregnancy through the rock's magical essence. However, the cupules at these sites tend to be outnumbered by incised grooves, and Hedges (1983b) rightly emphasises that the ethnographic explanation of the Pomo 'baby rocks', as they are called, should not be extended to other cupule sites (McGowan 1982). Nevertheless, one cupule site used in fertility rituals has also been reported from New Mexico, Mother Rock on To'wa yäl'länne (Corn Mountain) near Zuni Pueblo (Stevenson 1887: 539–540; also Fewkes 1891: 9–10). There, the pregnant woman would collect the mineral powder 'into a tiny vase made for the purpose' and deposit it in a wall cavity, if she desired a daughter (Stevenson 1904: 295).

The parallel development of the concept of a fertilising effect of the mineral powder resulting from pounding cupules is certainly an interesting observation, but it can easily elicit unwarranted extrapolation to other sites. Other ethnographic indications in the western United States provide very different explanations. The Klamath of southern Oregon are said to have renewed cupules in order to summon the wind to change the weather (Spier 1930: 21). Similarly, the Shasta of California sought to influence the weather: they incised straight parallel grooves into selected 'rain rocks' to increase or decrease snowfall, and they pounded cupules to induce rainfall and wind (Heizer 1953). This also brings to mind the northern Australian custom of cutting sub-parallel grooves into bedrock to 'make Old Man Rain bleed' (Arndt 1962: 171). Again, it is evident how similar cultural practices can be developed independently, without any contact. Parkman (1992: 367) speculates that the percussion sound of pounding cupules could have been intended to 'attract or replace thunder'. He notes, in support of this contention, that 'among the Kashaya Pomo, women grinding acorns in their mortars took special precautions to prevent unwanted rain'. Apparently they prepared shelters to muffle the sound, so as not to summon rain unintentionally (Alvarez and Peri 1987: 12). Similarly, the Shasta covered their rain rocks in order to prevent rain (Heizer 1953). Parkman (1988) offers one further explanation for cupules, in describing rock slabs at Takimitlding and Medilding, California, as Hupa 'calendar stones'. It appears from his description that contemporary Hupa believe the stones to have had some astronomical role, but the consultants were unable to explain the actual function of these features and the interpretation, like others listed here, cannot be regarded as secure.

Another correct ethnographic interpretation of cupules I can offer is illustrated in Figure 5. Here, a properly knowledgeable person demonstrates the use of a cupule, one of several dozen at the site that were still being renewed

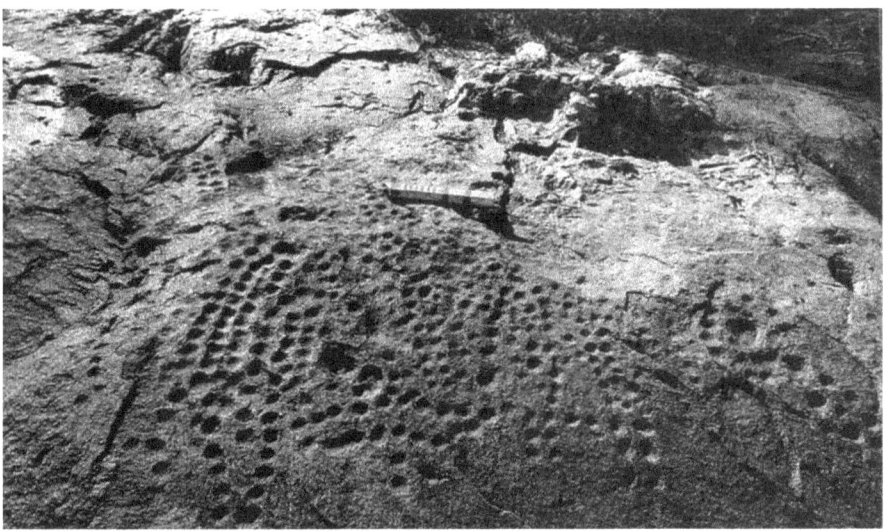

Figure 6. Kebaroti site 1, southern Kenya. Photograph by O. Odak.

used to render a barren woman fertile. Lombry also mentions the preparation of war paints (*nbuka vura*) in Congolese cupules.

A further, but different ethnographic interpretation concerns the Kebaroti site complex and the Lanet site in southern Kenya. Here, Odak (1992) reported a number of cupule pavements which the local Kuria people have interpreted to him as *boa* game boards. It appears, however, that the cupules predate these people and that their interpretation is not that of the makers, but is one imposed on pre-existing rock art (Figure 6).

recently. The elongate quartzite rock he squats on is a lithophone, the use and purpose of which were explained and demonstrated to me. In this instance, the cupule is again incidental, and — as was the case in the previous examples — its relative position to other cupules is irrelevant; it does not represent astronomical observations or whatever else ethnocentric observers like to invent. Another ethnographic interpretation of cupules as marking lithophones is reported from Burkina Faso (formerly Upper Volta, western Africa; Trost 1993: 94). On the other hand, there is anecdotic information suggesting that along the Ganges, especially in Punjab, Indian women desiring to become pregnant pour sacred water into cupules, once again linking the rock art to fertility. A similar observation has been made by Lombry (2008) who reports from the Congo the use of cupules to mix red paint made from haematite powder derived from a *mangwa gumba* (a polished haematite axe), which was then

The notion of the use of some cupules in board games is, however, promising elsewhere. In NNE Congo, Lombry (2008) observed the use of cupule arrangements in a pursuit game called *mangara* as recently as in the 1950s. In relation to geometrically arranged cupules in Nepal, Pohle (2000: 199–202) discusses the possibility that they were used in *uluk* and *rama rildok* games, and she accepts that many of the cupule arrangements relate to the latter game (Pohle 2000: Tafeln 1.1, 14–16, 18.1, 28.2). *Rama rildok* is a mancala game, to which Bandini-König (1999) also attributes cupules at Hodar, in the uppermost Indus valley, and Fu (1989: 179) mentions the same for Chinese sites. Cupules supposedly or actually used in board games form geometric alignments or groupings (cf. Lombry 2008: Fig. 4) and occur on horizontal rock panels. The ethnographic foundation of interpretations as elements of board games requires further investigation, but it appears to have been demonstrated in some cases.

Figure 7. Cupules at Moda Bhata, Rajasthan, India, examined by microerosion analysis in 2002.

There is scientific evidence from numerous sites that cupules were re-used after they were first created (Steinbring and Lanteigne 1991; Huber 1995), sometimes many millennia later. For instance, one specific cupule at Moda Bhata, India (Figure 7), which was initially pounded about 9000 years ago was briefly re-worked about 7200 years later (Bednarik et al. 2005: 182). Many similar examples are known, and it is clear that pre-existing cupules were often incorporated in the beliefs or practices of later people. This raises yet another warning, namely that it would be premature to equate the perceived 'age' of a cupule with its full antiquity: many cupules were no doubt initially created long before their most recent retouch event, and if the latter is extensive enough, no traces of earlier surfaces are likely to remain within the cupule. It is therefore then wrong to refer to the age of such marks, it is better to think of it in terms of its most recent use evidence, and in terms of this being a minimum age. Many cupules, especially the oldest known in the world, occur on particularly erosion-resistant rock types, such as quartzite, gneissic granite and even crystalline quartz (Bednarik et al. 2005).

One more ethnographic interpretation of cupules is available from Zimbabwe. Several granite lithophones are described by Huwiler (1998: 148), who reports that they are locally called *mujejeje*. These occur near burial places and were still used recently to communicate with ancestors interred in the vicinity.

Of these very few ethnographic interpretations of cupules, only the Australian example, some of those from the western United States, and those regarding lithophones can be regarded as fully secure. Interpretations as game boards may be plausible in some cases but need to be investigated more comprehensively. Other than that, we lack adequate ethnographic information to establish the former meanings of cupules, and all those explanations formulated by archaeologists lack scientific credibility.

In summary, we have limited ethnographic information that in some of the tens of thousands of cultural traditions that can be said to have existed since the first known cupules were made, they served for purposes related to fertility and to increase rituals, and we know with certainty that many cupules designate lithophones (see chapter on these phenomena). However, faced by the immensity of numbers of cupules ever made (very probably many times their surviving number) and of the enormous time span accounting for them, it is obvious that these glimpses are of very limited value in explaining the general phenomenon. Rather, these snippets of explanations appear to be incidental to some other principle. In particular, they raise unanswered questions that imply some unknown cultural dimension in these extremely limited cases we have reasonable explanations for. In all the secure ethnographic interpretations, there is no obvious need for the marks to assume precisely the very specific form of cupules. There is some merit in the assumption that, for lithophonic cupules, impact was focused on a very specific point because it yielded the best sound. However, even this is limited to some specimens, whereas on most lithophones there are numerous markings, all consisting of perfectly formed cupules, i.e. percussion was not just *focused* in their production, but was *highly focused* and quite intentionally so. None of the rare ethnographic explanations we have offers a reason for cupules to take the specific shape they have, or the fact that many or most of them seem to follow the principle of achieving greatest depth with smallest possible diameter. In short, the available ethnography of cupules does not explain the phenomenon satisfactorily.

REFERENCES

ALVAREZ, S. H. and D. W. PERI 1987. Acorns: the stuff of life. *News from Native California* 1(4): 10–14.

ARNDT, W. 1962. The interpretation of the Delamere lightning painting and rock engravings. *Oceania* 32: 163–177.

BANDINI-KÖNIG, D. 1999. *Die Felsbildstation Hodar*. Materialien zur Archäologie der Nordgebiete Pakistans 3, Mainz.

BARRETT, S. A. 1908. The ethnogeography of the Pomo and neighboring Indians. *University of California Publications in American Archaeology and Ethnology* 6(1): 1–332.

BARRETT, S. A. 1952. *Material aspects of Pomo culture*. Bulletin of the Public Museum of the City of Milwaukee 20 (Parts 1 and 2), AMS Press, New York.

BEDNARIK, R. G., G. KUMAR, A. WATCHMAN and R. G. ROBERTS 2005. Preliminary results of the EIP Project. *Rock Art Research* 22(2): 147–197.

FEWKES, J. W. (ed.) 1891. *A journal of American ethnology and archaeology*. Houghton, Mifflin, New York.

FU, C. Z. 1989. *The rock arts of China* (in Chinese). The Jiang Photographic Art Press, Beijing.

GIFFORD, E. W. and A. L. KROEBER 1937. Culture element distributions: IV. Pomo. *University of California Publications in American Archaeology and Ethnology* 37: 117–254.

GRANT, C. 1967. *Rock art of the American Indian*. Promontory Press, New York.

HEDGES, K. 1983a. A re-examination of Pomo baby rocks. *American Indian Rock Art* 9: 10–21.

HEDGES, K. 1983b. The Cloverdale petroglyphs. *Rock Art Papers* 1: 57–64.

HEIZER, R. F. 1953. Sacred rain-rocks of northern California. University of California Archaeological Survey, Report 22. *Reports of the University of California Archaeological Survey* 20: 33–38.

HUBER, A. 1995. Die Fussabdrücke am Schalenstein auf der Schöneben. *Mitteilungen der Anisa* 16: 52–62.

HUWILER, K. 1998. *Zeichen und Felsen*. Freemedia, Germany.

LOEB, E. M. 1926. Pomo folkways. *University of California Publications in American Archaeology and Ethnology* 19(2): 149–405.

LOMBRY, G. E. 2008. Congolese uses of cupules. *Rock Art Research* 25: 207–208.

MCGOWAN, C. 1982. *Ceremonial fertility sites in southern California*. San Diego Museum Papers 14, San Diego.

MOUNTFORD, C. P. 1976. *Nomads of the Australian desert*. Rigby, Adelaide.

ODAK, O. 1992. Cup-marks patterns as an interpretation strategy in some southern Kenyan petroglyphs. In M. Lorblanchet (ed.), *Rock art of the Old World: papers presented in Symposium A of the AURA Congress, Darwin (Australia) 1988*, pp. 49–60. IGNCA Rock Art Series 1, Indira Gandhi National Centre for the Arts, New Delhi.

PARKMAN, E. B. 1988. The Hupa calendar stones at Takimitlding and Medilding, north-western California. *Rock Art Research* 5: 72–74.

PARKMAN, E. B. 1992. Toward a Proto-Hokan ideology. In S. Goldsmith, S. Garvie, D. Selin and J. Smith (eds), *Ancient images, ancient thought: the archaeology of ideology*, pp. 365–370. Proceedings of the 23rd Annual Chacmool Conference, University of Calgary, Calgary.

POHLE, P. 2000. *Historisch-geographische Untersuchungen im tibetanischen Himalaya*. Giessener Geographische Schriften 76/1 and 76/2, Institut für Geographie der Justus-Liebig-Universität, Gießen.

SPIER, L. 1930. Klamath ethnography. *University of California Publications in American Archaeology and Ethnologie* 30: 1–338.

STEINBRING, J. and M. LANTEIGNE 1991. The petroglyphs of West Yorkshire: explorations in analysis and interpretation. *Rock Art Research* 8: 13–28.

STEVENSON, M. C. 1904. The Zuni Indians: their mythology, esoteric fraternities, and ceremonies. *Twenty-third Annual Report of the Bureau of American Ethnology*, pp. 3–634. Washington

STEVENSON, T. E. 1887. The religious life of the Zuni child. *Fifth Annual Report of the Bureau of American Ethnology*, pp. 533–555. Washington.

TAÇON, P. S. C., R. FULLAGAR, S. OUZMAN and K. MULVANEY 1997. Cupule engravings from Jinmium-Granilpi (northern Australia and beyond: exploration of a widespread and enigmatic class of rock markings. *Antiquity* 71: 942–965.

TROST, F. 1993. *Ethnoarchäologie in Südwest-Burkina Faso. I. Das Fundmaterial*. Akademische Druck-u. Verlagsanstalt, Graz.

ABOUT LITHOPHONES

Robert G. Bednarik

Abstract. Cupules occur commonly on lithophones, and there is thus no sharp discrimination possible between such markings on lithophones and other cupules, because the two form part of a single continuum. Rather, one needs to determine whether a particular clast may have the acoustic qualities essential to yield the appropriate sound, and if that appears to be the case and the typical percussion marks occur on it, we can safely assume that it was used as a lithophone. Therefore this presentation focuses on recognising lithophones without damaging them, by examining their physical properties.

Keywords: Lithophone, Cupule, Europe, India, Africa, U.S.A.

Phenomena that certainly do fall within the definition of cupules often occur on lithophones, in many parts of the world. As a generic term, 'lithophone' defines a musical instrument consisting of a number of rock pieces (usually discs or slabs) that produce musical notes when struck (Figure 1). The use of lithophones appears to have considerable antiquity. One of the most suitable natural features are stalactites in limestone caves, and impact traces on series of such speleothems in caves of the Franco-Cantabrian region containing also other Upper Palaeolithic activity traces have been interpreted as evidence that these were used as lithophones, e.g. at Nerja, Les Fieux and Pech-Merle (Dams 1984, 1985). Each stalactite yields a particular tone when struck, its acoustic properties being determined by its dimensions and material properties.

However, such assemblages of a number of stones yielding different sounds are not readily available in nature, except in some limestone caves. The far more common kind of lithophone occurs in the form of individual rocks found to have good acoustic properties, i.e. yielding a high-pitched metallic sound when struck. Such lithophones or rock gongs (Montage 1965) have been used widely around the world, but have been reported most often from Africa, Asia and North America. They can be of many different rock types, but there does appear to be a preference for granitic stones. It is important to note that the crucial characteristics are not those of the material, but those of shape and contact with the supporting mass. Irrespective of rock type, the best lithophonic sound results are always obtained from rocks that are thin, discoid or elongate, and only supported at very limited contact surfaces. Ideally, they are long and slender, and supported only at one end, which is why stalactites are excellent candidates. To function best, the stone must be as free as possible to resonate unhindered when struck, which allows it to increase the intensity and prolongation of sound by sympathetic vibration. This is achieved through minimal contact with other rocks, often less than 5% of the boulder's total surface area, and some of the best sound effects seem to be generated by free-standing stone spires attached to bedrock at one end. However, these are susceptible to breakage, precisely because of their resonant characteristics: if the build-up of the sympathetic vibration exceeds the stone's mechanical strength, it can snap, a fate manifested in many broken stalactites. Figure 2 shows two lithophones side by side, one still in use, and the other, to the right of it, broken off relatively recently (as evident from the fresh fracture surface), almost certainly because it was overtaxed. This site, located on the eastern shore of the Ghandi Sagar Reservoir in India, features several lithophones, some consisting of long, finger-like rock spires measuring almost 2 m length. The rock type is in this instance a well-metamorphosed quartzite, and the site features substantial deposits of Acheulian and Mesolithic artefacts. Lithophones at the Kinderdam site in South Africa, illustrated by Coulson (2007), appear to be of the same morphology and bear similar large cupules.

Figure 1. Modern lithophone made from Solnhofen limestone discs.

Figure 2. Two quartzite lithophones at Pola Bhata, Madhya Pradesh, India. The one on the left bears a single large cupule at its point which is still being used, the one on the right has broken off recently.

Figure 3. Granite lithophone boulder in the Serengeti Plain, near Banagi, northern Tanzania, featuring both patinated and recently used cupules.

Numerous stones formerly used as lithophones may be difficult to detect, the only traces of their use being faint impact markings that may have weathered away or may go unnoticed. For instance, clusters of random percussion marks are found in many parts of southern Africa, thought to be the residue of 'rituals at which the production of percussive sound such as hammering or drumming was required' (Ouzman 1998: 38). Those of interest in the present context are specimens that bear cupules. They occur frequently in sub-Saharan Africa (Singer 1961), for instance in Nigeria (Conant 1960), Uganda (Jackson et al. 1965) or Tanzania (Figure 3). Trost (1993: 94) mentions two cupule lithophones near Daramandugu in Burkina Faso, used ethnographically for communication purposes. Several granite lithophones from Zimbabwe are described by Huwiler (1998: 148), who reports that they are locally called *mujejeje*. These occur near burial places and were still used recently to communicate with ancestors interred in the vicinity. Other rock gongs in Zimbabwe are mentioned by Robinson (1958) and Cooke (1964). A superb slab lithopone with distinctive rows of deep cupules from Lewa Downs, Kenya, graces the front page of the *TARA Newsletter* No. 6, March 2005. It is quite probable that the considerable cupule concentrations of Twyfelfontein in Namibia and Spitskop in South Africa (Viereck and Rudner 1957; van Hoek 2004) are the result of the use of boulders as lithophones. Coulson (2007) illustrates a rock gong from Kinderdam, a petroglyph site near Vryburg, South Africa.

There can be little doubt that the gneissic rock disc at Morajhari near Ajmer, India (Kumar et al. 2003: Fig. 2; Bednarik et al. 2005: Fig. 42), is a rock gong (Figure 4), and there are many other instances known in India. An excellent example is the large rock flake at Jhiri Nala, located about a kilometre from the ancient cupule site Bajanibhat, east of Kotputli, also in Rajasthan. Bajanibhat in fact means 'Rock that gives sound'. The lithophone of Jhiri Nala is a thin flake measuring several metres length that split from a huge granite boulder by natural agency (probably natural impact, as there is no discernible evidence of lightning; see Bednarik 2007: 62), remaining in vertical position but standing almost free (Figure 5). It is therefore an excellent candidate for use as a lithophone,

Figure 4. Lithophonic gneiss boulder covered on both sides by cupules, at Morajhari, Ajmer, India.

Figure 5. Two large cupules on the tip of a granite lithophone at Jhiri Nala, near Kotputli, Rajasthan, India.

and even though it is in a most inaccessible location, it bears two very large cupules attesting to its use.

Numerous 'ringing rocks' have been reported from the United States, and some limited ethnographic evidence is available. In southern California, DuBois relates them to girls' puberty rites of the Luiseño (1908: 115) as well as to the boys' ant ordeal ritual (DuBois 1908: 92, 95, 121). Roberts (1917: 110–117) provides a narrative relating the use of a Kumeyaay ringing stone in an apparent supplication ritual, although in this case Hedges (1993) reports no cupules from the site. In another case, in Tulare county, California, Hedges did locate cupules on a Yokut lithophone site reported earlier (Latta 1977: 196). Bell Rock, a 7-tonne granite boulder moved to the Bowers Museum in Santa Ana, bears numerous cupules (Knight 1979), and Hedges (1990) has also reported cupule sites from Menifee valley, some on lithophones.

The significance of sound to pre-Historic societies, and in particular the possible connection between some rock art and the acoustic qualities of rock art sites has been extensively investigated by several scholars, especially by Waller (1993). In the case of lithophonic cupules, the connection is indisputable. But to produce the required harmonics frequency in the stone, it merely has to be struck, there is no need to produce cupules. Replication has shown conclusively that the striking precision required to achieve sharply demarcated cupules involves very deliberate targeting (see my chapter on technology, as well as the paper by G. Kumar, both in this volume). It therefore needs to be explained why the users of rock gongs did in certain cases not just strike the rock indiscriminately, or even restrict their blows to specific areas, but instead very deliberately produced cupules that may be several centimetres deep. One utilitarian explanation is that once a location on a lithophone was determined to yield the best possible sound, subsequent use focused on that particular spot, which eventually, after generations of use, resulted

Figure 6. The use of a cupule lithophone demonstrated at Pola Bhata, India.

in a cupule. This appears most plausible where only one cupule occurs on a large lithophone, appearing to occupy its optimal position (as in Figure 6). However, this is not usually the case, and where numerous cupules appear to be randomly arranged over a boulder it is more likely that the convention of making cupules is not purely utilitarian. This question is certainly in need of further and much more detailed empirical investigation. The subjective impression I have formed from my observations is that distinctively delineated cupules are made very deliberately: the impact blows have to be aimed at a very small area. This would suggest a conscious connection between the production of sound and the act of creating the cupule.

Judging from the few recorded instances it seems the utilitarian role of lithophones or rock gongs relates primarily to the communicating or carrying ability of the produced sound, and the metallic sound of effective lithophones can carry over distances of several kilometres. As mentioned above, in one report it serves to communicate with ancestors. The local villager shown in Figure 6, who offered spontaneously to demonstrate the traditional use of the large and very deep cupule, has provided a detailed explanation. The purpose of sounding this rock gong is to prompt all local villagers to assemble at a predetermined location. The man explained that several cupules at the site are still in regular use today for this purpose, and this was confirmed by the very recent use traces observed in them (Figure 7). Trost (1993: 94) has provided a similar explanation from

Figure 7. Recently used/renewed cupules at Pola Bhata, central India.

western Africa, noting that modulation of sound and rhythm correspond to spoken language and form a language similar to that produced with drums.

The remaining question is, how does one distinguish between cupules on a rock gong and 'general cupules', or how does one recognise a rock gong from its cupules? To be effective as a gong or lithophone, a rock must have quite distinctive physical characteristics as described above. However, it is highly possible that there is no hard and fast discrimination, because one class effectively grades into the other. Perhaps the audible aspects of cupule making were of significance even when the boulder being worked upon had relatively poor lithophonic qualities, at least in specific traditions. We do know, however, that there were at least some circumstances where the acoustic side effects of cupule production were apparently of no consequence, from the other recorded ethnographic productions of cupules mentioned in the chapter on ethnography.

REFERENCES

BEDNARIK, R. G. 2007. *Rock art science: the scientific study of palaeoart* (2nd edn; 1st edn 2001). Aryan Books International, New Delhi.

BEDNARIK, R. G., G. KUMAR, A. WATCHMAN and R. G. ROBERTS 2005. Preliminary results of the EIP Project. *Rock Art Research* 22(2): 147–197.

CONANT, F. 1960. Rocks that ring: their ritual setting in Nigeria. *Transactions of the New York Academy of Sciences*, Series 2, 23(2): 155–162.

COOKE, C. K. 1964. Rock gongs and grindstones: Plumtree area, southern Rhodesia. *South African Archaeological Bulletin* 19: 70.

COULSON, D. 2007. Rock art recording in South Africa and Botswana. *TARA Newsletter* 9: 9.

DAMS, L. 1984. Preliminary findings at the 'organ' sanctuary in the cave of Nerja, Malaga, Spain. *Oxford Journal of Archaeology* 3(1): 1–14.

DAMS, L. 1985. Palaeolithic lithophones: descriptions and comparisons. *Oxford Journal of Archaeology* 4(1): 31–46.

DUBOIS, C. G. 1908. The religion of the Luiseño Indians of southern California. *University of California Publications in American Archaeology and Ethnology* 8(3): 149–405.

HEDGES, K. 1990. Petroglyphs in Menifee valley. *Rock Art Papers* 7: 75–82.

HEDGES, K. 1993. Places to see and places to hear: rock art and features of the sacred landscape. In J. Steinbring, A. Watchman, P. Faulstich and P. S. C. Taçon (eds), *Time and space: dating and spatial considerations in rock art research*, pp. 121–127. Occasional AURA Publication 8, Australian Rock Art Research Association, Melbourne.

HUWILER, K. 1998. *Zeichen und Felsen*. Freemedia, Germany.

JACKSON, G., J. S. GARTLAN and M. POSNANSKY 1965. Rock gongs and associated rock paintings on Lolui Island, Lake Victoria, Uganda: a preliminary note. *Man* 5: 38–40.

KNIGHT, L. C. 1979. Bell Rock and Indian Maze Rock of Orange County. *Pacific Coast Archaeological Society Quarterly* 15(2): 25–32.

KUMAR, G., R. G. BEDNARIK, A. WATCHMAN, R, G. ROBERTS, E. LAWSON and C. PATTERSON 2003. 2002 progress report of the EIP Project. *Rock Art Research* 20: 70–71.

LATTA, F. F. 1977. *Handbook of Yokuts Indians*. Bear State Books, Santa Cruz, CA.

MONTAGE, J. 1965. What is a gong? *Man* 5: 18–21.

OUZMAN, S. 1998. Towards a mindscape of landscape: rock art as expression of world-understanding. In C. Chippindale and P. S. C. Taçon (eds), *The archaeology of rock art*, pp. 30–41. Cambridge University Press, Cambridge.

ROBINSON, K. R. 1958. Venerated rock gongs and the presence of rock slides in southern Rhodesia. *South African Archaeological Bulletin* 13(50): 75–77.

SINGER, R. 1961. Incised boulders. *South African Archaeological Bulletin* 16: 27.

TROST, F. 1993. *Ethnoarchäologie in Südwest-Burkina Faso. I. Das Fundmaterial*. Akademische Druck-u. Verlagsanstalt, Graz.

VAN HOEK, M. 2004. New cupule site in the Free State, South Africa. *Rock Art Research* 21: 92–93.

VIERECK, A. and J. RUDNER 1957. Twyfelfontein — a centre of prehistoric art in South West Africa. *South African Archaeological Bulletin* 12: 15–26.

WALLER, S. J. 1993. Sound reflection as an explanation for the content and context of rock art. *Rock Art Research* 10: 91–101.

THOK'OS OR THOKETOS (CUPULES)

David Camacho

Abstract. This paper refers to concepts about cupule-like features within the fieldwork carried out by the author. It also includes present Andean indigenous concepts concerning rituals, astronomy, and the views of sapient or wise people related to anthropic and natural concavities. The paper also refers to the author's personal ethnographic experiences on the subject.

Keywords: Cupule, Rock hole, Andean astronomy, Aymara, Traditional interpretation, Bolivia

During my fieldwork I found different types of cupule-like features, which I interpret as ritual, mortars for astronomical mirrors, mortars for domestic use, and natural depressions.

Rituals are carried out in sacred places, where ceremonies (including religious ones) took place in order to show gratitude or ask for something, to the Mother Earth or Father Earth. But in these ceremonies, people carried out sacrifices and offerings to Janaj Pacha, Kay Pacha and Uku Pacha, which means, the God of Above, the God of this Earth, and the God of Below. For us, the condor is considered as something sacred that always lives in the heights.

In Kalatrancani (below the Tunari mountain, near the city of Cochabamba), cupules are connected by means of grooves to other cupules, and the grooves also descend down to the surrounding earth. Here we can see how ceremonies were carried out. The blood they offered remained in the cupules. Likewise they made offerings with *chicha* (maize beer) and other beverages. These were mixed and then the liquid flew downwards to the earth. Here it is necessary to explain the following.

The offering that remains in the superior part, in the cupule, is destined to Janaj Pacha and Kay Pacha, but the remaining part of the liquid, that arrived to the ground is destined to Uku Pacha.

Mortars filled with water and used for astronomical mirrors are situated far away from places where public ceremonies took place. These astronomical sites offered great horizontal amplitude in order to achieve more exact alignments. In other words, these sites were chosen to obtain precise references of celestial bodies, with which the passing of time and the seasons of the year were observed.

With reference to this subject of astronomical mortars, it is worth mentioning that many years before the cultural zenith of astronomers in Andean cultures, there already were in our territory such astronomical mirrors that were used by local indigenous communities.

This evidence is very interesting because I was able to deduce one of the techniques used by Andean astronomers since pre-ceramic times. For example, when we look at ourselves in a mirror, the objects situated to the right are seen at the left, and vice versa. This seems to be the case of large and small mortars of Trigal (Department of Santa Cruz, Bolivia) (Figures 1 to 5).

Within the variety of these large and small concavities in rocks, it is notorious that some of them could not have been mortars, and, instead, their characteristics adapt themselves to what we are investigating (astronomic observation).

This function was observed in the sky or cosmos, and analysed by Andean indigenous people who succeeded in

Figure 1. Mortar on top of the rock of Trigal, Department of SantaCruz, Bolivia.

Figure 2. Alignment of deep mortars on top of the Trigal mountain which the author believes were used in astronomical observations when filled with water.

Figure 3. Detail of the mortar alignment of Trigal.

establishing certain metaphysical laws. This led them to organise their mental structure and then relate it to rituals, creating in this way their science and religion.

Ancient Andean people had a powerful tool, which modern man lacks. This tool comes from our cultural roots, our millenary culture, and it is based on patient and methodical observation, necessary for survival.

In the ancient world, astronomy, by means of understanding the seasons of the year, optimised agricultural and livestock production, and natural resources. In the indigenous communities, until nowadays, people continue to observe the different seasons and moon phases. Seed-time cannot take place during a lunar change, because they say it could diminish the harvest. On the other hand, during full moon, harvests are initiated, because they say it leads to greater production.

Andean 'amautas' (wizards or sapient people), before being priests or chiefs, had to be scientists, and in order to provide astronomical information in the ritual observatories, they previously had to analyse their observations in sites distant from public ceremonies, which offered conditions of great horizontal amplitude in order to achieve more exact alignments.

These sites were selected on the base of the profile of hills on the horizon, which constituted a precise reference of the rise and setting of the sun and stars they observed in order to have control of the seasons of the year.

In order to have a good agricultural harvest, the *amautas* of the Andean world had to develop astronomical technology for observation of celestial phenomena and for the adequate use of these data. But their principal contribution was to organise scientifically their society, and this way, administrate and distribute the production surplus and try to attain equality without individualism.

We all know that in our Southern Hemisphere, in winter the sun rises and descends along the north-east to north-west line and projects the shadows towards the south. In summer, the contrary takes place. The sun has a south-east to south-west trajectory, and the shadows are directed towards the north.

Aymara culture in Bolivia conserves and uses its ancient Pre-Inca lunar calendar composed of thirteen months of twenty-eight days giving a total of three hundred and sixty four days. There is one day missing for three hundred and sixty five. This day is called 'huata' ('fastening') in Quechua. It means to fasten, which is the fastening between the old year and the new one. That day a double event is celebrated, because it coincides with the winter solstice or 'Inti Raymi', the Festivity of the Sun, the New Year in Andean culture.

Regarding mortars for domestic or utilitarian use I must say that they are usually found in habitable places. They are known as 'khonanos' and were used for grinding grains or cereals. In many indigenous communities they still use these khonanos, even for grinding clay for making pottery.

With reference to the use indigenous people today apply to

Figure 4. Another view of the mortars on top of Trigal mountain after their excavation.

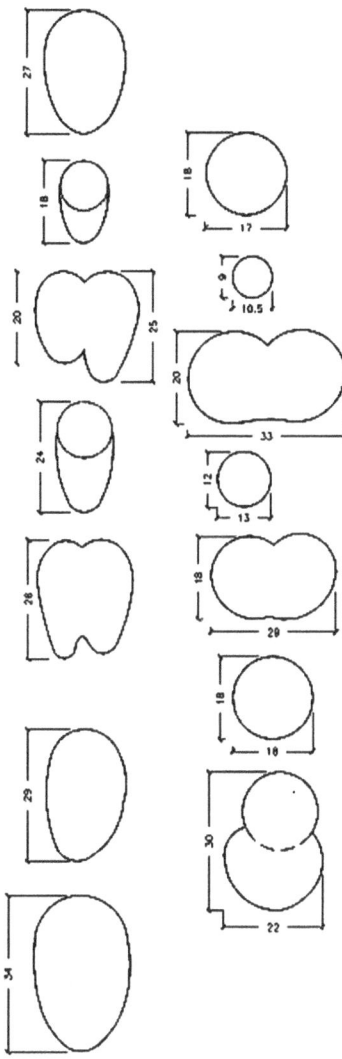

Figure 5. Dimensions and shapes of the mortars at Trigal, believed to have been used as astronomical mirrors when filled with water.

cupules I must tell about the following experience I had. Once I was following a footpath with an old indigenous man. The path was mainly used for donkeys carrying loads. On this path there are no houses, you can only find rockshelters and small caves. On a rainy day, while passing by one of these small caves, the old man showed me a cupule, situated a few metres from the deep rockshelter. He made me notice that the cupule was full of rainwater, and that the liquid overflowed continually. Then he said that it was worthless to continue walking because the river that was one kilometre from there was full of water and that it would be dangerous and impossible for us to cross it. He was right.

With regards to 'natural cupules', these are found in rivers, and with the passing of time, water and sand perforates the rock.

Finally, we must understand that without studying previously the symbolic geometric structures we will not be able to understand, neither use, the Andean symbols, and without the comprehension of these we will never have the possibility of reading the messages and teachings that are still engraved on rocks and rockshelters of our Tahuantinsuyo (the ancient territory that the Inca Empire conquered, divided in four regions). After having succeeded to translate the graphic expression that is disguised behind the symbol we shall find the text of the myths that our ancestors left us.

www.ingramcontent.com/pod-product-compliance
Lightning Source LLC
Chambersburg PA
CBHW041705290426
44108CB00027B/2856